ORGANISATIONAL BEHAVIOUR

ORGANISATIONAL BEHAVIOUR

K.C.S. RANGANAYAKULU

ATLANTIC®
PUBLISHERS & DISTRIBUTORS

Published by

ATLANTIC®

PUBLISHERS & DISTRIBUTORS

B-2, Vishal Enclave, Opp. Rajouri Garden,
New Delhi-110027
Phones : 25413460, 25429987, 25466842

Sales Office
7/22, Ansari Road, Darya Ganj,
New Delhi-110002
Phones : 23273880, 23275880, 23280451
Fax : 91-11-23285873
web : www.atlanticbooks.com
e-mail : info@atlanticbooks.com

Printed in India
at Nice Printing Press, Delhi

PREFACE

In an industrial environment Organisational Behaviour play a significant role. Organisational Behaviour deals with the study of what people do in an organisation, how their behaviour can affect performance of the organisation and highlight the ways for moulding these behaviours towards improving organisations' performance and effectiveness.

Twenty-first century unfolds with swift challenges at global level and as such OB professionals will have to unlearn their present strategies and be sensitive to the changing values, aspirations and attitudes that people, technologies and markets bring into the organisations. An *intelligent worker* will be ever demanding. Organisations that do not change immediately will be drowned by the tidal waves of change as a result of globalisation. This book is about human intellectuals who work in organisations—their needs, thoughts and emotions. Content has been streamlined and related to the activities of modern organisations. This book is not a research message. Students will become involved in learning about behaviour at workplace. There is no single theory or model that is said best, since organisational functioning is ever changing in these turbulent times and the calamities that are beyond the imagination of everyone/technology existing (for example, the recent "Tsunami" which has devastated the whole of Asia). Managers should scan the environment and organisational situations and predict the behaviour of people. Content of the book encourages students to relate their knowledge and experiences to the text and situations given. This book, written in an easy to understand language, is organised into sixteen chapters. I suggest the readers to use the search engines shown at the end for further information and dedicate this book to my college VRS & YRN College, Chirala, where I served for long time before going to Ethiopia. Readers may write me suggestions if any at surya@freemail.et

K.C.S. RANGANAYAKULU

CONTENTS

1

INTRODUCTION

Organisational behaviour and human relations—the emerging disciplines

According to Stephen P. Robbins, "Organisational behaviour is a field of study that investigates the impact that individuals, groups and structure have on behaviour within organisations, for the purposes of applying such knowledge towards improving organisation's effectiveness."

It is the study and application of knowledge about a human behaviour related to other elements of the organisation *i.e.*, Technology, Social System, Culture and Structure.

Modern society is organised in nature with complex organisations dominating every human activity. The success of organisation depends mostly on human factor, which is one among the production factors. This being a life organ needs better management than others, such as materials, money, and machines. As such distinctive branch of study developed which is known as Organisational Behaviour. Thus organisational behaviour is primarily concerned with the aspect of 'human face' or social face which is relevant for organisational performance. Therefore it studies social or human behaviour at individual level, group level and organisational level. It applies the knowledge gained about individuals, groups and structure on behaviour towards making organisations effective.

Human relations. Human relations broadly apply to the interaction and cooperation of people in groups. This can happen to any aspect of human activity. When human relation is used in the organisational contexts it means the integration of people into a work station which motivates them to work together effectively. Manager's role is to release and guide the inner drives of human beings who alone are capable of producing goods.

Organisational behaviour is an academic discipline concerned with understanding human behaviour in an organisational environment. It identifies causes and effects of the behaviour. Human relation applies behavioural knowledge in operating organisations to build human cooperation. It is action and goal oriented. While organisational behaviour seeks to gain understanding, human relations seeks to use it in operational situations. The difference in emphasis between the two terms is similar to the difference between a pathologist and physician who seek respectively to understand ills and use the knowledge to achieve results. Respectively the two approaches are two sides of the same coin which cannot be separated. Hence they are emerging disciplines of organisational study.

Nature and scope of organisational behaviour

It is a study of human behaviour in various times and situations. To organise the matters in modern times it is necessary to know about the organisational factors influencing the workers and *vice versa.* This 'soft discipline' reveals strengths and weaknesses of human factor.

Predicts human behaviour. It is not a study of emotional feelings of employee. It is to explain and predict human behaviour of people in organisations.

Rational thinking. Organisational behaviour is a rational thinking and action oriented.

Balances human and technical values. It seeks to balance between human and technical values of people working in an organisation.

Seeks to achieve productivity. It encourages higher productivity at work by building and maintaining employee's dignity, growth and satisfaction.

Inter-disciplinary. It is not a field of independent study. It integrates behavioural sciences such as Psychology, Sociology, Anthropology, Social psychology etc.

Science and art. It is both science and art being a branch of study which is applied in practical situation to yield results.

Results depend upon the 'art' *i.e.*, how best these skills are applied by the Managers.

Multiplicity. Organisational Behaviour deals with the behaviour of people at different levels *i.e.*, individuals, groups and organisations. Behaviour attributable at each of these levels can be both identified and isolated.

Does not exist in vacuum. Any organisation is made up of social system which is often changing due to changes in environment. Hence behaviour exists in organisation, but nowhere.

Normative science. Organisational Behaviour is a normative science. A normative science unlike the positive science suggests what are acceptable to people and society. This depends upon values of society which cannot be explained by a positive science that suggests only cause and effect relationships.

Humanistic. OB focuses the attention on people from humanist point of view. As a human being the individual is motivated by needs, feelings and wants. Hence behaviour depends upon these considerations.

Optimistic. There is optimism about the innate potentials of man who is social entity. The man will actualise these potentials in a given proper conditions environments. Man cannot achieve all those he wishes but he is only optimistic.

Objective oriented. Behaviour is rational and oriented to organisational objectives. Different objectives exist in organisations but OB tries to integrate them. Once the organisational objectives are achieved other objectives such as individual and group objectives are also achieved simultaneously.

Systems approach. Organisation is a system where different variables are linked to one another. The systems approach is an integrative approach which takes into account all the variables affecting organisational functioning. OB does not take man in isolation but as the product of socio-psychological factors. Behaviour goes by psychological framework, interpersonal orientation group influence, social and cultural factors. Thus man's native is quite complex and OB by applying systems approach tries to find solution of this complexity.

Adaptability. Individuals or groups adapt themselves to the changes occur in organisational environment. Their behaviour change with changes occurring in environment. OB considers this factor and develops suitable techniques that managers have to observe while supervising the human factor.

Pervasive. OB is all pervasive in nature since organisations do not exist without people. Wherever, people exist there changes occur hence managers have to ensure continuity in organisations by influencing their behaviour for successful accomplishment of objectives set for organisations.

Perceptual. Change of human behaviour is perceptual and continuous. Managers have to ensure welfare to people by implementing the changes that occur from time to time by moulding people to the overall system of organisations.

Different disciplines contributing to Organisational Behaviour

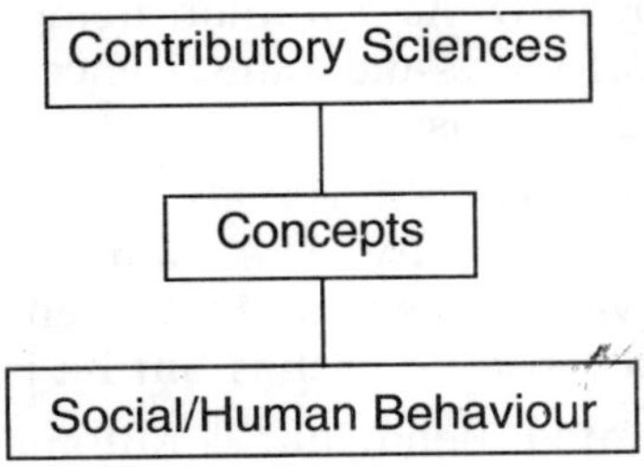

OB is not a discipline in itself but uses knowledge developed in the relevant disciplines. Basically it draws concepts and principles from core sciences of Psychology, Sociology, Anthropology and other Social Sciences such as Economics, History and Political Science.

Psychology. It is universally accepted science of behaviour. Psychology studies the behaviour of people in various situations. Manager should know the psychology of people before he takes decisions relating to organisation. There is a separate branch of industrial psychology which deals with the application of human psychology in organisation. In matters of selection, training, transfer, promotion, motivation, communication, work coordination and other situations psychology is of significant importance.

Sociology. It is the study concerned with social behaviour of a man. Social behaviour guided by society, customs, class, station, prestige, community and religion. Manager should take into consideration the said factors and act himself. Hence he should have the knowledge of sociology in the present industrial set-up.

Anthropology. It is concerned with behaviour of man in relation to value system, norms, sentiments, culture, biological needs etc., the behaviour is guided by these factors. Hence the Manager should understand their influence on individual or group training in different situations.

In addition Economics, Political Science and History have also contributed in understanding the behavioural process of individuals, groups and organisations.

Levels of analysis in OB Model and their interrelationship

The basic purpose of OB Model is to explain and predict the way people behave in organisations. The behaviour is influenced by many variables. These variables are grouped into dependent variables such as Productivity, Absenteeism, Turnover and Job satisfaction. Independent variables occur at individual level, group level and organisational system level.

The following diagram shows their relation and how independent variables influence dependent variables.

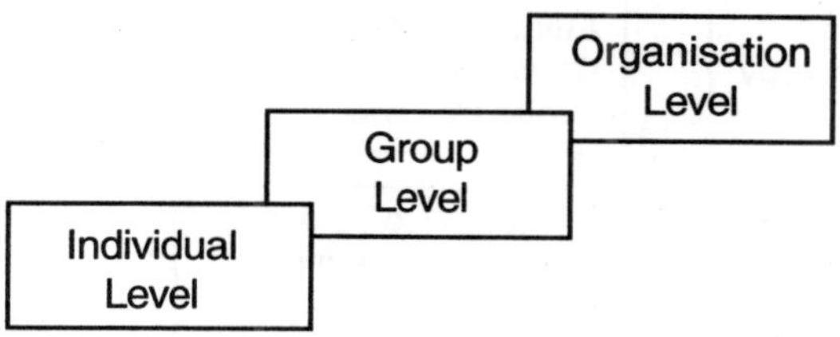

Basic OB Model Stage I

OB Model at Individual Level. Biographical characteristics such as personality, values, abilities influence perception, motivation and learning respectively which in turn influence individual decision-making. This individual decision-making influences dependent variables such as productivity, absence, turnover and satisfaction.

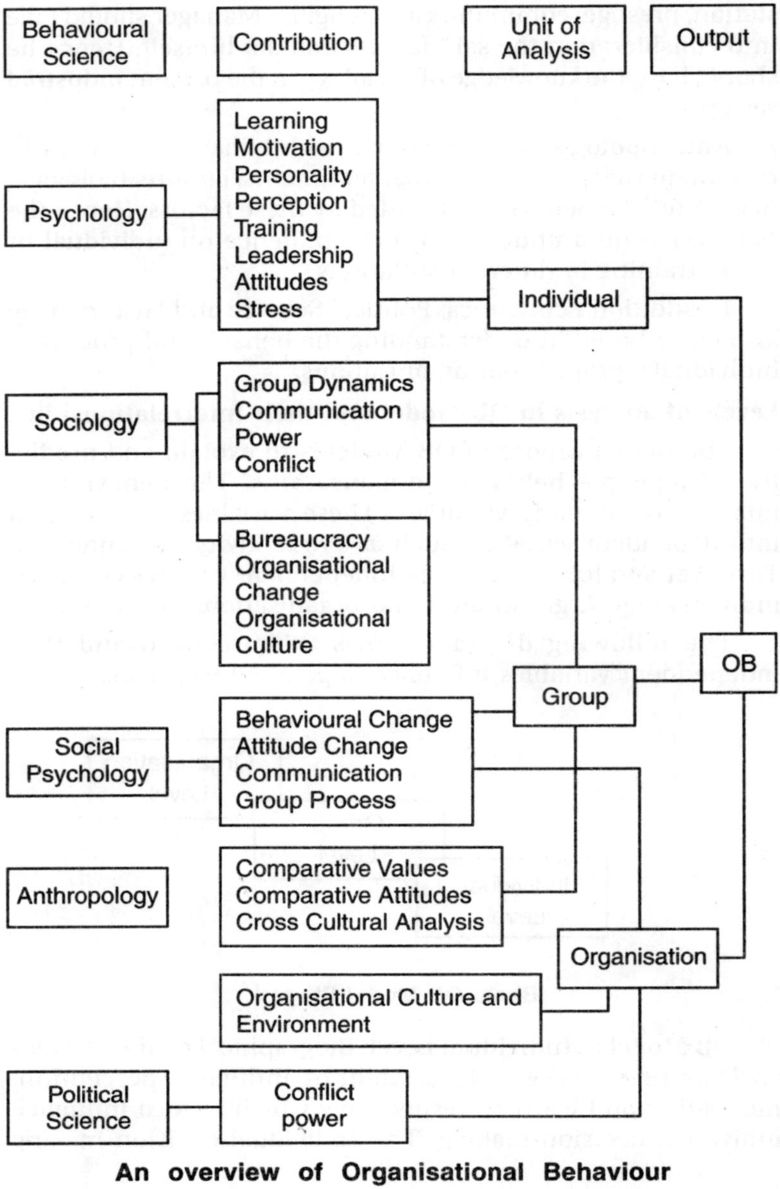

An overview of Organisational Behaviour

The following diagram shows the relationship.

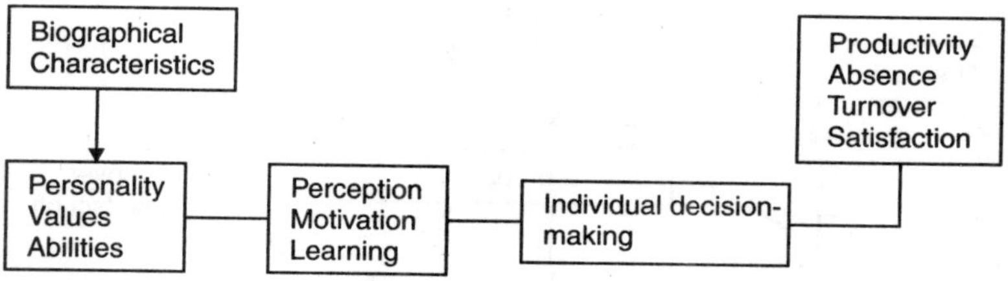

OB Model at Individual Level

The behaviour of people in groups is more than the sum and total of each individual acting in his way. The complexity of OB Model is increased when people are in groups. Here one should remember that group decisions, leadership, structure, communication, conflicts, power and politics influence the dependent variables. This is shown in the following diagram.

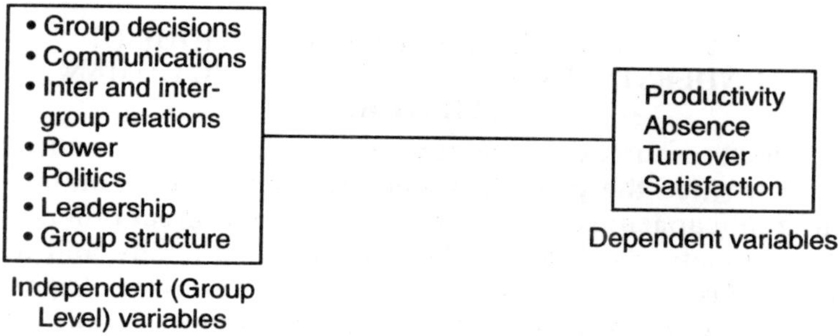

OB Model at Group Level

Organisation system level. Just as groups are more than the sum of their individual numbers. Organisations are more than the sum of their groups. Here organisation structure and design-work stress, human resources policies, organisational culture influence the dependent variables.

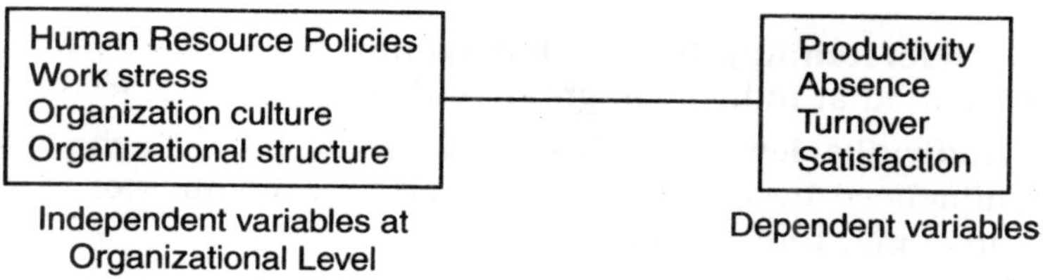

OB Model at Organisational system level

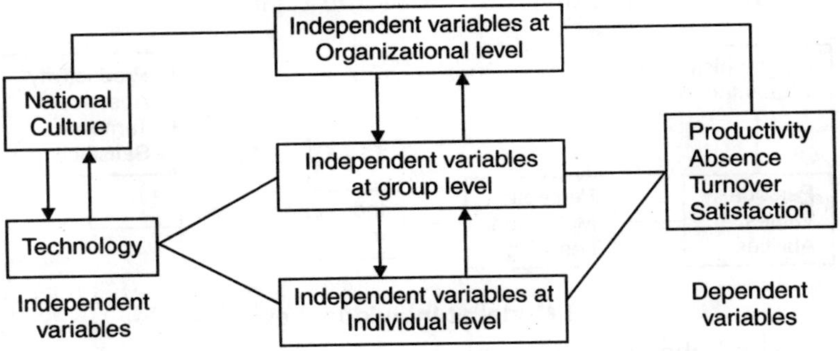

Adapted from Robbins, *Organisational Behaviour*, Prentice Hall of India, New Delhi, 1993.

Basic OB Model Stage II
(Contingency OB Model)

ROLE OF ORGANISATIONAL BEHAVIOUR IN UNDERSTANDING AND CONTROLLING HUMAN BEHAVIOUR

Of all resources man assumes vital role among production factors, since the prosperity depends upon men working in different capacities. It is easy to control and direct others but human factor is different. People think rationally and also selfish. It is necessary on the part of manager to create congenial environment where people release their energies. People work with commitment provided they are directed on the lines of Theory Y as described by McGregor. Thus human factor is quite uncertain and needs to be directed carefully to achieve the objectives set for the organisations. Here OB provides necessary insights of human beings for understanding and prescribing behaviour and means to achieve the organisational goals.

Understanding human behaviour. Behaviour is to be understood at individual, group and organisational level.

Individual level. Man is a social animal and his behaviour is influenced by working conditions, pay, methods of work, technology, groups, leadership etc.

Interpersonal level. In an organisation individuals interact with each other at work. Individual develops working relationship with others such as subordinates, superiors and colleagues. His performance depends upon how he establishes relationship with others and success depends upon sound relations he maintains. OB deals with understanding interpersonal relationships in the organisations. Role analysis, transactional analyses are some of the methods providing necessary insights.

Group level. Individuals form into groups on the basis of common interest, goals, habits, age, sex, language, religion and regional factors. They influence very much on the decisions of managers. So manager, should understand the people and their behaviour in groups. OB explains necessary skills and traits to deal with groups to increase morale and productivity.

Inter-group. In today's organisations Modern managers should know about the relationships between groups which are formed naturally. His efficiency depends upon his deep knowledge with groups and their relations since they influence organisational goals in turn. OB gives necessary inputs to managers for effective group cohesiveness.

Controlling and directing behaviour. Managers are required to control people at all levels. Their knowledge of OB helps them to communicate, coordinate, control and direct people in various situations of complex in nature. So that they can conform actual performance with that of expected one both in short run and long run.

1. Delegation of authority. Managers have to delegate authority to various individuals and groups for smooth functioning of the organisation. OB helps in discharging his functions by effective delegation.

2. Controlling. Managers are responsible for results, they should see the actual performance of people with whom they are in touch. OB helps them to control effectively by establishing better standards more acceptable to many at all times.

Communication. Managers communicate with people in groups and cliques. Knowledge of OB enables them to better communicate effectively without barriers. Communication is very important means for managers, to bring effectiveness at work. Communicating with individuals/groups is a tough task. Since the behaviour is influenced by the way they are communicated. Hence manager's job is made easy by their rich knowledge of OB.

Use of power. Sharing of power is one of the inputs the managers use while dealing with people in creating effective environment. He should know the feelings and fancies of people/ groups who assume or share his powers from time to time. Effective understanding of OB keeps the manager to feel ease in granting powers and revoking them.

Organisational climate. OB enables managers responsible for results in creating quite congenial or climate at work. They should see people release their energies at work with better motivation and morale. They should take all organisational conditions into consideration for creating overall climate where people work happily. This OB provides them necessary aids in keeping the organisational climate acceptable and objective oriented.

Motivation. Motivation of people is the responsibility of managers at work. People are motivated by unsatisfied wants and needs. People in different age groups are in need of satisfying their varying needs. Their behaviour is influenced by their state of condition in which they work. Hence managers should better understand their needs and their behaviour and satisfy them for better results. OB gives necessary talents to motivate people whereby their behaviour is influenced.

Cooperation. According to 'Barnard', Cooperation is voluntary and two ways. Unless worker cooperates, it is impossible to show progress. Behaviour depends upon cooperative spirit of the employees. Manager, should elicit cooperation and influence worker, for better performance. OB tutors managers by which they can establish spirit of cooperation among employees.

Coordination. Coordination of work and worker, needs sufficient knowledge of behaviour of people at work. Managers should learn required art of developing coordination. So that their work is made easy. OB ensures Managers sufficient information by which the employees' behaviour is streamlined.

QUESTIONS FOR DISCUSSION

1. Define organisational behaviour and human relations. Why they are regarded as emerging disciplines?

2. What is the nature and scope of organisational behaviour?
3. Explain different disciplines contributing to organisational behaviour.
4. What are the three levels of analysis in OB Model? Are they related? If so how?
5. Discuss the Role of Organisational behaviour in understanding and controlling human behaviour.

2

CONFLICTS

Definition of conflict and views on conflict

Life is not bed of roses. In life one has to struggle to live comfortably. Struggle comes from poverty or lackness. Individual does not live in isolation. He lives in association with others, when he coexists in a group or in an organisation *i.e.,* work place, differences will arise with others from time to time. These differences will result in 'Conflict'.

Definition. Conflict is a Process in which an effort is made by one person to further his interest by effecting other's interests.

According to **Robbins**, it is a process that begins when one party perceives that another party has negatively affected, or is about to negatively affect, something that the first party cares about.

It encompasses the wide range of Conflicts that people experience in organisations, incompatibility of goals, differences over interpretations of facts, disagreements based on behavioural expectations etc.

Features

1. Conflict occurs when two persons' interest are different.
2. Conflict takes place when perceptions of two persons vary.
3. Conflict arises when one interferes in other's activities wilfully.
4. Conflict begins when one starts to acquire resources before others start to act.

Different views. Different thoughts or views are developed over the role of Conflict.

Traditional view. Traditional approach viewed 'Conflict' as a dangerous one to organisation. Since conflict causes negative results such as anger, resentment, confusion, lack of cooperation etc. It disrupts smooth functioning of an organisation and creates disorder. Conflict is bad and should be avoided. It also says management should not permit conflicts to occur and resolve immediately.

Human relations view. Supporters of this view have accepted that Conflict is a natural outcome in any organisation since it is complex with many persons having various goals and interests. They also have felt Conflict is bad.

Interactions view. It is broad in scope. The supporters of this approach felt that Conflict is positive force and it is necessary for effective performance of a group or organisation.

According to this view:

1. Conflict is not organisational abnormality.
2. Conflict is inevitable.
3. Conflict is the integral part of change.
4. Conflict is desirable.
5. Optimum level of Conflict is healthy.

Difference between functional and dysfunctional conflict and determinants of functionality

Conflict is part of an organisation and inherently pathological and not always destructive. It is all pervasive and has many positive and negative outcomes. Hence Management has to create congenial atmosphere. On one hand conflicts are destructive and on the other they are constructive. They are neither desirable nor regrettable. They are neither eliminated nor created. They help in building empire and also in running organisation. Effective management has to keep them at optimum level by restricting at times allowing to play their due role.

Functional role of conflicts. Experts viewed that conflict is a potentially useful aspect of organisation. Conflict prevents stagnation and stimulates interest. It is the medium through which problems can be solved and solutions can be arrived at. It is the root of personal and social change. Without conflicts organisations would be apathetic and stagnant. Thus conflicts provide adequate platform wherein people can 'Blow of steam'. Khan *et al.*, viewed that one might well make a case for interpreting conflict as essential for the continued development of nature and competent human beings. Hence conflicts lead to positive consequences at times.

Some of the positive aspects of the conflicts are as follows:

1. Stimulant for change. Conflicts draw attention of the authorities for finding better solutions. It initiates a search for ways to derive objectives, methods and procedures.

2. Counteracts lethargy. Conflict counteracts the lethargy that often overtakes organisation. Sometimes group thinking prevents from making rational decisions.

3. Fosters creativity and innovation. It stimulates curiosity and interest. It prevents stagnation. In open confrontation people tend to put forward more practicable solutions. A climate of challenge compels individuals to think productively and creatively. It helps the people to test their capacities to learn and develop.

4. Cohesion. Conflict and competition drive groups go closer. Group membership and association with members gives satisfaction. According to 'Boulding', organisations are creations of their enemies and it is through a common hatred of the enemy they establish their internal unity.

5. Optimum level of conflict is desirable. Conflict is inevitable and also necessary for organisational life. It serves to balance power relationships between departments. It helps individuals to get relief from the tensions and ill feelings among them.

6. Rational actions. It provides opportunities to people and groups to think and act rationally.

7. Competition. Conflict brings cohesiveness in groups and infuses spirit of competition.

8. Draws attention to shortcomings. It draws the attention of management to the shortcomings in the existing system. Conflict is always not a medium to streamline problem and develop organisations. As discussed by traditional view and human relations view, conflict causes severe damages to the organisational health. The dysfunctional aspect of conflict can be visualised in the following ways:

1. **Creates stress on people.** Conflict generates feelings of anxiety and frustration. Winners face to injure the feelings of the defeated. Losers feel defeated. This causes stress on people.
2. **Increases distance.** Conflict causes a feeling of distrust and suspicion. It increases distance between people.
3. **Non-cooperation.** Loosers indulge in non-cooperation and pay scant attention to the needs and interests of other group members.

Diversion of efforts. Conflict completely distracts the efforts of groups and individuals from organisational goals. They always try to win over the competitors and rival groups, which gains them nothing more than, psychological satisfaction. Individuals and groups did not subordinate their goals to organisational goals.

Long-run goals loose importance. Due to conflicts long-run goals suffer as short-run goals gain importance. Too much energy is drained off in trying to put out the fires. In extreme cases sabotage, secrecy and even illegal activities occur.

Causes instability. Groups and individuals in warfare drain their energies for unproductive purposes. Tensions will continue and lead to communication breakdown. Conflict reduces the organisation into sub-units and small groups causing instability.

Conflicts beyond certain degree may lead to organisational dis-equilibrium. Hence management should understand the conflicts, their role and effects. Management should keep the conflicts to an optimum level and ensure congenial environment where people release their energies for the fulfilment of organisational goals.

The role of conflict at individual level and the ways to overcome these conflicts

Conflicts occur at individual, group and organisational level. At individual level two types of conflicts take place *viz.*, intra-individual and inter-individual.

The following diagram shows the conflicts at various levels.

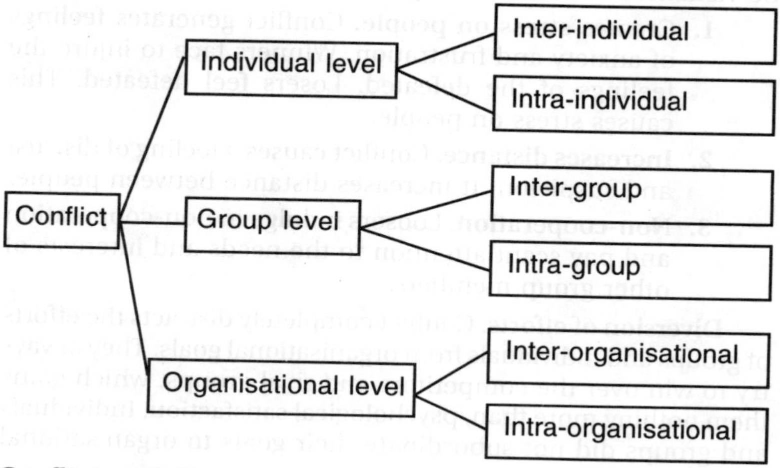

Conflict analysis

Intra-individual conflict. It is difficult to analyse, since it is internal to a person. Man works at home or at workplace only to satisfy his individual needs. Organisation is a place for individuals to satisfy his needs.

Goal conflict. An individual is exposed himself to various goals. Goal conflict occurs when two or more motives block each other. There are three alternatives of goal conflict — (1) Approach-approach. (2) Approach-avoidance and (3) Avoidance-avoidance conflict.

1. Approach-approach conflict. The goal conflict arises, when a person has two mutually exclusive alternatives but he can have only one. In this situation individual has to decide one or the other. According to this approach the individual gets satisfaction positively, equally in either of the two.

2. Approach-avoidance conflict. An individual has to choose or take decision which is characterised by both positive and negative features. When the goal is satisfying at one end and threatening on the other, the individual vacillates and unable to decide future course of action. Such conflict is called *approach-avoidance conflict.*

3. Avoidance-avoidance conflict. An individual has to take choice between two options which are mutually exclusive and equally not attractive. Such conflict is called *Avoidance-avoidance conflict.* In such situation the tendency is to stay unresolved. If the individual makes a decision one of the avoidance-avoidance options the closer he gets to implementing that decision, the more likely he is to be repelled by the negative characteristics of the choice, retreating towards the other decision. Ultimately he will be in dilemma again. Such a situation is painful if he does not have a third option.

Understanding of goal conflict is necessary to integrate individual goals with organisational goals. The management should resolve goal conflicts by building computability between personal and organisational goals.

Meaning of the role conflict? Causes of role conflict and methods to avoid the role conflict

An individual may perform different duties in different situations. In all the situations he is expected to behave in different manner. A District Collector may be an administrator, judge, husband, community leader, consultant etc. If we examine three roles emerge such as expected role, perceived role and actual role. The expected role is what others expect from an individual. The perceived role is what assumed by an individual that how he should behave to fulfil the expected behaviour. The enacted role is what an individual really behaves in an organisation. Thus individuals ought to play multiple roles in life as well as organisations, simultaneously. This type of role conflict is called *intra role conflict.* There are four types of such conflicts which are given below.

(I) Person-role conflict. It occurs when role requirements are contrary to the values and beliefs of the person. Sarbin said this role conflict occurs in three situations:

(i) When the individual occupies a role which is not consistent with the beliefs of self.

(ii) When the individual is biologically not capable to fulfil the role.

(iii) When the person fails to perceive the expected behaviour due to mental or physical deficiencies.

(II) Intra-sender role conflict. It occurs when expectations from a single member of a role set *may* be incompatible. *Ex:* A person is expected to complete a work in a given time but it is not possible to complete within the scheduled time.

(III) Inter-sender role conflict. This happens when the expectations sent from one sender are in conflict with those from one or more senders.

(IV) Inter-role conflict. This occurs when an individual occupies two or more different roles simultaneously and the expectations associated with those different roles are inconsistent.

Factors in role conflict. The factors responsible for role conflict are classified into three categories.

1. Role ambiguity. Role ambiguity exists when role expectations are not known and also not clearly defined. Role ambiguity increases role conflict. The role ambiguity will be intensified when the individual does not fulfil the job requirements due to his lacking.

2. Organisational position. Role conflict is inherent where an individual performs different roles both formally and informally which are incompatible mutually. Modern organisational positions are sources of role conflict. A supervisor while getting work done on behalf of management should play the role as representative of management. Simultaneously he should represent the workers and play the role on behalf of workers. Thus he belongs to both the parties and perform up to the expectations of both workers and management. Conflict arises in the mind of supervisor as to whose expectations he should fulfil.

3. Personal characteristics. Role conflict arises because of personal characteristics such as commitment, involvement, achievement orientation, flexibility, rigidity, emotional sensitivity etc., such persons often get into role conflict.

Impact. People facing role conflict will experience stress, tension and emotion which result in poor performance when manager's perception of work is not perceived by his subordinates, there tends to be poor motivation. Role conflicts have adverse impact on health and morale of employees. The employee will experience tension and undergo poor job satisfaction.

Resolve. The extent of 'Role conflict' depends upon (1) Awareness of role conflicts, (2) Acceptance of job pressures, (3) Ability to tolerate stress, (4) Personality make-up.

Management of role conflict should be to avoid the situations of role conflicts. Role conflicts can only be minimised but not be completely reserved. Organisations using participative methods of decision-making tend to minimise role conflicts. By persuasion individual goals can be brought closer to the organisational goals.

INTERPERSONAL CONFLICT

Interpersonal conflicts occur between two individuals. Such conflicts results in between two persons who hold polarised points of view. There may be several forms of interpersonal conflicts such as hierarchy conflicts (between superiors and subordinates), functional conflicts (between occupational and specialists) and professional conflicts. Inter-personal conflict takes place at horizontal level *i.e.*, among equals and at vertical level *i.e.*, between superior and subordinates.

The following are the reasons for interpersonal conflicts:

1. Personality difference. Two persons do not like to work together for reasons known to each other. This is purely psychological problem and it has nothing to do with their job requirements.

2. Perceptions. Varied backgrounds, experiences, education, training result in individual perceptions. These perceptions result in interpersonal conflicts.

3. Power and status differences. Conflicts arise from unequal distribution of power. Organisations operate by distributing powers and authority. Status inconsistencies also lead to conflicts. *Ex:* Lecturers give orders to professors.

4. Scarce resources. Interpersonal conflicts arise when two individuals fight for one item or facility. The conflicts go to un-manageable level and it is very difficult to manage interpersonal level.

5. Ego-states. Two persons often involve in these conflicts due to individual egos. People with personal egos will think and behave differently. These people do not know much about others.

6. Value systems. Value system is a framework of personal philosophy which governs and influences individual reactions. People with different value system think and interpret the same thing differently. Such differences become the basis of interpersonal conflict.

7. Socio-cultural factors. People with different socio-cultural backgrounds develop conflicts among themselves. Many interpersonal conflicts are based on caste, community, religion, region etc.

8. Interest conflict. People belonging to different groups see their interest differently. This is caused by situational factors not because of human tendency.

9. Role ambiguity. Role ambiguity is one of the reasons for role conflict. Sometimes inter-role conflict may happen because of organisation structure.

• **Group conflicts**

Two or more persons constitute a group. In an organisation group formation is inevitable. Groups normally occur on the basis of sex, age, linguistic differences, religion, interests, habits etc. Group will influence its members, other groups, members in other group and organisation too. In this interaction process, group conflicts occur at intra-group level and inter-group level.

Intra-group conflict. It is a conflict that occurs within the group or internally. It may occur between two persons of the same group or between group leader and followers. Thus when group interest is not compatible to members at a given time, conflicts arise.

Intra-group conflict arises in the following situations:

(i) When group faces a unique problem.

(ii) When the group leader plays role not consistent with group expectations.

(iii) When new values are imposed on the group by the environment.

(iv) When a person's extra group role comes into conflict with his intra-group role.

(v) When the group members are drawn from different sections of society.

Inter-group conflict. Inter-group conflict refers to conflict between an individual and a group or between two groups. When the groups exist in an organisation they should try to coexist with harmony to each other. But due to various reasons they fail to live in harmony with others. The following are the reasons where often disputes arise which the management should understand and streamline for cohesiveness and congenial atmosphere.

Goal in-congruence. The groups are formed on various reasons as said earlier. Groups try to prevail over others. The group interest when differs with each other they will influence and cause inhibitions, polluting the atmosphere ought to be in an organisation. A group should perceive the goals of other groups mutually reinforcing. Every group should design its goals in a way compatible to other groups. The achievement of a group's goal prevents or reduces the chances of attainment of other groups. Hence the management should integrate the group interest and see they will not be incompatible to each other.

Sharing of resources. Often conflicts arise in matters relating to distribution of benefits, incentives and other common benefits. Conflicts arise due to paucity of resources. Hence Management should look into these resource distribution matters rationally so that majority will be benefited by their decisions.

Task relationship. Groups are created through organisation structure. Groups are necessary through which organisational goals can be achieved. Such groups are sometimes dependent and independent. The group interaction depends upon how they are related to each other and work with functional relationship. Group clashes happen when two groups work jointly or dependently. Management should clearly define the authority of each group for smooth functioning.

Uncertainty. Conflicts arise in times of uncertainty. When groups are dependent they should work in harmony and upto the expectations of others. The groups should work without putting others to wait for them and ensure certainty. Thus group conflicts can be reduced by minimising the uncertainty among the groups.

Attitudes. Groups should have positive attitude to other groups. They should work with mutual respect and consideration for problems of others. They should not blame each other and come forward to assume responsibilities. In such situations groups work with mutual cooperation and less room for group conflicts.

Heterogeneity of members. The group conflicts will arise and depend upon the nature of members. If the members are more and drawn from different backgrounds the team spirit lowers and creates inter-group conflicts.

Reward system. Inter-group conflicts arise, when reward system is linked to group performance rather than overall performance. In such cases, groups work with the spirit of competition and try to overtake other groups resulting in communication gap, incompatibility in goals etc., followed by differences and conflicts.

Communication gaps. The groups work and ensure better performance only when they get necessary information to them timely. Absence of such information will lead to poor performance and conflicts because of suspicion and absence of correct information.

Absence of formalisation. In the absence of formalisation disputes arise and unrest is caused. Hence organisation should enforce rules and regulations with clear information to all.

Non-participation. Absence of group participation in decision-making is seriously disrupting the performance. Joint consultations will offer opportunities to resolve differences and develop mutual trust. Higher interaction facilitates coordination and cooperation.

Values and perceptions. Differences in attitudes and perceptions are responsible for disputes and conflicts. Highly qualified persons hesitate to assume small works, when they are assigned.

Status. Sometimes status incongruent will also lead to conflict. When individuals are assigned unrelated job they feel status and refuse to do. People also feel false status when they are assigned unsuitable jobs.

Line and staff. Line people are responsible for results and performance while staff are advisory only. They should work together but both due to wrong conceptions fail to understand others and put to conflicts.

CONSEQUENCES

Winners — within group

1. Members of a group develop 'we' feelings.
2. Members feel superiority over others.
3. Members experience high morale.

Winners — between groups

1. They develop negative feelings to other groups.
2. They feel they are great.
3. They treat loosers as enemies.
4. They assume that they are good and rival groups as bad ones.
5. Groups become more aggressive in their approach.
6. Groups overestimate their strengths.
7. Groups become well-knit units.

Losers — within group

1. Members blame each other.
2. Members develop inferiority.
3. Members lose morale.
4. Members fail to maintain unity within the group.

Losers — between groups

1. Groups develop tension and enmity.
2. Initially resists, defeat.
3. Communication breaks down.
4. Group disintegrates.

- **Intra-organisational conflicts**
- **Reasons for intra-organisational conflicts**

Conflicts in organisations are of many kinds. One such conflict is intra-organisational conflict. The following are such intra-organisational conflicts:

1. Horizontal conflict
2. Vertical conflict
3. Line and staff conflict.

Horizontal conflict. Horizontal conflict is called the conflict arising at the same level of two groups or departments which are interdependent and tend to act independently. Here the department people develop the spirit of competition and try to achieve their goal, at the cost of other groups or departments. The incongruity between group goals are responsible for such type of intra-organisational conflict. Failure of one department causes distortions in other departments since it has change effect and ultimately the organisation experiences the misfortunes.

Vertical conflict. Vertical conflict occurs between people at two levels, possibly between superior and subordinates. Normally these conflicts take place for the following reasons: (1) Inadequate communication, (2) Perceptional variations, (3) Attitudinal changes, (4) Distrust, (5) Differences in interests, (6) Lack of mutual understanding, etc. If superiors try to maintain more control over subordinates, subordinates tend to resist and avoid responsibilities which ultimately result in conflicts often.

Line and staff conflict. In an organisation people are divided into two categories: (1) Line, (2) Staff. They are perceived to have different approaches in their way of dealing with organisational matters. Since their nature of involvement in solving problems is different and they tend to act differently. In general Line people are held responsible for failures as they take decisions and responsible to solve problems of the organisation. Staff persons are expected to advise the line in solving problems. As long as they see the problems with equal perception, conflicts do not arise. Conflicts do come when the required perceptions fail between them towards the problem. The given below are the reasons for conflict of Line and Staff.

Grievances of line persons

1. Line people criticise Staff persons for their encroachment into the area of line persons.
2. Often Line reports that Staff gives advises of little practical utility.
3. Line fears that Staff may steal the credit which Line do not want to share with others.

4. Line remarks that Staff do not see the problem as a whole and lack the practical perspective.
5. Line feels that Staff may dominate them with their ideas on paper.
6. Line often resists the demand from Staff that they are superiors to Line.
7. Line refers to Staff as paper tigers and are only academic in their approach.

Grievances from staff persons

1. Staff claim that Line people are not recognising them.
2. Staff report that Line people are not using Staff in proper manner.
3. Staff demand that Line people do commit mistakes and approach Staff after the problem is turned out to be a crisis.
4. Staff criticise Line, for not receiving time-tested solutions.
5. Staff express that Line people do not implement the ideas advised.

Inter-organisational conflict

When conflict arises between two organisations operating under different ownerships, such conflict is called inter-organisational conflicts. Conflicts may arise between an individual and organisation also. Sometimes two different groups, belonging to different organisations may develop clashes. At times conflict may happen between a group and an organisation having different ideas in their minds.

Types of inter-organisational conflicts

1. Union-management conflict. Labour unions observe strikes, work sabotage, and absenteeism when they are in clash with management. Conflict is common for labour union and management. Since they want to win at the cost of others. Management tries to exploit workers and make profit, while unions want to get more benefits from management. Thus they are with two opposite ideologies operating under, hence conflict is natural.

2. Union and government conflict. Often unions of labour indulge in work sabotage, gheraos, strikes, work avoidance, absenteeism, etc., when they do not get benefits they are eligible for. At times Government agents have to solve the problem by mediation. Under such circumstances they both develop conflicts since their interests are divergent.

3. Inter-union conflict. Often unions working with different philosophies get in clash with each other in sharing the rights and privileges.

4. Inter-management conflict. Due to bitter competition prevailing in the industry managements representing different corporate units often get into clash with each other in matters such as patents, prices, capturing markets, securing licences etc.

5. Management and government conflict. Government supervises the industrial activities and takes disciplinary action against companies involved in anti-social activities or anti-national interests. Thus conflicts are common between company management and state.

Conditions. Following are the conditions to be fulfilled to claim to be a conflict:

1. Two parties know each other very well.
2. Two parties clearly identifies themselves with two interests they are serving.
3. A decision taken by one will affect the welfare of the other.
4. Two parties are divergent in their attitudes and perceptions.
5. Two parties are mutually exclusive and if one achieves the goal then other will definitely lose.

Purposes of inter-organisational conflicts. Conflicts are common and natural in this competitive world with limited resources and opportunities:

1. Organisations will lose very purpose for which they are existing in the absence of conflicts. Conflicts are necessary to develop spirit of competition and use the resources. Absence of conflicts will leave the industry into vacuum and weaken the ideals of organisation.
2. In the presence of conflicts people work with unity and will be alert.

3. Conflicts give new lease of a life and organisations work with new vigour and spirit.
4. Organisations will be dynamic in the wake of conflicts.
5. Conflicts infuses social control.
6. Conflicts make the organisational members to be aware of strategies.
7. Conflicts develop competition as such resources will be utilised productively.
8. People look at the things, rationally in the light of conflicts.

Conflicts are common in an organisation since organisation is a complex unit, where people fulfil their desires and aspirations. Some conflicts are desirable as they contribute for the development of the organisation. However, all conflicts are not so, as conflicts also do harm to the organisation. The conflicts which help in correcting the organisation are called constructive conflicts and others are destructive as they are not helpful in any manner. Managers should know the nature and effects of constructive and destructive conflicts.

Features and impact of constructive conflicts

1. Problems are brought to the notice and get clarified.
2. Develop group thinking.
3. Promote creativity.
4. Eliminate organisational lethargy.
5. Enable to think and act productively and constructively.
6. Offer a system of checks and balances within an organisation.
7. Stimulate individual efforts.
8. Build team spirit.
9. Strengthen the organisation.
10. Channel the efforts of organisation in right direction.

Features and impact of destructive conflicts

1. Conflicts replace co-operation by in-fighting.
2. Create stress or strain.
3. Kill group cohesiveness.
4. People will become shortsighted.

5. People fail to subordinate individual goals.
6. Morale of the employees is lowered.
7. Group cohesiveness and team spirit is destroyed.
8. People lose confidence in management.
9. Management loses credibility.
10. People rather play.
11. People lack initiative.

Structure. It means organisation structure which includes size, centralisation of authority, decentralisation, leadership, communication, reward systems, degree of dependence between groups, specialisation, etc. These variables influence organisational effectiveness and cause conflicts. Management should bring necessary changes in appropriate aspects of organisation structure to keep the organisational conflicts at optimum level.

1. Optimisation of inter-dependency between groups. In organisation, departments and groups are common. Conflict arises when dependency between groups is not balanced. The dependency should not be too much. And also the groups should not be losely linked. Management should reduce if over dependency is there and tighten where groups are losely attached. However the dependency cannot be altogether avoided. The management should adopt continuous surveillance to keep the parties at optimum distance depending upon the situation. Management has to pool the activities whenever necessary and separate physically depending upon the situation and conflict strength. The organisation be restructured to minimise conflicts depending upon the nature of conflict.

2. Distribution of resources. Resources or facilities should be rationally allocated keeping the need and necessity in the organisation. Since conflicts often arise when groups have to share the limited resources. Rich companies arrange separate facilities departmentwise so that conflicts do not occur. When resources are not enough management should educate or give orientation to divisions for optimum use of facilities.

3. Rotation of jobs. Conflicts often come when people act in rigid manner without flexibility. At times conflicts happen when supervisor is not properly understood by the members of the division. When understanding fails between individuals or groups conflicts happen. Here management should adopt job rotation by which all people realise the reasons and lapses existing in the system. However, job rotation has got its disadvantages. And it is not the sole and unique measure to minimise the conflict. Management should use this method wherever appropriate and suitable.

4. Appointment of integrators. Departments and divisions fight for more and better facilities, when resources are limited. Such conflicts can be minimised by the appointment of integrators who integrates and convinces the working groups in matters of space, time span, goal subordination, values, etc. The integrator should be seen as impartial and judicious in his approach.

5. Superior's interference. When two groups or individuals are in conflict superior's interference at appropriate time will solve the problem. Superior, who is common authority for both the groups should interfere and issue necessary orders.

6. Domination. The simple solution to solve the problem of conflict is to force the troublemakers to give up the fight. The superiors should fire the troublemakers, so that they shall keep quiet without creating conflicts further. At times the supervisors tell the fellows to maintain calm composure and get on to the job.

7. Separation. Conflicting groups are to be separated physically so that problems do not re-occur. Thus if groups are not allowed to interact with each other the conflicts get subsided.

8. Appeal. The warring groups or parties should bring the matters to the notice of higher authorities who would resolve by offering a solution acceptable to the groups.

9. Subordinate goals. The superiors should educate the groups to dilute their conflicts and orient themselves towards the common and organisational goals. They should further caution the groups not to develop further distance by disputing with each other. They should also suggest the groups to give up fighting attitude as they would not accomplish common goals if the groups work separately. Thus it is believed that when the disagreeing parties are brought to work together and subordinate their individual or group goals to common goals harmony will be easy.

10. Identify common enemy. Sherief illustrates that groups in conflict with each other temporarily resolve their differences to combat a common enemy. A common enemy unifies the divorcing groups. *Example*: Threat of Hitler combined Russia and Western powers temporarily.

Methods of resolving organisational conflicts

Conflict is managed by various methods, yet resolution is made by the following five methods as shown in the diagram:

(1) Competition, (2) Avoidance, (3) Accommodating, (4) Compromising, (5) Problem-solving.

The resolution and its success depends upon situations and parties in conflict. The five methods are five different combinations of cooperatives and assertiveness of groups to rivals.

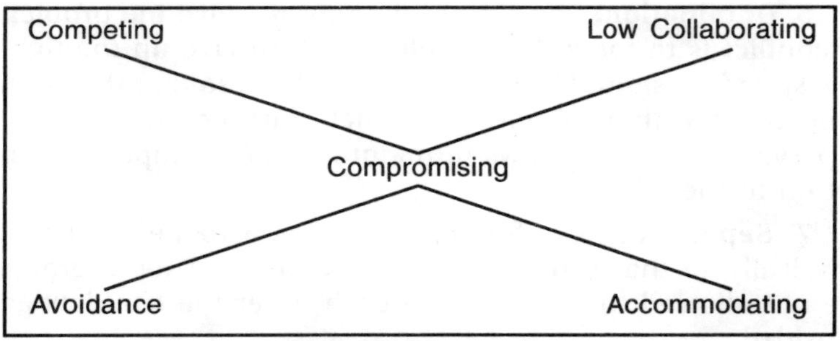

Degree of Cooperation

Dimensions of conflict handling approaches

Source: Stephen P. Robbins, *Organisational Behaviour*, Prentice Hall of India Pvt. Ltd., New Delhi. 7th Print, p. 452.

1. Competition. The group is highly assertive and less cooperative in this method of resolution. The group or individual will argue for his goal achievement. The party also uses weapons at times. Party argues for his goal achievement. The party goes in confrontation to win his chances as he is less corroborative. This type of confrontation occurs only when the two parties are rigid in their stand.

2. Avoidance. This method refers to the withdrawal from the conflict by which the confrontation can be avoided. When one party withdraws the other party takes the chance of winning. Thus one party goes on withdrawal indifference, evasion, apathy, fight relying on fate etc. Conflict may be resolved by mutually withdrawing from the field. Sometimes the conflict or incomparability is concealed, so that conflict does not arise and both parties will have equal position. However, conflict cannot be completely eliminated.

3. Accommodating. Parties will be highly co-operating and less assertive and sometimes parties do sacrifice for others. The parties emphasise on common interests and de-emphasise on differences. Self-concern is minimum with either of the group. Both parties try to go along with other without picking up conflict. They do not give chance to rise conflicts since they are afraid to clash in with others. This approach or method would help to find solution in short run but not in the long run.

4. Compromise. Both *parties* sacrifice and try to share the benefit. Here, groups work on give and take basis and go on negotiations. The important pre-requisite is that parties should be equal in strength. If one party is strong automatically the other party will have to yield to the pressure and dictation.

5. Collaborating. It proposes complete rethinking about the conflict situation. Groups with open mind share information, listen to others and discuss with objective look. Parties debate the issue considering different alternatives without personal feelings and try to solve the problem in collaboration. The parties will have objective solely in mind and they do not bother who is right or who is wrong. They do not like to know who will win or who will lose. Both parties play constructive role.

These approaches of conflict management state that no method is suitable and correct. Method of solving or resolving the conflict depends upon parties, situation, values, attitudes, culture, environment etc.

QUESTIONS FOR DISCUSSION

1. Define conflict and discuss various views on conflict.
2. What is the difference between functional and dysfunctional conflict? What determines functionality?

3. What are the goal conflicts at individual level? How to overcome these conflicts?
4. What is meant by role conflict? Discuss the causes and methods to avoid it.
5. What is interpersonal conflict? Discuss the reasons for interpersonal conflicts in modern organisations.
6. How does conflict arise at top level? What are the reasons and consequences and how to prevent such conflicts?
7. Explain the reasons for intra-organisational conflicts.
8. Examine Inter-organisational conflict. Mention types of such conflicts. Elaborate the conditions and purposes of such conflicts.
9. What is structural approach of conflict management? Is it possible to overcome conflict situation through this approach?
10. Critically examine the different methods of resolving organisational conflicts.

3

LEADERSHIP

"Leadership triggers a person's will-to-do and transforms lukewarm desires for achievements into burning passions for successful accomplishments."

"Leadership is the process of influencing people towards the accomplishment of goals."

"Leadership is interpersonal influence exercised in a situation and directed through communication process towards the attainment of a specified goal or goals."

The above definitions reveal the following ingredients:

1. Leadership is a personal quality.
2. Leader tries to influence people behaviour to fulfil predetermined goals.
3. Leader influences people to behave in a particular way.
4. Common goal establishes the relationship between leader and followers.
5. Leadership is a continuous process of influencing.
6. Situation variables influence the effectiveness of leadership.

Importance of leadership. Organisations are directed by managers. Managers should have leadership qualities to direct employees and other elements of organisation. Men by nature act selfish and try to give priority to their personal goals leaving the organisational goals to chance. Here manager by his leadership ability integrates the two sets of goals and make the human factor as desired and planned. Drucker opined that leaders are different. The utility of leadership can be discussed as follows:

Motivating employees. Employees by nature need motivation without which they will not perform duties as desired by the management. Here leader has to create congenial environment where the employees would like releasing their energies and work hard.

Creating confidence. Leader has to create confidence in the minds of followers that organisation will achieve goals and in turn their personal individual goals. Without such confidence people do not commit and use their potentialities.

Morale. Leadership builds morale of people who work for the organisation. Morale refers to the feelings of employees to their leader organisation and fellow employees. People with high morale will work efficiently and ensure productivity and stability.

Inspires employees. A leader creates strong urge in the minds of employees for higher performance. According to Terry, leadership triggers a person's will-to-do. He has to inspire his employees by setting himself as a model and example.

Secures co-operation. According C.I. Bernard co-operation is voluntary. Leader creates an environment where people readily cooperate to work in team spirit. He inculcates the spirit of collectivism among the employees. He further provides character to the group and paves the way for integrated effort at various levels of organisation.

Provides good working climate. Leader initiates necessary changes and brings unity among people by his judicious use of power and time. He utilises the resources in optimum manner and see benefits go equitably to all the employees depending upon their worth. He invites participation of people in solving problems rather than taking independent decisions. The leader creates a sound climate without jeopardy to any section of his followers.

Cohesive force. Leader acts as a cohesive force and keeps the group intact by his vision and disciplinary powers. He energises human action and transforms choose into order. He changes half-hearted behaviour into whole-hearted endeavours by going into the insights of people.

Functions of leaders. Leaders discharge various functions in the process of integration of organisational goals and group or individual goals.

Develops teamwork. For efficient organisation three elements are necessarily to be scanned: environment, group goals, and individual interests. Leader has to identify strength and weakness of organisation and try to integrate the three elements. He has to encourage inquisitive employees and prohibit insidious elements and create hygienic environment.

Represents follower's grievances. He is a linking pin between employees and management. The strength of the organisation depends upon how strongly he is linking the groups and organisation individuals and group. Leader takes personal risk, ensures better service, working condition, solve the problems of organisation and in turn ensure smooth functioning.

Counsels the employees. Leader should act as a friend, philosopher to his followers/employees by counselling them from time to time on their organisational problems which they encounter. He should go across the barriers and ensure effective performance. The employees are put to emotions and tensions while discharging their duties along with others in organisation.

Use powers judiciously. By his judicious use of powers he balances the groups and pressures they create to imbalance the organisation. Leader enjoys powers both formal by virtue of position and informal by way of personal contacts with people around him. He uses powers, to compel others sometimes and reward legitimately. Power acts as cement to develop relationship or bondage with people who work for his organisation. Leader cannot be effective if he does not know how to use his powers appropriately.

Strives for effectiveness. Leader takes decisions on several occasions of crucial nature. He should take right 'decision' at right 'time' to keep the effectiveness intact. He should reward and punish people. He should balance the relationship by appropriately fixing responsibilities and sharing authority. By and large he should get along with people to reach the predetermined goals.

• Is Leader Born!

In general it is felt that leaders possess qualities by birth and not developed. A leader by birth or by experience gains qualities that are uncommon in many. Terry gives the following leadership qualities.

1. Energy. He is energetic both mentally and physically to carry out his duties successfully.

2. Emotional stability. It enables a leader to act with self-confidence, avoid danger and deal with his follower subordinates with an understanding.

3. Knowledge of human relations. He should have requisite knowledge of behaviour of people of various backgrounds in different situations.

4. Empathy. It enables him to look at things objectively.

5. Objectivity. He should not get emotionally invòlved and not loose sight of organisational and national objectives.

6. Personal motivation. He should have enough enthusiasm to get the job done.

7. Communication skill. A leader should be able to communicate clearly that other should not have any ambiguity.

8. Social skill. He should understand people and be approachable. He should be friendly with others.

9. Technical competence. He should have complete knowledge of all the operations under his guidance and know the consequences of things either way.

Field Marshal Viscount Slim gives the following six basic essentials primarily for Military leadership, namely:

(1) Courage,

(2) Will power,

(3) Judgment,

(4) Flexibility,

(5) Knowledge, and

(6) Integrity.

Some more qualities the leader should possess are as follows:

Emotional balance. Leader should not lose control over himself especially in times of crisis. He should have tolerance capacity and free from bias. He should be logical in actions and refrain from emotions such as impatience, anger or contempt for any of his followers.

Inner drive. The leader should set goals for himself and should have intense urge to accomplish them. He need not be complemented or praised or rewarded to stay motivated.

For that matter he should be self-motivated and take the matters as a challenge.

Leadership styles

The way leader influences groups in a particular situation are called leadership style. It depends upon three important elements such as leader, follower and situation. Different leaders act differently in different times or situations. The existence of various styles suggests that there cannot be single best style which is suitable.

Positive leadership. The leader wishes to create an environment where the followers would get their needs satisfied. Leader identifies the needs and wants of subordinates and fulfils them, so that the followers can work happily in the organisation. This is how a leader will have positive view towards the subordinates, so that they can release their energies and work efficiently. Leader further opines that unless individual needs are satisfied organisational goals cannot be accomplished.

Negative leadership. In this approach, leader uses fear and force to influence followers. Leader relies mainly on controlling and use of formal authority where, he thinks it is possible to accomplish organisational goals.

Basic leadership styles

Feudal. Leader considers the subordinates as necessary part of an enterprise and compensates them for performing tasks.

Paternal. The leader sees his relationship with employees as parent and son and takes care of the welfare of people.

Dictatorial. Leader gives order and tries to follow up rigidly for completing the organisational goals.

Contributory. The leader tries to seek participation of people in decision-making thereby gives satisfaction to them having contributed their views.

Developmental. The leader tries to offer development to subordinates by using their potentialities. There are various ways in which leadership style can be classified.

These types have been divided into five abroad divisions arbitrarily:

1. Autocratic or Authoritarian.
2. Democratic or Participation.
3. Laissez-faire or Free-rein.
4. Paternalistic.

1. Autocratic or Authoritarian leadership. Here manager centralises decision-making power. He designs the work situation and employees to do what is told to them. Followers are afraid and feel insecure of superior. Leader makes subordinates to act as he directs. He uses fears, threats and insists on getting his own way.

Edwin B. Flippo divided the autocratic into three types, namely: (a) Hard-boiled, (b) Benevolent and (c) Manipulative.

(a) Hard-boiled. Leader uses negative approach heavily and influences through order, which results in employees becoming resentful.

(b) Benevolent. Though decision-making power is kept in his hands, the leader uses positive approach by praising followers to receive personal acceptance of his own decisions.

(c) Manipulative. Manager takes decision by himself and makes the subordinates to feel that they are really participating in decision-making.

Autocratic people (leaders) presume that people are generally lazy, will avoid work and shrink responsibility. It stresses that people work basically for money. Basing on this assumption leader exercises tight control over subordinates who are driven by fear than through job satisfaction. Over use of authority results in strikes. Further it causes frustration among people who work just to escape punishment.

Advantages

1. There are many subordinates who work under strict supervision only, for them it is good.
2. It provides strong motivation and reward a manager exercising this style.
3. It permits quick decisions.
4. Incompetent subordinates work well.

Disadvantages

1. People dislike if negative approach is in excess.
2. Employees do not subordinate their goals to organisational goals.
3. Employees lack motivation and keep low morale.

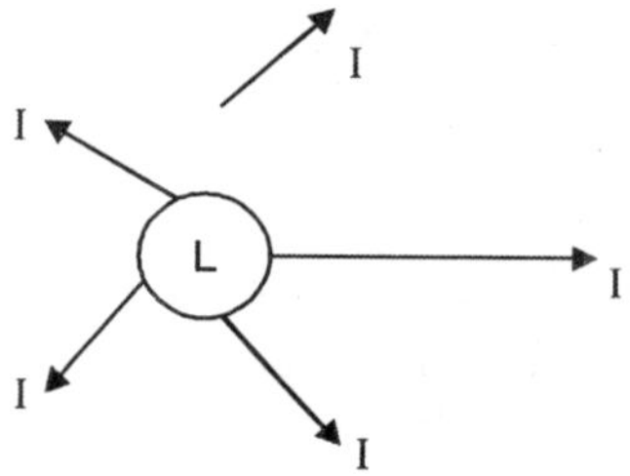

2. Democratic leadership. Leader persuades and encourages participation of people in decision-making. Duglas McGregor labelled this style under Y theory that subordinates involve in decision-making and assume responsibility. Instead of taking his own decision leader emphasises participation of followers in decision-making. Leader who wishes to seek the welfare of subordinates, which in turn enables him to achieve organisational goals. The subordinates can better utilise their energies and potentialities for the sake of organisations.

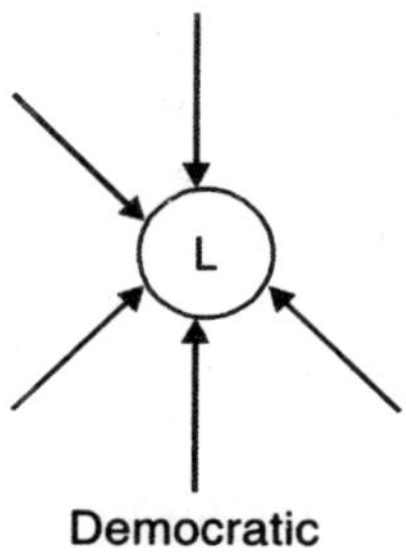

Democratic

Benefits

1. Followers are motivated to work when their suggestions are going into the decision-making.
2. Employees will work productivity since they implement decision whole-heartedly.

3. The follower strengthens the hands of superior.
4. It enhances the morale of employees to new heights and upholds the attitudes of employees.
5. It provides organisational stability.

Problems

1. Subordinates may view superior as incompetent to handle the situation independently.
2. There is some danger of misinterpretation of decision sharing.
3. Participative decision-making is time consuming.
4. For some leaders participative leadership means passing the decision to the subordinates.

Participative style is appreciated when:

1. Leader wants the subordinates to develop decision-making abilities.
2. Leader has so much to hear people and problem.

3. Laissez-faire or free-rein leadership style. In this style leader does not exercise control over people and gives no direction. Leader tries to pass the responsibility on to the subordinates. The leader prefers to lead his group with loose rein allowing his subordinates a great deal of freedom. Here, leader completely delegates powers to subordinates who have to plan, motive and control themselves otherwise they will be held responsible for their own actions. The leader relinquishes powers to the followers.

Free-rein style would be desirable under the following conditions where:

- the organisational goals have been communicated well and are acceptable to the subordinates.
- the leader is interested in delegating powers fully.
- the subordinates are well trained.
- the followers are knowledgeable and ready to assume responsibilities.

4. Paternalistic leadership. Leader adopts parental attitude as the right one for the relationship between himself and followers. He wishes to keep them happy as family members.

He emphasises good working conditions with a desire to be good with them. Leader's philosophy is that 'happy employees work harder'.

Trait approach to leadership

Early contributors have concluded that leadership is largely a matter of personality and a function of specific traits. Supporters of this theory suggest that leader possess specific qualities and key traits different from others. These traits do not change in a leader. This theory attempts to suggest that successful leader possesses peculiar traits, many organisations, to select leaders, will look for traits which help to predict their failure or success. Traits help organisations to select suitable personalities in appropriate roles.

According to 'Ghiselli', following are the generally accepted list of traits which contributed to a leader:

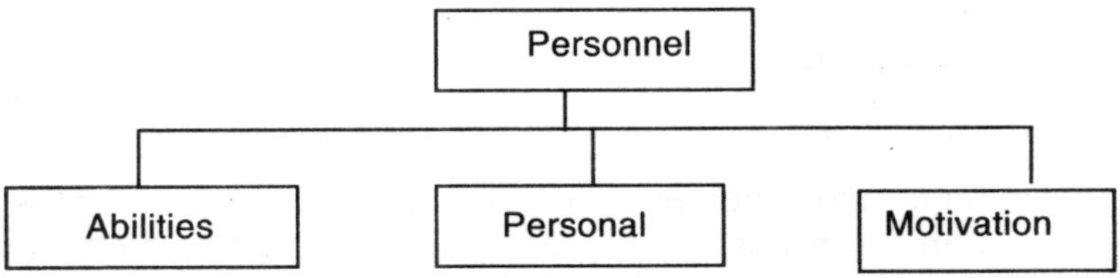

Abilities	Personal	Motivation
- Supervisory ability	- Self-assurance	- Need for occupational achievement
- Intelligency	- Decisiveness	- Self-actualisation
- Initiative	- Faminity	- Power over others
	- Maturity	- High financial reward
	- Working class affinity	- Job security

'Keith Davis' has advised the following four traits possessed by most of the leaders.

(1) Intelligence,

(2) Social Maturity,

(3) Achievement Drive,

(4) Human relations attitude.

Criticism

1. Among many leaders Traits are not consistent.
2. There is no universal list of traits for successful leaders.

3. Leaders cannot be seen differently from the followers.
4. Traits need not be there in leaders.
5. Extremes in personality are not usually associated with leadership.
6. It is difficult to define Traits.
7. Traits cannot be measured quantitatively but can only be inferred from the behaviour.
8. It is not clear how much a leader should score on a given trait to become effective.
9. Effective leadership is not a function of traits alone.
10. It is ridiculous to assume that traits are uniformly distributed at all managerial levels.

Managerial Skills Mix

	Human	Technical	Administrative
Top Management			
Middle Management			
Lower Management			

A leader normally possesses 3 different skills such as Human, Technical and Administrative. These skills are not uniform in all executives at all levels. The proportions vary, if one moves from lower level to higher level.

Trait is defined as an enduring quality of an individual. According to "Stog Dill", the following traits make people as leaders:

1. Physical
2. Intelligence
3. Self-confidence
4. Sociability
5. Will Power
6. Dominance
7. Urge to achieve

According to Ghiselli the leader should possess:

1. Supervisory ability
2. Achievements motivation
3. Self-actualising

4. Intelligence
5. Self-assurance
6. Decisiveness

Qualities are of two kinds: one innate and second 'acquirable'. Innate qualities are natural and possessed by birth. As such leader is said to be born and not made. Acquirable qualities are those which can be acquired by training or through experience. As child one learns many behavioural patterns through socialisation. After some time by training they can be developed.

Following are some of the major innate and acquirable qualities of a leader:

1. **Intelligence.** A leader should be intelligent and capable to decide and judge the matters. It is a natural quality, however it can be enhanced through various training methods.

2. **Emotional stability.** A leader should have emotional stability and refrain from anger and bias. He should have self-confidence and meet situations successfully.

3. **Human relations.** Leader should know how to maintain sound human relations to get voluntary cooperation from people and extract work from them.

4. **Empathy.** He should be able to see from the viewpoint of others and objectively. Leader should respect the feelings of others, their rights, beliefs and values.

5. **Objectivity.** Without prejudice, a leader should do biasing on facts and information. He should not get involved emotionally in any decision that affects the prosperity of people and organisations.

6. **Motivating skills.** Leader should be able to motivate others and enable them to achieve higher performance. He should stimulate the inner drives of people and activate them.

7. **Technical skills.** Technical competence is most essential factor that a leader should possess to think and supervise the operations at his disposal.

8. **Communicative skills.** A leader should be able to communicate with followers and others in order to convince, persuade, and stimulate them. It is a great skill necessary for his success.

9. Social skills. A leader should be accessible and sociable with people. He should conduct himself very well so that no one can work with others and take cooperation from them. It is not necessary that a leader should possess all these qualities, in high proportion. The said qualities are only suggestive but not comprehensive. Possession of these qualities help managers to become successful.

Critical analysis

1. All these qualities need not be present in all the leaders.
2. Leaders may have some qualities in different proportions.
3. Measuring is not possible, but traits can be felt by the way the matters are handled by the leaders.

Trait theory is simple and fails to produce clear-cut results. Trait is one of the factors of the environment to which the leader is exposed to. Generalisation cannot be drawn about the traits in a leader as leader and non-leaders cannot be discriminated on the basis, of just traits.

MANAGERIAL GRID AND LEADERSHIP STYLES

An important approach to leadership style developed by *Blake and Mouton* in Managerial Grid. They suggested that leader behaves in two ways—one production oriented and secondly people oriented in varying degrees. Production orientation means attitudes of supervisors towards work efficiency, standards and targets fixation, quality decisions, creativity and research aspects etc. people orientation means—attitudes of supervisors towards human relations which include—personal commitment, maintaining higher order level needs of workers, trusting people, satisfying personal relations.

1,1 Exertion of minimum effort to get required work done is appropriate to sustain organisation membership.

1,9 Thoughtful attention to needs of people leads to a friendly and comfortable atmosphere and work tempo.

9,1 Efficiency results from arranging work in such a way that human elements have little effect.

9,9 Work accomplished is from committed people with inter-dependency through a common stake in organisation purpose and with trust and respect.

5,5 It implies balancing the needs to get work with maintaining morale.

Each style implies relative concern for people and production. Most acceptable position is 9.9 maximum concern for production and maximum concern for people. It is often referred to as 'super leader style' and organisations have been using training programmes to develop 9.9 leadership.

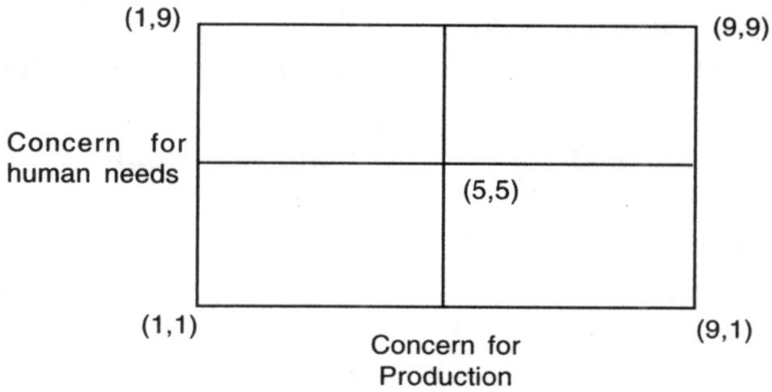

Managerial Grid

Evaluation. Grid approach is attractive and instructive. It serves as a useful framework for the leadership training. Though the programme is popular among practitioners, it is highly controversial among theorists because it lacks empirical evidence.

PATH GOAL THEORY

The theory is an important landmark in the development of 'leadership'. Path goal theory predicts leadership effectiveness in different situations. Leaders are effective because leader smoothens the path to reach goals. The model proposes that individuals are satisfied with their jobs it leads to desirable outcomes. The theory focuses on how leader influences employees, perceptions of valence, instrumentality and expectancy. This theory takes into consideration situational variables and characteristics of subordinates.

Propositions

1. Leader is acceptable to followers when they see him as source of satisfaction.
2. Leader's behaviour is motivational, if he satisfies the needs of subordinates and complements the environment

of workers by providing the guidance, clarity direction and rewards necessarily for effective performance.

Leader should

1. Clear paths
2. Clarify goals
3. Provide support
4. Provide rewards
5. Analyse the situation.

According to Path Goal theory, Leader should perform the following functions.

1. Supportive. Leader should be friendly and approachable to the subordinates.

2. Directive. Leader plans, organises and directs people. He defines standards of performance and let subordinates know as to what is expected of them.

3. Participative. Leader solicits the views of subordinates and give them room in decision-making.

4. Achievement oriented. Leader sets challenging goals and expects the subordinates to perform them better.

LEADER Vs. MANAGER

Leader and Manager are the two different terms used interchangeably. Leadership normally exists in unorganised fields or activities, while Managers do exist in organised institutions. A Manager should possess leadership qualities. But Leader need not be a Manager. A Manager has to lead subordinates. The following table summarises the said points.

LEADER	MANAGER
(i) Exist in unorganised and organised groups.	(i) Exists only in organised groups.
(ii) No organisation structure is necessary.	(ii) Requires organisation structure.
(iii) Influence people to strive for group goals.	(iii) He has to plan, organise, direct people to achieve group goals.
(iv) Get the authority by virtue of their skills, abilities and situational demands.	(iv) Exercise formal authority.

1. Leaders have followers.
2. Leaders have emotional appeal.
3. Leaders meet the needs of followers.

Thus leaders have different orientation and bent of mind towards their followers.

BEHAVIOURAL APPROACH Vs. TRAITS APPROACH

Trait theory is based on great men theory. Great men theory, holds that historical events are the creation of outstanding personalities. 'Thomas Carlyle' stated that 'history is bibliography of great men'. Jesus, Alexander, Caesar, Churchill, Gandhi, Nehru, Kennedy etc., come under this category. Now Trait theory presumes that a leader possesses uncommon qualities by birth or experience for successful leadership. Leaders differ from followers in terms of traits such as fairness, achievement drive, vision, creativity, technical competence.

Critical appraisal. Mere possession of qualities do not ensure success and many leaders did not become good managers. It is difficult to define traits. It is often difficult to measure traits also. Though leader possess traits, to what extent he should score on a given 'trait' to become effective. Mere possession of traits does not ensure success because situational factors influence leaders' traits. Trait theory forgets followers' importance and situational factors. Since many factors affect leadership, trait alone would not contribute to effectiveness. Situational factors determine the success over and above personal qualities. Trait theory does not give prominence to followers and situations. Success depends upon how and what traits are attempted in which situation and when and *vice versa* and there is no universal list of leadership qualities that are approved.

Behavioural approach. Success of a leader does not go with mere presence of skills in a leader. But it depends upon how they are used in a given situation. As such it is concluded that ultimately 'behaviour' of leader decides the success but not simple existence of traits in a leader.

Ohio state studies. Ohio State University studies identified two models of behaviour of leader. First model leader is employee oriented and establishes mutual respect and two-way communication. He is also friendly with followers, approachable and listening to employees. Secondly leader is structure (task) oriented and defines the work of subordinates and expects the goals of organisation to be fulfilled. The studies found that in first case absenteeism and grievances are many. In second model the performance was poor. Finally both models are clubbed and leader used both the models in his approach which resulted in high performance and more job satisfaction.

Employee orientation		Structure oriented: Low	Structure oriented: High
	High	High consideration for employee and low consideration for structure.	High consideration for employee and high consideration for structure.
	Low	Low consideration for structure and low consideration for employee.	Low consideration for employee and high consideration for structure.

Low ← Structure oriented → High

Michigan studies. Michigan University has studied behaviour of high performing and low performing groups. They too formed two distinctive styles of leadership similar to Ohio-studies *i.e.*, job centred and employee-centred. Here job centred leaders emphasised the technical aspect of the job, work standards, etc., on the other hand employee centred leaders were witnessed showing concern for their well-being, participation in goal setting etc. The conclusions strongly favoured the leaders of employee oriented in their behaviour since their performance is far better than the other leaders (job centred).

The behavioural studies have accepted behaviour of leader as the key for success. It is the behaviour that makes difference in success not traits. Here the Manager behaves in suitable manner taking followers, capabilities and situational factors into consideration.

Employee Centred Leader	Production Centred Leader
- Treats subordinates as human beings. - Seeks the welfare of employees. - Involves the employees in goal setting.	- Emphasises work standards. - Closely watches at the job. - Employee is seen as part of a machine in the production process.

LIKERT'S MANAGEMENT SYSTEM

To understand leader behaviour Rensis Likert, University of Michigan USA has developed certain concepts and approaches. He gave a continuum of 4 systems of Management taking the leader behaviour with three different variables. He referred to four leadership styles such as Exploitative autocratic (System-1), Benevolent autocratic (System-2), Participative (System-3), Democratic (System-4) the partial adaptation of Likert's continuum is shown here. Likert has shown that high performers are marked by System-4 (democratic). He attributes the success to the leadership behaviour maintained by adopting supportive relationship with subordinates and giving them complete chance of participation. In this, Likert states that all subordinates should feel sense of personal worth and importance. He has taken variables which includes motivation, communication, interaction, decision-making process, goal setting and control process.

- **Tridimensional Grid**

"William J. Reddin" is the father of the three dimensional theory of leadership. He is the first person to introduce effectiveness as another dimension. Thus he uses task orientation, relationship orientation and effectiveness. A leader is he who uses a 'style' suitable to the situation is called effective leader. Taking Robert Blake and Mouton's managerial grid as a useful flat form, Reddin added effectiveness as third dimension.

Task orientation is defined as *'efforts to direct people for achievement of goals'* when Manager plans, organises and controls subordinates. Relationship orientation is defined as maintaining cordial relationships with subordinates, wherein Manager respects the suitable style appropriate to a given situation. Leader uses one of them or both. On this basis there are four leadership styles.

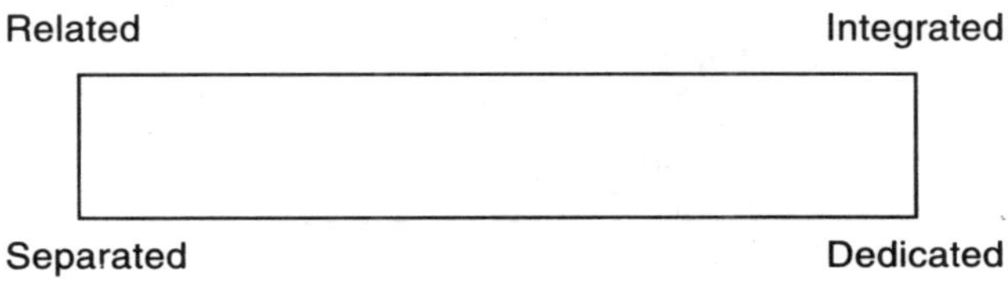

Separated. Manager corrects the deviations. He enforces Rules and policies.

Related. He likes involvement of others in decision-making and seeks voluntary cooperation.

Dedicated. Leader does not want to identify himself with people and integrated in production.

Integrated. Leader develops team work and involves people in the organisation with two-way communication.

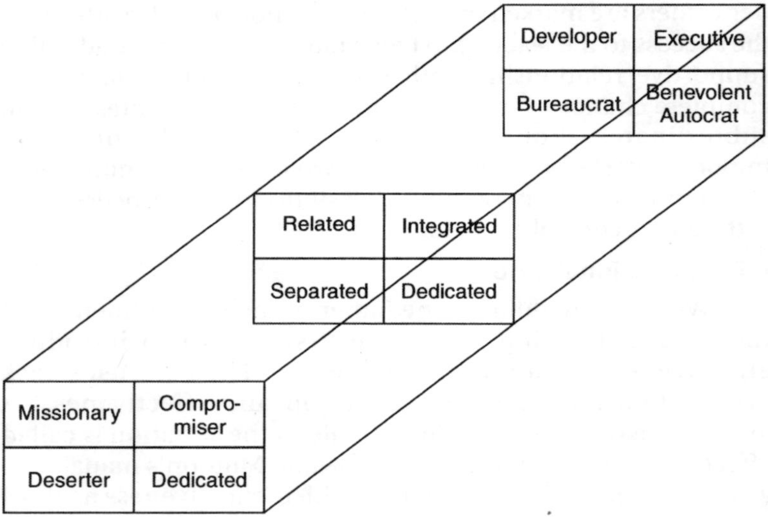

The basic four styles result into eight styles. These styles result from the eight possible combinations of task orientation, relationship orientation and effectiveness as shown in the above figure.

Basic Style	Less Effective Style	More Effective Style
Integrate	Compromiser	Executive
Dedicated	Autocrat	Benevolent Autocrat
Related	Missionary	Developer
Separated	Deserter	Bureaucrat

Ineffective styles

1. Deserter. Leader works to rule and believes in minimum output with low commitment and less involvement. He has both low task orientation and low people orientation. He is completely alienated from organisational life.

2. Missionary. Leader wants to keep the subordinates happy. He wants to maintain harmony with superiors. He avoids conflicts and does not take initiatives.

3. Autocrat. Leader is concerned with task. He takes unilateral decisions and show no concern to subordinates. He adopts negative approach.

4. Compromise. He uses high task and relationship orientation. He is poor decision-maker and avoids decisions. He is weak and yields to various pressures and allows others to influence him too much.

Effective styles

1. Bureaucrat. The leader shows minimum concern for both people and work. He wants to control the situation by rules and often disliked by subordinates. He produces few ideas and less initiative in his approach.

2. Developer. Leader gives maximum importance for people and minimum concern for work. He trusts people. He allows subordinates to express their feelings and respects their sentiments.

3. Benevolent autocrat. He pays more attention to work and less attention to workers. He knows what to be done without causing resentment. He follows feudalistic approach in managing people and adopts positive economic motivation to get things done by the followers or subordinates.

4. Executive. He gives maximum importance to both people and work. He sets high standards and utilises team work. He integrates task and team to motivate people. Reddin maintains that all the styles have good and bad elements and it depends upon the situation as to which style is appropriate and best. He further states that basic styles become effective if used in appropriate situation and *vice versa*.

Reddin model is accepted on two basic points:

1. He integrated behaviour with situation.

2. He introduced third dimension to the model developed by Blake and Mouton who said task and people are the two elements to be oriented.

Fielder's contingency model of leadership effectiveness

Both Trait and Behavioural approaches fail to provide comprehensive theory of leadership. These theories have attempted in simplifying the leadership which is multi-dimensional. So far no attempt is made for establishing relationship between leadership and performance indicators such as production, efficiency satisfaction etc. This Fielder's contingency theory adopts one best-way style *i.e.* scanning the situation before optimum leadership style can be selected. Situational theory is challenging, highly fascinating. Leaders should be flexible and adapt to the situational changes in attitudes, perceptions, power, tasks of subordinates. Fielder is the first scholar who bases his leadership study on situational variables. His model rectifies the deficiencies in Trait and behavioural studies. Fielder developed a contingency model assuming that effectiveness depends upon his ability to act in changing situations.

Situational factors. Fielder's model is called 'contingency' model because the leaders' effectiveness depends upon situational variables. They are (1) leader-member relation, (2) task structure, (3) leader's position power.

Leader-member relation. It refers to the cordial relationship and mutual trust both leader and subordinates share. It indicates the leader's ability to influence them. If the followers have trust in his leader, the leader can depend upon task or structure. The situation is less favourable if followers do not have confidence in leader.

Structure. Here job requirements are clearly defined. Here individual goals and groups are clearly defined and interlinked.

Position. Leader secures powers by virtue of his position in an organisation to reward his followers. He enjoys package of powers, rights and authority. He exercises his authority to ensure work done by the subordinates.

Favourableness of situation. Fielder has developed various situations—eight possible combinations varying from highly favourable to highly unfavourable situations. A favourable situation is when the leader-member relationships are good, the task is clearly defined and leader has complete power to influence his subordinates. The other extreme situation is where the said factors are completely opposite in their nature.

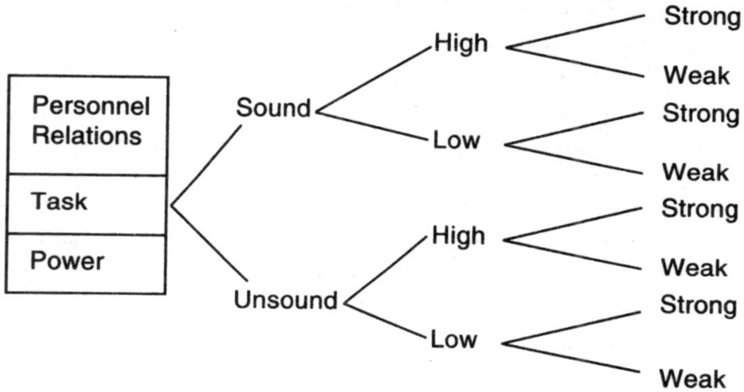

Fielder has developed an instrument known as LPC (least preferred co-workers) questionnaire to measure his style whether task oriented or relation oriented.

Fielder's study covered 1200 groups where he compared task Vs. relation oriented styles. The manager is asked to describe his co-worker. The high LPC leaders described their co-workers positively and favourably and low LPC leaders described their co-workers negatively and unfavourably. Thus high LPC leader style is termed as relationship oriented leaders and low LPC leader style is described as task oriented leader. Fielder concluded that task oriented leader, tends to perform better in situations favourable to them and relationship oriented leader performs better in moderately favourable situations.

Critical analysis. We cannot label a Manager as efficient or poor. A Manager who performs well in a situation may not in other situations. The effectiveness depends upon not on style but on situational variables. Fielder suggests that it is desirable to modify and make the situation more favourable than modifying a leader.

Hersey-Blanchard's Theory of Maturity

The theory is focused on the followers. Successful leadership is achieved by selecting the leadership style which is a contingent theory that focuses on the level of the follower's maturity. Theory identifies two leadership dimensions—task behaviour and relation behaviour. The researchers believed that leadership style should change with employees maturity. According to them effectiveness of leadership depends upon the actions of the followers who accept or reject the leader. This dimension is overlooked in many leadership theories. Maturity refers to the ability and willingness of people to take responsibility. It has two components *viz.* job maturity and psychological maturity. Individuals, who are high in job maturity have required knowledge, ability and experience to perform their jobs without direction from others. Psychological maturity refers to the motivation to do something. Individuals high in psychological maturity do not need external encouragement. Blanchard and Hersey has explained four leadership styles.

1. Telling—(high task—low relationship)
2. Selling—(high task—high relationship)
3. Participating and (low task—high relationship)
4. Delegating (low task—low relationship)

1. Telling (high task—low relationship). Leader emphasises directive behaviour. He defines the roles and tells people what, how, when and where to do various tasks.

2. Selling (high task—high relationship). Leader provides both directive behaviour and supportive behaviour.

3. Participating (low task—high relationship). Leader and follower share in decision-making with the main role of the leader being facilitated and communicating.

4. Delegating (low task—low relationship). The leader provides little direction or support.

The theory devides employees maturity into four stages:

Stage 1: People are neither capable nor willing to take responsibility to do something.

Stage 2: People are unable but willing to do the necessary job tasks.

Stage 3: People are able but unwilling to do what the leader wants.

Stage 4: People are both able and willing to do what is asked.

The following figure shows that integrated situations and leadership styles. Leader withdraws his control over activities and followers as they raise in maturity. Leader also withdraws his relationship when the maturity level of employees at stage 1. Follower needs clear and specific directions hence high task and low relationship is advised. At second stage, people are unable and willing to do the necessary job tasks hence high task—high relationship style is needed. High task behaviour compensates for the followers' lack of ability and high relationship behaviour tries to get the followers psychologically to get into leader's desires. Stage 3 creates motivational problems

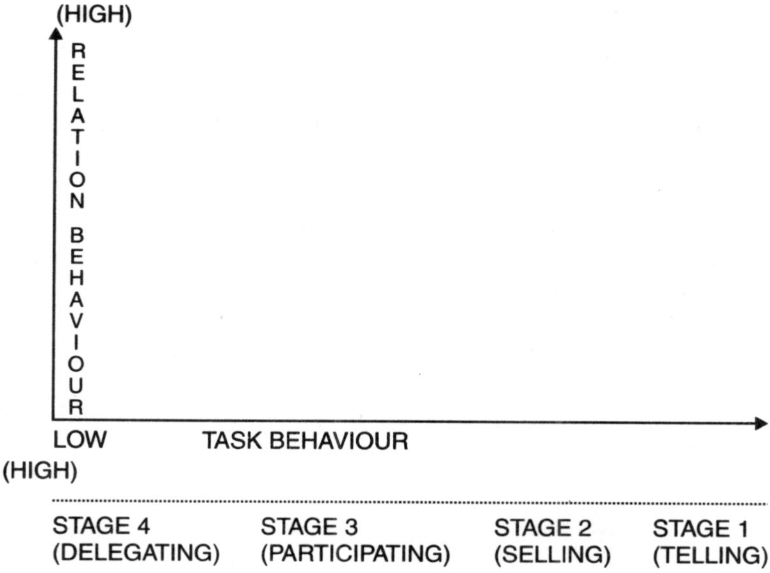

that are best solved by a supportive, non-directive and participate style. Finally at stage 4, the leader does not have to do much because followers are both willing and able to take responsibility.

The model is easy to understand when compared to others. It suggests several alternatives for leader behaviour that emphasises adaptive and flexible. The leaders also suggest that leaders can influence both employees and the work situation by building skills and confidence in subordinates.

QUESTIONS FOR DISCUSSION

1. Define leadership. And it is said that an individual contributes 60 per cent of his own and the balance 40 per cent is induced by leadership. Explain how this is achieved by a leader.
2. "A leader is made but not born". Explain.
3. Explain the characteristic features of various leadership styles.
4. Discuss the strengths and weaknesses in the trait approach to leadership.
5. Explain various leadership styles using managerial Grid.
6. Explain Path Goal Theory.
7. 'A Leader is not necessarily be a good manager'. Discuss.
8. How trait and behavioural approaches are different? Explain.
9. Explain Likert's Management system. How is it best and why?
10. What is Tri-dimensional Grid? Explain.
11. Critically examine Fielder's contingency model of leadership effectiveness.

4

MOTIVATION

Introduction

Motivation is the process of including persons to experience needs for certain desired behaviour so that organisation efficiency is achieved. '*Webster*' defines 'motivates' as to provide with a motive. Motive is that within an individual which incites him to action. It is an organic state of man that prompts him to an action.

Motivation Process. Performance can be described as a function of an individual ability (A), knowledge (K) and motivation (M) which may be depicted schematically as:

$P = M (A + K)$

Here ability and knowledge do not guarantee that the individual will work and perform duties. There is another factor motivation (M), which determines the effort expected of him. Motivation is the resultant of incentives and disincentives which play active role. This can be expressed as

$M = I \sim DI$

Thus performance is ultimately resultant of the above two equations.

$P = (1 - D1) (A + K)$

Thus a higher (A + K) would result in a faster change in performance with the same motivation factor. And even high (A + K) would not ensure performance in the absence of motivation.

MASLOW'S THEORY OF NEEDS AND MOTIVATION

Needs and its nature

Need is the state or condition of man. It prompts people to action. It is the primary energiser of behaviour. Needs are 'whys' of behaviour and mainsprings of action. They represent mental condition of human beings. They cause behaviour in many ways. They arise continuously and determine the general direction of an individual's behaviour. No single need determines behaviour rather a number of needs operate at the same time. Needs form hierarchy. Lower level needs should be satisfied first then comes of higher order needs. A need satisfied will not motivate people. Usually people seek the satisfaction of needs of higher order.

A.H. Maslow proposed and has shown the needs in same order. The figure below gives schematic version of needs.

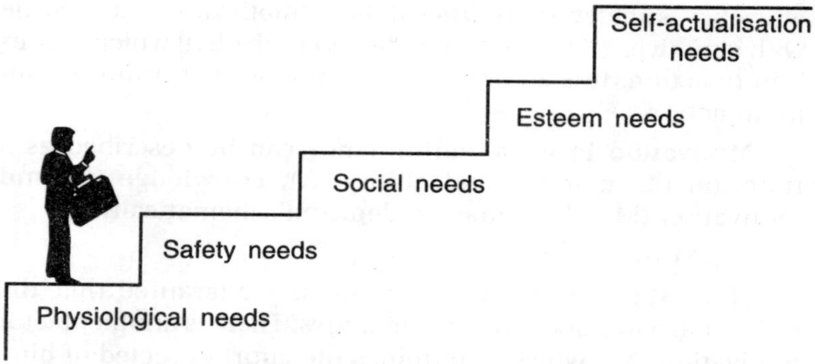

Maslow's hierarchy of needs

1. Physiological needs. Physiological needs include food clothing and shelter. They exert tremendous influence on behaviour. They are the most powerful and one must satisfy them in order to survive. Maslow says that man lives by bread alone. Physiological needs dominate when all other needs are not satisfied.

2. Safety needs. Once physiological needs are satisfied, the safety needs dominate human behaviour. These include protection from dangers such as fire accident and economic security such as fringe benefits, health and insurance. These needs are concerned with protection from hazards of life, from danger, deprivation and threat. Managers can influence by providing job guarantee, insurance plans, pension schemes etc. According to *McGregor* security needs may serve as motivators.

Organisations provide elaborate fringe benefits, health, accident insurance etc., to motivate employees.

3. Social needs. After the above needs are satisfied social needs arise. Man being a social animal wants to associate with, to make friendship. They are stronger in some situations.

4. Esteem needs. They are two fold—self-esteem and esteem of others. Self-esteem needs include self-confidence, achievement, competence, self-respect, knowledge, independence and freedom. The others include status, recognition, and appreciation. These needs are rarely satisfied. Modern organisations offer few opportunities for the satisfaction of these needs. These needs' satisfaction generates feelings of self-confidence, worth, strength and capacity.

5. Self-actualisation needs. It is the desire to become what one is capable of becoming. These needs motivate continuously and are infinite. They are self-realisation of one's own potentialities for continued self-development. These needs differ from person to person. The conditions of modern life give limited opportunities to fulfil these needs.

MOTIVATION AND ITS IMPACT ON BEHAVIOUR

Motivation causes goal-directed behaviour. Need of a person causes him to behave in a particular manner that he tries to satisfy himself so that he does not feel lacking.

Desire is the state of condition of lacking something, which he needs. This develops tension in his mind. Man takes advantage of incentives and facilities existing in the organisation and takes relief. There is difference between the two States *i.e.*, before and after desire fulfilment. In between the behaviour is the concern when man undergoes frustration and tension. At this stage different people behave differently, until the desire is fulfilled.

The individual undergoes frustration until the desire is fulfilled during which time he attempts to be aggressive or withdraw or compromise. These three cause different behaviours.

1. Aggression. It is a more common reaction to frustration—an act against someone or something who/which is responsible for his frustration. The aggression takes different forms such as displacement, negativism, and fixation.

2. Withdrawal. Alternatively, overcoming frustrations withdrawal from the scene causing frustration, anxiety or conflict. This frustration may be causing physically or physiologically. So individual attempts are different forms of withdrawal—fantasy regression, repression and flight.

3. Compromise. When the individual fails to achieve the goal, it causes frustration. When the frustration cannot be reduced by aggression or withdrawal, the individual tries to compromise with the situation. The forms of compromise are identification, projection and rationalisation.

The theory of defense mechanism helps in understanding human behaviour in the organisation. Human beings cannot tolerate frustration for a long time and adopt defense mechanism to fulfil the needs. Managers should understand the mental state of people and influence their behaviour so as to fulfil organisational and individual needs simultaneously.

4. Examine the Herzberg's Hygiene theory of Motivation. Herzberg has conducted a study by interviewing 200 accountants and engineers in different companies in Pittsburgh area, USA. He concluded that there are two categories of needs affecting behaviour. According to him some job conditions called Hygiene factors if absent would dissatisfy employees. He identified another set of job conditions called 'motivational factors' which if present will build strong motivation but their absence dissatisfies employees.

Hygiene factors. Herzberg identified ten factors such as company policies, administration, supervision, personal relations with supervisors, relations with peers and subordinates, salary, job security, working conditions and status. These are parts of the job, under which the job is performed. These factors are necessarily to be maintained at a particular level.

Motivational factors. Herzberg identified five factors such as recognition, advancement, work itself, possibility of growth, responsibility. These are related to job contents. Any increase in these factors will satisfy the employees. Any decrease would not affect their level of satisfaction. Hence they can be used to increase the output as such they are called motivators.

Maslow's theory *Vs.* Herzberg's theory

Herzberg's theory is compatible with Maslow's theory. Both deal with same problem. While Maslow expressed in term of needs, Herzberg attempted in terms of goals and rewards. Herzberg attempted to refine and cast new light on this content of work motivation. Herzberg recommended Hygiene factors to use them for meeting lower level of needs and identified motivators to imply the satisfaction of higher order needs.

Both models show some similarities close and examination of two models reveal that 'hygiene factor' match with Maslow's lower level needs and motivation imply higher order needs of Maslow's theorem.

Limitation. Maslow has built his theorem on the basis that unsatisfied needs which motivate employees and satisfied needs would no longer motivate. Thus it is considered to be universally applicable. It is only applicable in advanced countries. But in underdeveloped countries physiological, safety and social needs are acting as motivators, since people lack them in highly populous and backward countries.

Critically evaluation of Maslow's theory

Maslow assumes that needs arise one after the other and in escalating order. Thus he categorised needs into lower level and higher order. He presumes that unless lower order needs are satisfied higher order needs do not arise. If the order is rigid the solution is very simple to managerial problems of motivating people. But practically speaking the needs do not arise in given order and also differs from person to person depending upon situation.

Limitations

1. Some people, even if deprived of lower order needs, try for higher order needs satisfaction.
2. For some persons self-esteem needs are more powerful than basic needs.
3. Even in organisations physiological, safety, social and esteem needs need not be in order all times.
4. In some cases the order of needs may be discontinued. And all the needs need not be relevant.

Need hierarchy is not as simple as said by Maslow. Also the behaviour of persons differ from one to another though need is same. Hence Managers should be careful in influencing. It is difficult to understand the needs of all others from their behaviour. A person may try to achieve higher order needs satisfied even of lower order needs are not fulfilled. In practice the needs do not arise one after the other. In fact all the needs exist but their impact varies.

The solution is not common in all cases. The recourse for need satisfaction in one case may be different from other. Also it varies from situation to situation. There is no confirmed approach to motivate people by satisfying needs unsatisfied. A contingency approach would be developed and applied to solve the problem of people which is complex.

- **Achievement motives**
- **McClelland's theory of motivation**

Similar to Maslow, McClelland focused his theory on needs. He proposes that organisation offers opportunity to satisfy 3 needs (i) achievement, (ii) affiliation, (iii) power.

Need for power (n-pow). Need to dominate others is an influent need for some people who want to influence or control people. It speaks about the ability to manipulate activities of others to suit one's own purposes. Such people seek leadership positions. Thus n-pow helps Manager to understand employees' behaviour. There are two types of 'n-pow'—one personalised power and second socialised power.

Need for affiliation (n-aff). Man is a social animal. He wishes to seek company of others and support for which he develops meaningful relationships. They see organisation as an opportunity for establishing and satisfying relationships. They frequently interact with co-employees. They cannot perform things in isolation often they seek affiliation because they want to share their ideas or beliefs. Thus effective managers have stronger need for affiliation.

Need for achievement (n-ach). People take personal responsibility for finding solutions to problems. They try to effort and win but not by chance. They take calculated risks and set moderate goals. They like to know how they are performing. They are not motivated by money.

Developing achievement motivation. They see nation's economic success goes with achievers. Unfortunately only few had to bear the whole risk and push through the system. He offered a course of action executives and suggested four important points:

(i) Achievers should strive to get feedback.
(ii) They should watch and emulate those who have performed well.
(iii) They should be realistic and set goals moderately.
(iv) They should control daydream by talking and thinking positively.

McClelland adopted TATs—Thematic Appreciation Tests. He presented ambiguous picture and ask for an interpretation of what he sees and presumes. Such themes are counted, ultimately the subjects final score represents the individual's desire for high achievement.

Evaluation. McClelland sees very low n-achievement factor among people. He says country's economic advancement depends upon the extent of such people in population. Thus entrepreneurial success depends upon his desire to achieve. They can be backbone of many organisations. Hence organisations should establish conducive environment for high achievement. Managers have to raise, the achievement need level of subordinates by creating proper environment—permitting subordinates authority, increasing responsibility and gradually making tasks more challenging.

Limitations. Yet the theory is not well received due to certain limitations:

(i) The technique is objectionable.
(ii) The evidence in support of this theory is doubtful.
(iii) Achievement motivation can be taught.
(iv) Motivation is temporary feeling but not a permanent feature as it changes from time to time.
(v) Achievement through training is expensive and time consuming.

However, McClelland holds his theory practicable and ensure work motivation.

• Nature of men

McGregor: Human scientist developed certain assumptions in predicting human behaviour. These assumptions are crystallised to enable managers to understand people and motivate them. However, assumption differs from man to man and time to time, because of complexity of factors influencing this behaviour. McGregor characterised man from two viewpoints.

Theory "X". This is the traditional theory of human behaviour. McGregor has made some set of assumption about man and his behaviour. The assumptions are as follows:

1. Management is responsible for organising production factors like men, machinery, materials and money.
2. In respect of people—Management has to train, direct, motivate and control their behaviour.
3. Without Management intervention people would be passive. They must be persuaded, rewarded, punished, controlled and directed.
4. Man by nature is selfish and avoids work.
5. He lacks ambition, dislikes responsibility and prefers to be led.
6. He is indifferent to organisational needs.
7. By nature he resists change.

First three are managerial concern and the other four deal with human nature. Manager is negative in this approach to man. Managers who believe this attempt to control their employees closely. They believe that external control is appropriate for dealing with irresponsible employees.

Theory Y: Mc Gregor has assumed from other viewpoint the following in dealing with people:

1. The average human being inherently does not dislike the work. For man work is a source of satisfaction.
2. Man will exercise self-control and self-direction to achieve the objectives, set for him.
3. Men wishes to achieve the higher order needs satisfied from commitment to objectives.
4. Average man learns the work and assumes responsibilities.

5. In modern industrial world, the potentialities of man are partially utilised.
6. High degree of imagination and creativity in the solution of organisational problem, is widely distributed in population. Mc Gregor has viewed people positively.

• Comparison of Theory X and Theory Y

The assumptions made by McGregor under Theory X and Theory Y are mutually exclusive and represent two divergent points of view. The difference between the two can be visualised from the following table very clearly:

Comparison of Theory X and Theory Y

Theory X	Theory Y
• Autocratic (Leadership style)	• Democratic (Leadership style)
• Close Supervision	• Liberal supervision
• Stick approach	• Carrot approach
• Emphasis on coercion and punishment	• Emphasis on freedom and liberty
• People are lazy	• People enjoy work
• People like to be directed	• People have self-direction
• People are motivated by economic considerations	• People are motivated by self-development
• Managers are result oriented	• Managers are welfare oriented
• People are immature	• People are mature

1. Theory X assumes that man inherently dislikes to work. Theory Y assumes man enjoys work and learns.
2. Theory X proposes that man avoids responsibility but it is quite opposite in Theory Y.
3. People do not have creative thinking according to Theory X. But in the case of Theory Y the assumption is that creativity is largely distributed among employees.
4. In Theory X people lack self-motivation, but in Theory Y people possesses the skill of self-direction and capable of controlling by themselves rather than controlled externally.
5. In Theory X leader adopts autocratic style and it is

quite opposite in Theory Y, as leader invites democratic style of function by inviting more participation.

6. People are immature in Theory X and mature in Theory Y.
7. Man is basically economic concern in Theory X while it is different in Theory Y.
8. Men are motivated by lower order needs according to Theory X, while higher order needs play and influence the behaviour of people according to Theory Y.

Thus Theory X and Theory Y reflect two sides of the same coin. The approaches are different in looking at the human factor most potential of all the production factors. Modern Management control techniques such as MBO, decentralisation, job enrichment assume that man is self-motivated, self-directed and self-controlled as such freedom and autonomy are proposed in Theory Y. Thus Theory Y is more refined than Theory X which was proposed in olden days when technology was not well developed.

• **Features of Theory Z**

Of all the contemporary motivational theories, Theory Z attained great deal of importance. This has originated from Japanese Philosophy of Management. An important feature of Japanese management is that managers seek to better utilise human factor. They are successful in industrial front due to 3 apparent reasons such as Technology, Culture and Management system. Of the three, management system has added substantially to the success stories of Japan industries. Actually their system integrates both organisation and individuals to produce efficiency

W. Ouchi and A. Jaeger have been responsible for this new theory of Z. They have identified the following seven major and important dimensions which constitute Theory Z.

1. Employment. In American firms employees move frequently through different organisations for better pay and service conditions. Sometimes highly specialised people go fast. This is really causing unrest in many employees. This typical feature is balanced by Japanese management which proposes to hire employees on long term basis that too permanently. By this employee feels more commitment and firm capitalises in time by training him. The worker tries to develop attachment and integrate his goals with the organisational ones. This system is similar to marriages in Indian system which are permanent and bondage continues until they die. Due to business cycles the production suffers and if workers are hired and fired on the basis of economical changes the workers do not develop loyalty to the organisations. Theory Z proposes to hire the worker permanently without retrenchment in off season. Here the worker is asked to work on overtime basis without additional remuneration during boom conditions and he will be asked to work less number of hours/days when market conditions are poor.

2. Decision-making. Decision-making is not made by individuals as is in American set up nor by groups. In Japan the problem is left for discussion at all levels of organisation for a reasonable period of time and the decision will be taken on the basis of opinion of all in organisation irrespective of his concern. So that all the employees are in know of its implications and will implement whole-heartedly without any hesitation or indifference to it.

3. Responsibility. In American management the responsibilities are felt by individuals. But in theory Z model of management the responsibility is collective and all the employees at various levels are held responsible for failures as well as successes. And the managers will be demoted to handle less dignified job if not performing satisfactorily.

4. Evaluation and promotion. Since the employment is a lifetime commitment their promotion is based on seniority. In such cases the employees perform by integrating their goals with organisational goals effectively. In case of American style of management where employees move frequently the evaluation is also fast to check the mistakes and failures.

5. Control. The employees are controlled by formal and explicit measures through rules, regulations and procedures. But according to Theory Z the employees are not measured by formal standards and current performance, but by his traits, cooperation, etc. The mistakes of the employees are broadly taken as errors in the process of leaving since managers too commit mistakes because they do not have to show results instantaneously say before the financial year closes.

6. Career paths. In American model employees seek to develop specialisation. But in Theory Z the employees are rotated laterally so that they learn different aspects of plant and diversified knowledge allows him to learn all aspects of organisation. Therefore it suggests career paths in non-specialisation areas too rather than simple functional area.

7. Concern. Theory Z tries to produce typical man who reflects all cultural, economical and social aspects of the organisation. According to theory Z the employee will be socialised and indoctrinated thorough orientation/training for about six months. The employee is expected to commit himself to the organisation. In Japanese management approach the employee is not subject to fire hence he is willing to contribute more in the long term interests of the organisation.

The informal controls, non specialised career paths, evaluation, collective responsibility and permanent employment are acting as inputs going into theory Z.

Theory Z retains American cultural values of individualism and entwined with collective approach to decision-making. Combination of these provide the framework for theory Z philosophy.

• Features of immaturity-maturity theory

According to Argyris seven changes should take place in the personality of individuals if they have become mature people. These changes reside on a continuation and the healthy personality develops continuously from maturity to immaturity.

Immature Characteristics	Mature Characteristics
Passive	Active
Dependence	Independence
Capable of behaving in a few ways	Capable of behaving in many ways
Shallow interest	Deep interest
Short term perspective	Long term perspective
Subordinate position	Superior position
Lack of self-awareness	Self-awareness and control

1. Individual moves from passive state (as a child) to active (adult) state. As child, he does not have control over environment and series of events occur without

his choice. Contrarily adult knows how to control the environment and can control the occurring of events.

2. Man develops from a state of dependence as child to a state of relative independence as an adult.
3. Individual as child, behaves in a few ways but as an adult he is capable of behaving in many ways. The adult is more adaptable than the child who is more predictable.
4. Individual has shallow interests as child, but develops deeper interests as adult.
5. Individual, as child, is concerned with the present and his time perspective is very short. As he matures his time perspective increases to include the part and the future. He is highly concerned with the future events that may or may not happen.
6. Individual, as child, is subordinate to every one. As time passes he moves to equal or superior positions to others. As adult, when he is working with others he does not feel himself to be a follower.
7. Individual, as child, does not have self about. As he grows and reaches an adult state, he thinks, himself and develops ego and tries to protect himself.

Implication of the theory. Argyris says that very few persons develop to full maturity. He feels that immaturity tends to exist in individual not because of their nature of laziness but because of management practices. When they join organisation, they are given little opportunity and computed to be dependent and hence they tend to behave immaturely. People tend to be immature because of built in mechanism of formal organisation where leadership span of management, unity of direction, organisation structure, operative procedures, budgetary controls act as boundaries and restrict the creativity and initiative of the individuals. Argyris suggests that human factor is the valuable resource of any organisation and then should be proper integration of individual and organisational goals. He suggests organisation structure to humanist system from the existing management system, to be more flexible and participative. Such system provides to individuals opportunities and keep them satisfied beyond physiological and safety needs.

Role of non-financial and financial incentives in motivation

Individual's needs are of two types—financial needs and non-financial needs. Manager has to identify these needs and satisfy them so that employees can be motivated and their behaviour can be influenced in desired manner.

Non-financial incentives. Monetary incentives do always not motivate people. They should be accompanied by non-financial incentives such as recognition, promotion status, increase in responsibility, etc.

Status. Status refers to the position of an individual in reference to others. Positions refer to the rights, privileges, powers attached to him in order to discharge responsibilities entrusted to him. Thus people would like to be ranked. Especially middle level and high level managers are status conscious which is more important than money.

Promotion. It refers to the upward movement of employees in hierarchy. People with better performance by their skills and capacities are promoted to high positions. Thus when employees are moved to vertical positions they are associated with better package of powers and rights in addition to pay.

Responsibility. Increase in responsibility is one kind of incentive to some people who are challenging and enthusiastic in work. It is always not liked to do monotonous, dull and boring tasks. So people having strong performance and achievement drive should be given additional responsibility.

Recognition of work. Employees working hard expect recognition of their work and performance. It is an inherent feeling by nature that man would like to be acknowledged for better performance he is showing. Such appreciation and word of encouragement would console the employees and work more.

Job security. To ensure performance the employees prefer job security. The secret of Japanese success in industrial front is the way the employees are hired on permanent basis. So that they can develop loyalty to organisation work with more commitment. However, it is not denied that yet times employees become complacent if they know that they are not thrown out.

Importance. The employees should feel a sense of importance in their work. Managers should give credit where it is due and show interest in. For this reason the managers should praise people in public and criticise privately. Satisfaction of this need to feel important can be provided by asking for opinions and suggestions.

Identify individuality. No two persons will be motivated in the same manner. People differ in tastes and feelings. Managers should identify them and satisfy, so that employees can show better performance than taking the group as one entity.

Participation. Wherever necessary and whenever possible employees should be given the opportunity of participation in decision-making particularly where they affect them. Participation provides them opportunity of knowing the impact of decisions.

Openness. Wherever necessary the managers should act openly with people. Being secretive induces frustration in the minds of people. Motivation requires creation of feeling of belonging. Team spirit and group cohesiveness have to be inspired which cannot be done by secretive practices.

Confidence. Confidence in people would instil confidence in themselves. Managers should adopt the attitude that employees do their best. In such atmosphere people are motivated to integrate individual goals with organisational goals.

Role of financial incentives. People work in organisations for money which provides livelihood for them. Managers propose appropriate strategies to motivate people at work. Further incentives and reward schemes are established to benefit employees. Incentives are of two kinds—financial (in terms of money) and in kind (non-financial). Financial incentive is that cash payments and cash linked schemes such as Bonus, profit sharing retirement pay, vacation pay, overtime pay, wages and salaries paid periodically. Non-financial incentive motivates man to work hard and encourages assuring additional responsibilities without seeking monetary benefit. They are in the form of status, position, promotion, recognition etc.

Financial incentives. Money is the sole motivator for employees as it provides livelihood and it is a common medium for all employees to buy necessary items and acquire facilities to live comfortably. As such it is said as reinforce. It is not to deny the simple fact that money influences the way an employee works. But pay and merit system has lost its effectiveness due to the following reasons:

(i) Pay is not perceived as being related to job performance.

(ii) Performance ratings are viewed as biased.

(iii) Rewards are not viewed as rewards.

Present reward message is not taken as a reward in positive sense because of 5 major reasons.

(a) Conflicting reward structures are in force.

(b) Employees perceive inequity in pay.

(c) The merit increase may be perceived as threat to the employee.

(d) Trust and openness about merit are low.

(e) Some organisations view money as the primary motivator ignoring the importance of job itself.

Some rules for making effective use of money as a motivator

According to Dubin:

(i) Money should not be treated as primary motivator without due regard to other factors such as challenging work, managerial and organisational climate.

(ii) Money is a secondary reinforce.

(iii) Money should be directly related to performance.

(iv) Money is potent motivator when it is used to reduce tension and worry.

(v) Money should be perceived as equitable in comparison to one's own efforts.

Comparison of Maslow's theory of needs and Alderfer's ERG theory

Maslow has categorised needs into five categories which are already shown in the diagram on page 58.

1. Physiological needs
2. Safety needs
3. Social needs
4. Esteem needs
5. Self-actualisation needs.

Alderfer of Yale University has reworked Maslow's model of hierarchy of needs and assigned them closely. His model is known as ERG theory. According to him, needs are grouped into three sets—Existence, Relatedness and Growth. Existence needs concerned with basic material requirement for a man to exist or survive. They include what Maslow considered for physiological and safety needs. The second group related needs are the desire for maintaining important personal relationships.

Ex: Social and status needs. Maslow's social and external component of esteem classification comes under this category. Lastly Alderfer isolates growth needs i.e. desire for personal development. This includes Maslow's intrinsic component of esteem category of needs and self-actualisation needs.

Alderfer differ from Maslow on the following grounds:

1. Contrary to Maslow's opinion, Alderfer feels that more than one need may operate at the same time.
2. If the gratification of higher level need is stifled the desire to satisfy lower level need increases.

Maslow's need hierarchy is step like progressive. ERG theory proposes that rigid hierarchy does not exist. A person can be working on growth needs even if existence and relatedness needs are not satisfied or Alderfer opines that all the three need categories could be operating at the same time.

ERG theory contains regression, frustrations, dimension. Maslow viewed that an individual stays at a particular level of need until he is satisfied. But ERG theory counters that when higher level need is not satisfied the desire to increase lower level need arises.

In summary Maslow says that satisfied lower order needs lead to the desire for high order needs. But according to Alderfer multiple needs can be operating, as motivators at the same time and frustration to satisfy higher order needs causes regression to a lower level needs.

- **Social information-processing model**

Social Information-Processing (SIP) model of motivation theory emphasises that people respond to their jobs as they perceive them.

SIP model argues that employees adopt attitudes and behaviours in response to their social perceptions. Regularly employees meet friends, relatives, co-workers, supervisors and customers. They comment upon the job and work environment of the employees. Thus employee's motivation and satisfaction can be manipulated by the comments of co-workers, friends etc. So managers should give more attention to employees perceptions of their job, as to the actual characteristics of those jobs. They should spend more time telling the job how interesting it is. By this they can motivate employees and influence them to work better.

QUESTIONS FOR DISCUSSION

1. Define motivation and describe motivation process.
2. Briefly explain Maslow's theory of needs and motivation.
3. Explain, how does motivation affect Behaviour.
4. Examine the Herzberg's Hygiene theory of Motivation.
5. Compare and contrast Maslow's theory of needs and Herzberg's theory of motivation.
6. Critically evaluate Maslow's theory of needs hierarchy.
7. Can achievement motives be developed? Explain McClelland's theory of Motivation.
8. Theory X and Theory Y are concerned with the nature of people. How does the job situation affect the application of these theories? What are its implications for motivational process?
9. Compare Theory X and Theory Y and write their implications on behaviour of employees.
10. Explain the main features of Theory Z and what are its implications on managers?
11. Explain the main features of maturity-immaturity theory. How can manager motivates a mature person?
12. Discuss the role of non-financial and financial incentives in Motivation.
13. Compare and contrast Maslow's theory of needs with Aldfer's ERG theory.
14. What is social information-processing model? What are its implications?

5

ORGANISATIONAL EFFECTIVENESS (OE)

Organisation theory is built around the concept of 'effectiveness'. Organisational effectiveness has gained vital importance in modern industrial scenario. Every manager is expected to enhance the effectiveness of his organisation by knowing reasons effecting it. The concepts visualised by behaviour lists at various ways of achieving it.

Definitions

Paul E. Mott defined organisational effectiveness as the ability of an organisation to mobilise its centres of power for action—production and adaptation.

RM Steeves has expressed organisational effectiveness to the adaptability-flexibility, productivity, job satisfaction and profitability of an organisation.

Organisational effectiveness is a label to which an organisation has performed according to its capacities, potentials and general goals.

Amitai Etizioni has defined OE as the degree to which organisation realises its goals. Kimberly has seen OE in terms of survival of an organisation.

According to Basi and Arnold OE is the extent to which an organisation, given certain resources and means, achieves its objectives without placing undue strain on its members.

Effectiveness *Vs.* Efficiency. These two are different terms which are interchangeable. The term efficiency in engineering and economic sense refers to the relationship between input and output. While effectiveness refers to goal achieving behaviour and its results. From decision-making point of view efficiency refers to selecting best course of action among several alternatives. But effectiveness refers to taking right decision at right time. Thus the decision though appears to be right, it will not ensure results if not taken at right time. Effectiveness is a broad term and takes into account several factors inside and outside the organisation. OE refers to the degree to which pre-determined goals are achieved. Efficiency refers to the way in which the resources are put to use, whereas effectiveness refers to the accomplishment of organisational goals and objectives. In terms of Chester I. Bernard, when unsought consequences are trivial, effective action is efficient.

Goal attainment approach to organisational effectiveness

Amitai Etizioni defined OE as the degree to which organisation realises its goals. Thus OE is referred to goal achievement. An organisation exists to fulfil its goals. Hence its attainment is the only criterion to measure OE. C.I. Bernard too said that OE means accomplishment of recognised objectives of cooperative effect. OE is appraised in terms of accomplishment of ends rather than means. Thus goal attainment criterion has gained lot of acceptance from common sense point of view to measure OE. Thorndike has noted that OE as productivity, net profit, the extent to which the organisation accomplishes its missions and the success of the organisation in maintaining or expanding itself. Campbell suggested that attainment of goals as quality, productivity, readiness, profit or return, utilisation of prevention of stability, turnover, accidents, morale, motivation, satisfaction internalisation of organisational goals, conflict cohesion, flexibility, adaptation and evaluation by external entities, for measuring organisational effectiveness. Bass, a psychologist suggests that effectiveness of an organisation should reflect the worth of the organisation to its individual members and society.

Assumptions of the approach. To make this approach meaningful the following assumptions are made:

1. Organisations should have goals well-defined and understood.
2. Progress towards these goals should be measurable.

Problems of the goal approach. Goal approach has some limitations, however it is an accepted yardstick to measure the effectiveness of an organisation.

1. Goal approach is not compatible to organisations that do not produce tangible output.
2. Goals are plenty such as long run and short run; personal and group; group and organisational, etc. The question arises as to which goal is to be taken as criterion to measure?
3. Who will measure the goals?
4. Various groups interpret goals in different ways, under such conditions consensus among different groups is impossible.
5. More serious problem is about the evaluation of performance.

In spite of the above problems 'Goal attainment' is considered as the sole criterion to measure the OE in modern industrial system. Richards is of the opinion that achievement of organisational goal plays significant role in strategic decision-making.

Following are the steps to be taken to operationalise goal attainment:

1. Explore various goals of an organisation.
2. Select one appropriate goal.
3. Device the yardstick to measure it.
4. Compare it with other organisations.

Price states that effectiveness depends upon five important factors such as Productivity, Morale, Institutionalisation, Adaptiveness, Conformity. Further he stresses that five systems such as political, economic, ecology control, population system and continuity system will finally determine the organisational effectiveness.

Difference between goal optimisation and goal maximisation

Goal maximisation. It refers to getting higher goals and achieving maximum results in a given situation.

Goal optimisation. Goal attainment depends upon several things in an organisation such as raw material availability demand for product, labour availability, technology, competition, power availability etc., as their supply is not in the hands of management. Goal achievement is subject to several conditions

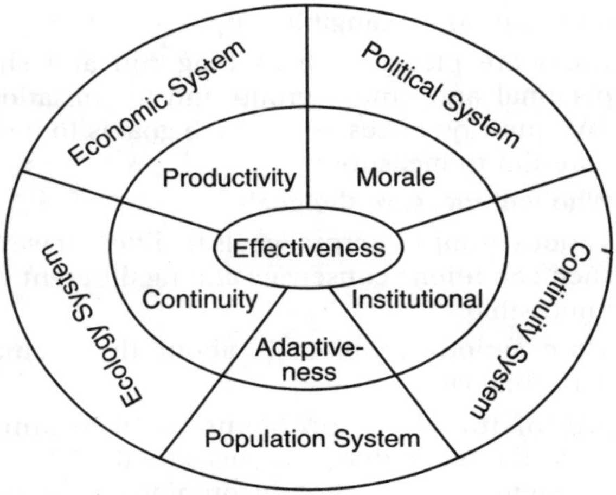

Abridged from James I. Price, *Organisational Effectiveness*, Homewood, Ill, Irwin, 1968.

prevailing at a point of time. Hence management should optimise goals rather than maximising goal. Richard M. Steeves advocates the following points in support of goal optimisation:

1. Sometimes goals are conflicting to each other. For instance production maximisation and maximisation of job satisfaction are not possible. To resolve this, compromisation may be made in terms of goal optimisation.
2. Goal optimisation allows differential weights to be placed on different goals. For example, the weight of the profit goal may be twice the weight of job satisfaction.
3. Goal optimisation is desirable since goal achievement depends upon several other factors and subject to market conditions, leadership, financial convenience, technological constraints, etc., as such optimisation is only the alternative.
4. Since the environmental forces, economical factors and social conditions change in course of time, goals also should be made flexible. Thus goal optimisation is inevitable.

5. Goal optimisation will enable long range planning and help in planning resource allocation efficiently.

Mostly common decision-making is concerned with discovery and selection of optimal alternatives. Maximisation approach is referred to economic man approach and optimisation is referred to administrative man approach.

Maximisation approach/Economic man approach. Economic man is completely rational and tries to maximise his returns. The economic man decision is based on:

1. *Means and ends relationship*: Manager identifies clearly the ends to which he wants to reach and follows the means available to him.
2. He is fully aware of information and alternatives out of which he has to choose. In the Organisation decisions are directed towards maximisation of goal achievement, for example, profit maximisation. It is achieved where marginal cost is equal to marginal revenue.

Maximisation is destructive. Maximisation of profit or production is possible only when the environment is exploited to maximum. Under such conditions depleted environment will be unable to supply required resources in the long run. Also the people who are exploited will become strong opposition in the long run. Hence an organisation should not utilise the resources in the environment to a maximum extent. Hence, one should utilise them optimally. Thus one should not go beyond which organisation endangers itself and generate countervailing forces in the environment to weaken the organisation. As such the alternative is optimisation.

Optimisation. Administrative Man approach.

Administrator always emphasises optimisation in decision-making which satisfies him.

Simon says administrator adopts the following behaviour in decision-making process:

1. He develops alternatives without high estimations.
2. He chooses an alternative which satisfies him very well.
3. He recognises everything is not available in plenty.

Thus administrative man tries to be rational by satisfying rather than maximising. This model is based on reality, since social, economical and technical factors put barriers on the capacity of maximisation. Hence optimisation is desirable. Thus, optimisation represents real situation of decision-making. That is why Gordon, Cyert and Chamberlin emphasised satisfactory profit, rather than maximum profit respectively.

Systems theory of organisational effectiveness

Goal attainment approach concentrates on output. It speaks about efficiency of the organisation to reach the target at a point of time. But systems approach calls for judging the ability of an organisation in acquiring inputs and transferring them into output. System is an assemblage of variables which are integrated and inter-dependent. Accordingly, the effectiveness of an organisation depends upon the performance of all its branches. The organisation is closely related to open system, which emphasises the relationship between elements of organisation and its environment as they jointly influence the effectiveness.

The systems view aims at continued and efficient receipt of input and efficient transformation into output. The effectiveness was in the flexibility of response of the organisation to the changing environment. The most effective organisations are those that successfully adapt structure, work, technologies and policies with the changing environment to facilitate goal attainment.

Seashore and Yachtmen repeat that highest level of organisational effectiveness is reached when the organisation optimises its resource procurement.

Georgopolous and Tamnenbaum emphasises that organisational structure includes sub-systems called 'stations'. These stations will be effective when they are more productive, lower in inter-group conflicts and flexible than non-effective stations.

Friedlander and Pickle attempted to say that OE is determined by the degree to which the societal and employees' needs are fulfilled.

Schein contends that effectiveness of an organisation depends on the scanning and use of feed-back from the environment.

Caplan uses four variables to measure effectiveness which are stability, integration, voluntarism and achievement.

S.B. Prasad says that effectiveness depends upon 3 sub-systems such as economic, social and technical. He further says that organisation is said to be effective only when equilibrium is maintained among these three sub-systems.

Distinction between managerial effectiveness and organisational efficiency

Organisational effectiveness refers the degree of success at which the organisation is working. And there are many indicators to reflect the way the organisation is successful. They are productivity, profitability etc.

Managerial effectiveness is one of the variables of OE. Managerial effectiveness is commonly defined in terms of goal achieving behaviour. According to Guion, success of a manager lies in attaining goals of organisation.

Managerial effectiveness is too optimised. As an optimiser a manager utilises the available economic, technical and financial resources towards its sustained long term functioning. The managerial effectiveness depends upon three elements such as personal qualities, process and product which are inter-dependent.

Personal qualities. Personal qualities will decide the effectiveness of a manager. Jargenson has advised the following qualities to distinguish effective and less effective managers.

Effective Manager	Less Effective Manager
Decisive	Amicable
Aggressive	Confronting
Self-starting	Neat
Productive	Reserved
Well-informed	Agreeable
Determined	Conservative
Energetic	Kindly
Creative	Mannerly
Intelligent	Cheerful
Responsible	Formal
Enterprising	Courteous
Clear thinking	Modest

Process. Success depends upon managerial efficiency involved in managing the affairs of the organisation.

1. Setting of goals
2. Decision by consensus
3. Delegation by results
4. Trust in people in solving problems
5. Communicating effectively
6. Consistent behaviour

Product. Managers work for goals, goal attainment varies from industry to industry, though manager is nice in qualities and decision-making process. Managerial effectiveness depends upon achievement of the goals by managers. Following are some of the goals which indicate the managerial effectiveness.

Goals

Productivity
Organisation
Leadership
Welfare of employees
Profit Maximisation
Growth
Stability

Relationship among the causal, intervening and end-result variables in organisational effectiveness

Likert has identified three sets of variables which are useful in discussing OE. Grouping the variables would help in interpreting the data and for diagnosing the OE.

1. Causal variables.
2. Intervening variables
3. End-result variables

1. Causal variables. They are independent and influence the organisation. These are controllable and management can change as and when they like. For example, structure, policies, procedures, strategies etc.

2. Intervening variables. These reflect the internal state of an organisation. For example, loyalties, attitudes, motivation, perception of members of an organisation. These variables are influenced by causal variables. The intervening variables are divided into two categories *i.e.*, (i) attitudinal, (ii) behavioural.

These variables are responsible for the development and effectiveness of organisation both in short-term and long-term.

3. End-result variables. These are dependent variables such as profit, sales, costs, production etc. These are caused by the causal and intervening variables. Managers are very much interested in these matters as they reflect the achievement of organisational effectiveness.

Inter-relationship. The inter-relationship among the above variables is shown in the following figure.

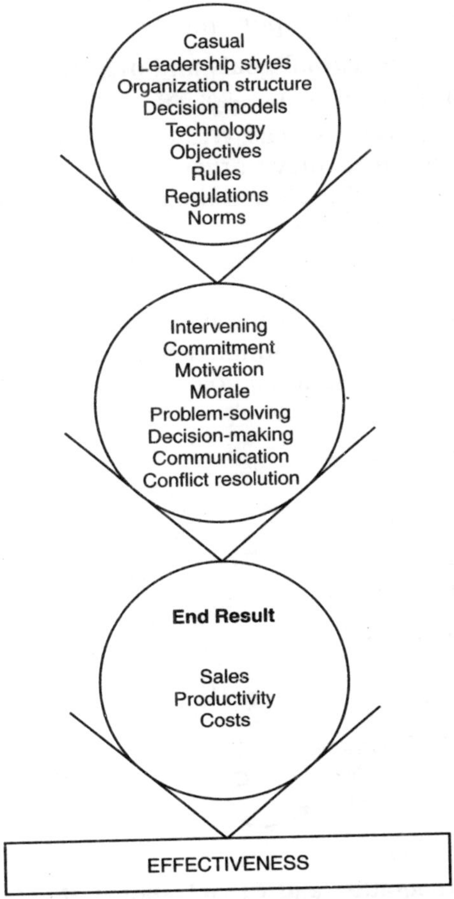

Inter-relationship among causal, intervening and end-result variables

The above figure shows that existence of causal variables influence the intervening variables which in turn result in end-result variables. These three finally result in organisational effectiveness. Likert stresses that any attempt by management to improve intervening variables without paying necessary attention to causal variables will not enhance end-results. Hence management should influence intervening variables through causal variables to reach end-results effectively. Thus to improve the OE, attempts should be made to improve first causal variables which will automatically improve the intervening variables followed by improvement in end-result variables. Thus causal variables act as stimuli upon intervening variables.

Integration of individual goals and organisational goals

Amitai Etizion has defined OE as the degree to which organisation realises its goals. Without realising individual goals it is impossible to achieve organisational goals. It does not mean that individual goals and their fulfilment alone will speak about organisation effectiveness. Here the reader should understand that management should fulfil individual goals, while fulfilling organisational goals. Clearly to say an organisational goal which does not fulfil the individual goal is not worth to achieve. Since it is individual, who will be instrumental in achieving the organisational goals.

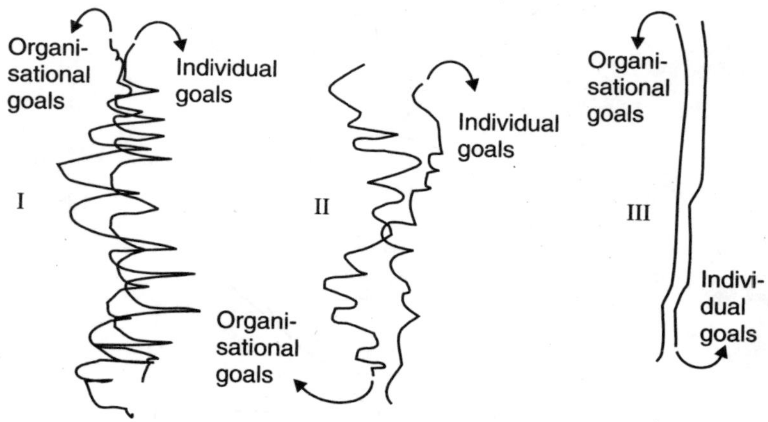

Goal integration and Organisational effectiveness

Hence management has to integrate the two sets of goals to make its existence meaningful. Neither organisation nor individuals fulfils their goals ignoring the goals of others. An individual trying to fulfil his goals without honouring organisational goals will be caught by the management. Hence individuals simultaneously fulfil the organisational goals. Similarly organisation will fail to achieve its goals if it ignores individual goals fulfilment, since it has to function through the individuals.

The integration process of two sets of goals are discussed in three situations.

In the first situation the organisational effectiveness is low due to loosely linked goal situation. In this situation members are opposed to the organisational goals. Organisation is ignoring the welfare of the members and members do not have regard to organisational goals which do not benefit them at all. In such situation only one set of goals can be fulfilled and other will have to adjust. Some these individuals leave the organisation or organisation will quit the individuals. At times, organisation may go out of action depending upon the external environment.

In the second situation both organisational goals and individual goals are integrated moderately as such the effectiveness is moderate. Here neither organisation nor individual is capable of ignoring others and individuals wish to fulfil their needs.

In third situation, there is high degree of intersection between the two *i.e.*, organisation goals and individual goals. No one can escape from others. No one wishes to ignore the other. Since they have mutual respect and regard to each other. Both organisation and individualy go together without hurting others' interests. As such the organisational effectiveness is high. Its end results such as productivity and profitability will be high.

Adaptive coping cycle and various stages

An effective organisation adapts itself to the changing conditions of environment. Schein suggests that an organisation can do this through the technique of adaptive coping-cycles. Hence an organisation, to be effective, should interact properly with environment. There are six stages to be followed for effectiveness.

1. **Sensing change.** Change is common in external environment of organisation. External environment includes, market, technology, economy etc. These aspects change from time to time and manager should sense them in advance.

2. **Collect relevant information.** In second stage the member should collect all relevant information relating to the change perceived. Organisation receives technology, information, materials and workers from environment and produce goods. These goods again will be sold in the market. The success of an organisation depends upon how it collects relevant and useful information to take decisions and find solutions in solving the problems and producing goods economically.

3. **Conversion process.** The organisation has to change the production method as per the requirements of the market and produce goods suitable to the markets.

4. **Stabilising internal changes.** When organisation converts the existing method of production it will affect other sub systems. So organisation has to stabilise the undesired changes and stabilise the organisation.

5. **Export new products or services.** At this stage, the organisation has to export new products or services in accordance with the environmental or market requirements. If the organisation fails to adopt new methods of distribution (say) it will be ineffective.

6. **Welcome feedback.** The organisation should invite feedback from the environment about these changes incorporated in the organisation. The manager should know how the organisation is integrated with the environmental requirements. This is the most important stage.

Conditions for effective coping. For effective coping with environmental changes the organisation should fulfil the following conditions:

1. Organisation should have effective communication network to collect timely and valuable information required.
2. The organisation should have flexibility and change to new methods or procedures.

3. The people of the organisation should have willingness to change.
4. The organisation should be able to integrate the organisational goals and individual goals.
5. There should exist supportive climate in the organisation.

Edger Schein a notable social scientist contends that effectiveness of an organisation depends upon its ability to sense and use feedback from environment.

Organisational effectiveness in relation to time

'Time' is universally accepted dimension and unique variable in relation to which organisation has to maintain effectiveness. Management has to keep the organisation effective in all the times to come.

Gibson *et al.* have developed criteria to measure the effectiveness of organisation in short-run, intermediate and long-run. The relationship between time dimension and effectiveness criteria is shown in the following figure.

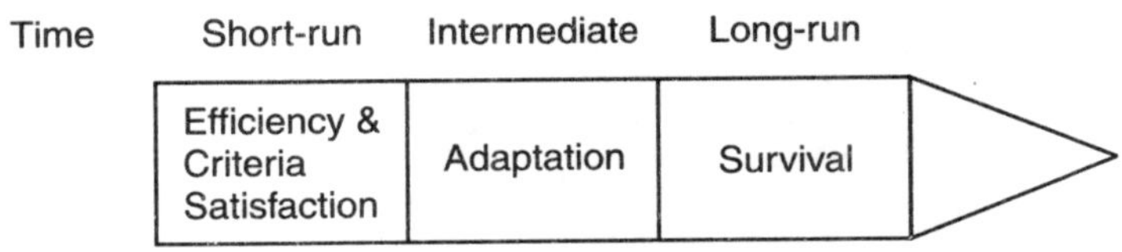

Management should have adequate predicator to test the effectiveness. According to Gibson to check the effectiveness in the long-run 'Survival' is appropriate criteria. 'Adaptation' is appropriate criteria to study the effectiveness in the intermediate period followed by short-run measures such as efficiency and satisfaction.

QUESTIONS FOR DISCUSSION

1. What is organisational effectiveness? How it is distinguished from organisational efficiency?
2. What is goal attainment approach to Organisational Effectiveness?
3. What is the difference between goal optimisation and goal maximisation?

4. Examine the systems theory of organisational effectiveness.
5. How you distinguish managerial effectiveness from organisational efficiency?

   Or

   What is the difference between organisational effectiveness and managerial effectiveness?
6. What are the causal, intervening and end-result variables in organisational effectiveness? Discuss their relationships.
7. Why individual goals, organisational goals are not congruent? Elaborate.

   Or

   What criteria are used for judging the effectiveness of an organisation? How does the degree of integration of goals effect organisational accomplishment?
8. What is adaptive coping cycle? What are its various stages?
9. In relation to time, how organisational effectiveness is explained?

6

Group Dynamics

Definition of Group

According to Smith, a group is the set of two or more individuals who are jointly characterised by a network of communication with a shared sense of collective identity and one or more shared dispositions with associated normative strength.

A group is defined as two or more individuals, integrating and interdependent who have come together to achieve particular objectives.

A group is collection of people having common interest, interaction, and awareness of one other.

A group is that its members have common goals.

A group is one that the members of which have ties and relationship among them.

A group is that the members in it interact with each other.

Shaw defines group as two or more persons who are interacting with one another in such a manner that each person influences and is influenced by the others.

A group is the aggregation of small number of persons who work for common goals, develop a shared attitude and are aware that they are part of a group and perceive themselves as such.

Group dynamics implies the kind of interactions that the members come into.

Features of Group

1. More persons. A group consists of two or more persons. There is no maximum limit of members.

2. Shared interest. The members subscribe for group objectives. It is not necessary that each member agrees with all the objectives. But each member subscribes to at least one objective. The shared objectives bind them together.

3. Aware of group. In a group, members know personally each other more closely. They are aware their membership, each member believes that he is a participant in some specific group.

4. Interaction. Members of the group interact with each other. They have the opportunity to communicate with others face to face, in writing or through telephone or network.

5. Enduring relationship. The members endure tighter social relationships. They are less organised.

6. Rules and regulations. Group starts with mutual awareness and establishes rule for comfortable coexistence.

7. Interdependence. The members are often dependent on each other to serve common purpose.

Types of groups. People form into groups under various circumstances. The group tendency depends upon the circumstances, size, objectives of the institution.

Formal group. Group is defined by the organisation's structure with designated work assignments establishing tasks. The behaviour of the members are directed by the organisations.

Informal group. It is an alliance among people that are neither formally structured nor organisationally determined. These groups are natural formations in the work environment in response to the need for social contract.

Common group. It is determined by the organisation chart. It is composed of the subordinates who report directly to a given manager.

Task group. It is organisationally determined. It represents those working together to complete a job or task. Group's boundary is not limited to its immediate superior. All command groups are task groups and not *vice versa.*

Interest group. People may affiliate to attain a specific objective with which they are concerned. People form into an united body to further their common interest.

Friendship group. Groups often develop because the member have one or more common characteristics. Social alliances can be based on similar age, habit, political views, etc.

Apathetic group. Low paid workers form into group because of discontentment.

Erratic group. The behaviour of erratic group is unpredictable. Semi-skilled workers who require interaction work together. Their relations with management are erratic.

Strategic group. In the plant, skilled workers who perform key jobs form into groups. They are always interdependent.

Conservative group. People at the top of the organisation are highly specialised and form into group. They display self-confidence. They can influence the functioning of the organisation.

Primary and secondary groups. In a primary group members have opportunity of discussing face to face. The group is also small in size. The membership is based on intimate relationship. The secondary group is more formal and members may not have any interest in the problems. The intimacy, interaction, association and cooperation may not be found in secondary groups.

Reference group. It is a group to which the member really belongs. An individual may be a member of several groups but he may not actively participate in all such groups. Member would like to participate in a group where norms are attractive to the individual. Such group norms become more influential in determining behaviour.

Membership group. It is a group with which member identifies himself. His association ceases the moment individual stops paying subscription towards the membership.

In-group. The in-group represents a cluster of persons having values in a society or dominant place in social functioning.

Purpose of Group

There is not single reason that compels individuals to join groups. Individuals form into groups for several purposes.

The most popular reasons are:

1. **Security.** Few individuals like to stand alone. Generally individuals at work wish to associate with others, to feel stronger by being together. By forming into groups one can reduce the feeling of insecurity. Being part of a group individuals get reassurance from interacting with others.

2. **Status.** Inclusion in a group viewed as important by others. Group provides recognition and status for its members.

3. **Self-esteem.** Membership provides people feeling of self-worth. Self-esteem of an individual is bolstered.

4. **Affiliation.** Group feeling provides workers a feeling of job satisfaction and fulfil their needs of friendship and social relations.

5. **Power.** What cannot be achieved individually becomes possible through group action. By the formation of groups employees can increase their bargaining power with management. Informal groups provide additional power to influence others. Groups also provide necessary confidence so that individual can influence others which he cannot do by formal position and authority

6. **Goal achievement.** Group helps in achieving a goal that would be difficult if pursued by a single person. There are times when it takes more than one person to accomplish a particular task. Thus there is a need to pool talents, knowledge or power in order to get the job completed.

7. **Economic benefits.** Economic reasons also cause group formation and individuals believe that they can derive greater economic benefits if they form into groups.

8. **Relieves boredom.** Mutual interaction relieves people from boredom and monotony on the job.

9. **Mutual interaction.** Groups help people to interact with each other.

10. **Opportunity to learn.** Group provides opportunity to members for exchange of ideas, thoughts, attitudes on-and-off the job.

11. **Source of information.** Groups help others (individuals) to know about others and give information when they are sick.

Benefits of groups to organisation

Groups make or mar growth of the organisations. On one hand groups establish the organisations by their militant nature and selfishness. Groups impede the work of the organisation and become barrier to smooth functioning. As such managers try to divide the people and rule them in order to achieve organisational goals. Sometimes managers do transfer the arrogant people to different departments. And also management separates people physically to minimise their interference in the work.

On the other hand groups help the organisation in a big way and individuals by and large. Employees have strong need for affiliation. Lack of interaction among employees lead to turnover, absenteeism, accidents, low productivity, etc. Management should understand the group philosophy as they help in an organisation. If they are used properly results of an organisation can be bettered.

Groups perform the following:

1. Socialism. Every organisation has its own culture and work environment with traditions and norms, besides rules and regulations. These groups help employees (new) by giving necessary orientation and educating them to adjust with the norms of the organisation.

2. Getting the job done. In principle the organisation has to provide training and orientation before the work is done. In any situation on behalf of organisation, groups help and enable the employees in carrying out their duties carefully. These groups enable management in implementing policies.

3. Decision-making. Groups help in better decision-making. Two brains are better than one. It is possible to pool excellence and intelligence through groups. And decision-making is easy through groups.

• **Functions of groups in modern organisation**

The groups in an organisation serve two vital functions:

1. Task functions.
2. Group maintenance functions.

Task functions. Groups help in completing tasks.

1. Initiative. Group advises its members new ideas and ways to complete the activity. Thus groups help to take initiative.

2. Seeking information. Groups enable the organisation in collecting and pooling information from all concerned.

3. Making suggestions. Groups help organisations and individuals in advising others while carrying out their duties.

4. Clarifications. Members take necessary suggestions or clarifications from their group members on doubts or suspicions which occur from time to time.

5. Summing. Groups help individuals to sum up the views of all concerned on a problem under consideration.

6. Consensus. Group members enable the organisation to arrive consensus decisions on problems of the organisations.

Group maintenance functions: Groups help its members in building group feeling and attitudes.

1. Harmonizing. Differences are common in between leaders and departmental heads. Then groups and group members try to reconcile the differences and bring harmony.

2. Gate keeping. Group helps its members to participate in decision-making. Groups also invite others to give suggestions.

3. Encouraging. Groups encourage members through friendly, warm and other facial expressions.

4. Follow up. Groups help the members in representing their individual problems.

5. Standard setting. In establishing standards, procedures, etc., groups would enable the organisation.

- **Group development**

Groups pass through sequence of five stages as shown below:

1. Forming,
2. Storming,
3. Norming,
4. Performing and
5. Adjourning.

1. Forming. In this stage so much uncertainty prevails about the structure, purpose and leadership. Members tend to test the waters to decide what type of behaviour is acceptable.

2. Storming. Here are members accept the existence of the group but afraid of discipline imposed on them by the leader. And at this stage the members will be in conflict with each other in declaring the leader, who will control them.

3. Norming. At this stage group demonstrates cohesiveness and people feel a sense of identity. The group solidifies and defines member behaviour.

4. Performing. At this stage the structure is fully functional and accepted. Group members move to know and understand each other to perform the tasks ahead.

5. Adjourning. For temporary work groups, members have to undergo adjourning stage. At this stage the group prepares for its disbursement. Attention is given towards wrapping up activities, however responses of the members vary.

Group becomes strong and effective as it passes through the first four stages. It is not necessary that every group formation passes through all the stages precisely. Sometimes several stages go simultaneously.

Stages of Group Development

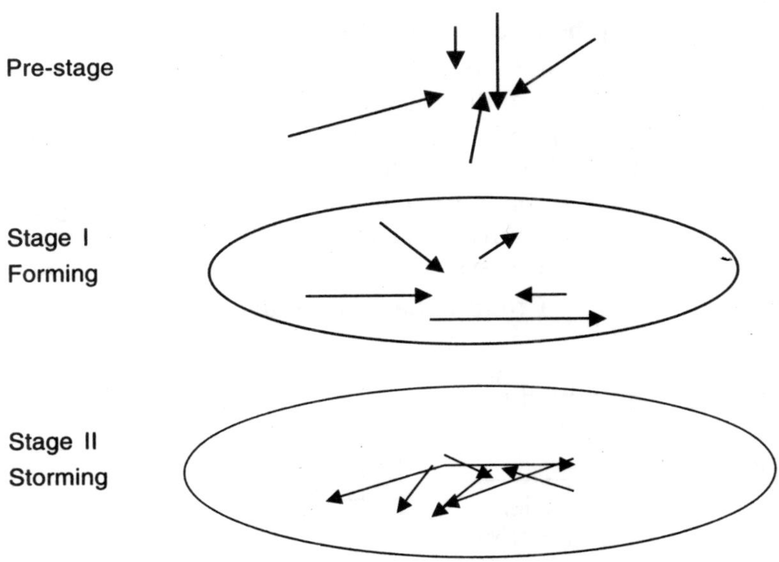

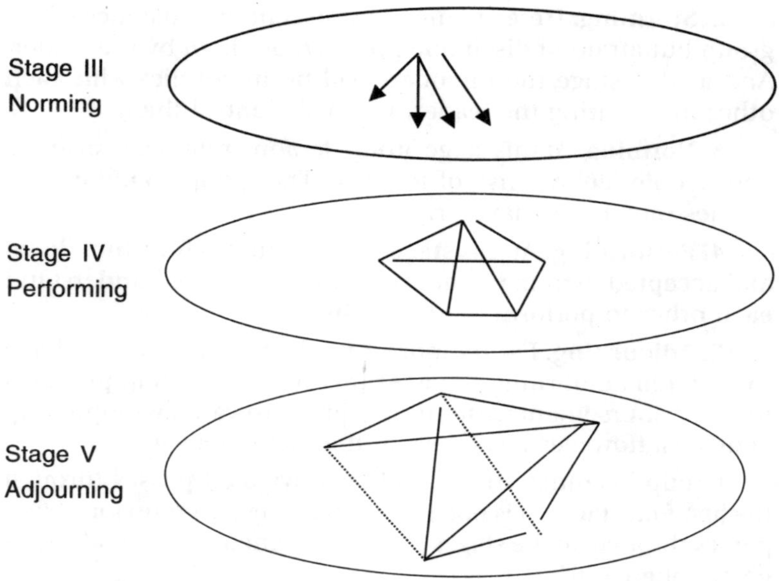

Source: Stephen P. Robbins, *Organisational Behaviour*, Prentice Hall of India, New Delhi.

- **Relationship between a work group and the organisation**

Some groups in their efforts are successful than others. It depends upon the ability of members, group size, level of conflict, internal pressures, etc. Following diagram shows the major components determining group performance.

Work groups do not exist in isolation. They are part of organisation. Every work group is influenced by the external conditions. Thus a group is a sub-system embedded in a larger system.

Group Behaviour Model

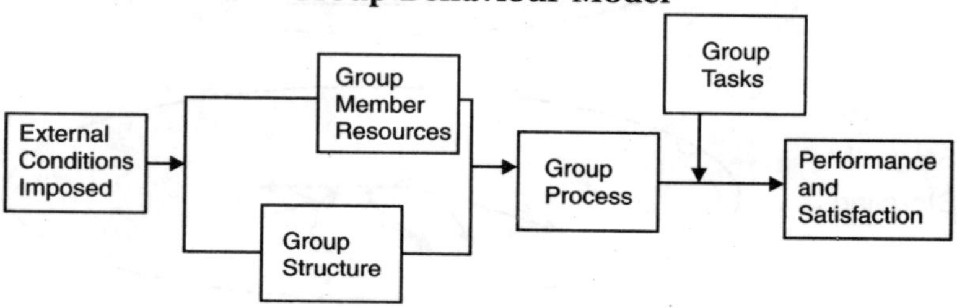

Source: Stephen P. Robbins, *Organisational Behaviour*, Prentice Hall of India, New Delhi, p. 291.

Determinants of relationship

Organisation strategy. Strategy outlines the goals of an organisation and the members for attaining them. The strategy that an organisation is pursuing at any given time will influence power of the work group(s). The ability of work group depends upon the resources allocated to the work group.

Authority structure. A group or individual has to work under a manager who exercises authority for work completion. Authority structure means deciding who reports to whom. Also it is concerned with who will take what decision at what time. However informal leaders also emerge to influence decisions of the group and organisation. There is strong relationship between the group and group leader (informal) and also formal (leader).

Regulations. The behaviour of a group can be predicted with the help of rules, regulations and procedures laid down by the organisation. These factors will influence the work group performance.

Organisational resources. Group behaviour depends upon time, money, materials and equipment allocated to them. If more facilities/resources are available, more the performance and *vice versa*.

Personnel selection. Group behaviour depends upon the ability of employees in that group. Ability depends upon the selections made by the personnel department.

Performance evaluation system. Behaviour of group depends upon the method of evaluation of its performance. The way the performance evaluated should reflect true pictures of performance. Also group behaviour depends upon the rewards the organisation gives to its people or groups. Thus rewards influence the achievement of group goals.

Organisation culture and values. Every organisation has its own unwritten culture that decides employees' behaviour. Every employee should understand the culture and values of the organisation and follow. Sometimes sub-groups will have different culture and standards by which their performance is evaluated. Thus groups behaviour is influenced by the organisational values and culture.

Physical work setting. The working conditions also influence group performance. Physical work setting includes, layout of employees' work place, ventilation and lighting, tools, distance between worker and boss, distance between co-workers, noise etc., cause and contribute to group performance.

Resourcefulness of group members

Group effectiveness depends upon the resourcefulness of its members. There are two important areas where members are resourceful.

Abilities. Group performance depends upon members' intellectual abilities. Mere abilities do not ensure group performance, but how effectively the member will perform in a group decides the group achievement. The members with original abilities will emerge as group leaders.

Group efficiency also depends upon the task related abilities that the members possess. Again what qualities or abilities members possess is not matter but how will the members interact in a group. However, the abilities also depend upon size of the group, type of task, leader's action and level of conflict within the group, etc.

Personality characteristics. Group behaviour depends upon individual traits, group attitudes and behaviour. The attributes with positive connotation such as sociability, self-reliance, independence, etc. tend to be positively related to group productivity, morale and cohesiveness. Negative qualities such as authoritarianism and dominance tend to influence negatively on group performance. These personality traits on the part of members affect group performance.

Single characteristic does not influence the group in a predictable manner. But personality characteristics together play an important role in influencing the group behaviour.

Formal groups *Vs.* Informal groups

In an organisational setting there are many types of groups. The groups are broadly divided into two kinds. One, formal groups and the other informal groups.

Formal groups. Formal groups are created and maintained to accomplish specific and predetermined tasks. They are wilfully formed. Sometimes they may be permanent. Temporary groups cease as soon as their purpose is over. They work in terms of rules and regulations. The group is structured with boundaries in terms of space and time. They are very much linked to organisation.

Informal groups. Informal groups develop to fulfil unwritten purposes as a result of social and psychological forces operating at the work place. They always work in terms of needs and go beyond organisation structure. Their function is not governed by the rules and regulations of company management. They do not have physical or written boundaries. Formal and informal groups differ from each other on the following grounds:

1. **Origin.** Formal groups are defined by the organisation while informal groups are evolved on likes and dislikes of the people at work place.

2. **Purpose.** Formal groups are created to serve specific objectives of the organisation while informal groups do form to serve the social and psychological purposes of people which are not served by the former.

3. **Size.** Formal groups are formed by the member representing different sections of the organisation, sometimes too large in size as it is mandatory. While in the case of informal groups members are too small in number since they work not in terms of rules but in terms of social purposes.

4. **Nature of groups.** The formal groups tend to exist as long as organisation survives. Sometimes members also change to keep the members alert.

Informal groups are proposed temporarily to serve specific and temporary purpose, not fulfilled by the formal groups. They are closed quite immediately after the purpose is fulfilled. Members may wind up the existing one and form into new ones depending upon the changing tastes and purposes.

5. **Number.** Formal groups can be imagined basing on the length and breadth of the organisation. But in the case of informal groups their number will be beyond imagination. Since they are formed taking likes and dislikes of people into consideration.

6. **Authority.** Formal groups derive authority from organisations. They may be granted powers and withdrawn.

But in the case of informal groups powers are assumed by the members as long as the group serves their interests. In the case of formal organisation manager enjoys only limited powers, while in the informal organisation leaders enjoy unlimited powers since they are formed out of curiosity.

7. Behaviour. In the case of formal groups, member behaviour is checked by rules and regulations of the organisation. But in informal groups members behaviour either positive or negative depends upon their confidence in the group. They may withdraw their support when group fails to fulfil their expected interest.

8. Communication. Formal groups communicate in a prescribed manner and only through hierarchy. In the case of informal groups there are no such restrictions and methods prescribed.

9. Control. Management does not have control over informal groups as they are the products of natural feelings. But it is different in the case of formal groups as they are constituted by the organisation. They cease their operation soon the management feels to wind up.

- **Nature of informal groups**

Informal group is the cluster of people having common ideas and interests. People come together to serve their peculiar interests not fulfilled by the formal groups constituted by the organisation. Thus informal groups work in terms of needs of people and go beyond the formal groups. They are not seen or shown in organisation structure designed by the organisation. But management recognises the existence of informal ones on the following reasons.

Reasons

1. Quest for social satisfaction. Man is a social being and would like to associate with people who appreciate his ideas. Thus people with common interest come together to discuss and socialise themselves on organisational, professional and personal matters.

2. Avoid Boredom. In a formal organisation men are divided on the basis of their specialisation and as is demanded by the job. It is not possible to feel relaxed with colleagues prescribed by the formal organisation. But in the case of informal groups people get a lot more satisfaction by sharing their personal ideas and feelings. As said by Davis along with technical imperative, there is also social imperative to work together. Thus informal groups are the natural ones that advise out of natural likes and dislikes.

3. Release of tension. People in modern organisation are governed by super specialisation in any profession. The employees work with high concentration of mind at work place under conditions designed by the management to improve quality and production. There, the employees do not get complete satisfaction since they cannot interact with people around as they like. Under such conditions informal association of people give them job satisfaction as they can interact with others without any reservations.

4. Leisure time. Personnel wish to spend their leisure time with people of their choice. It is possible only in informal associations of people.

5. Freedom. Employees are governed by hierarchy relations *i.e.*, superior subordinate relationships. Informal groups individually forget such barriers and enjoy freedom to speak, clarify and take advice on personal and professional matters.

Types of groups

1. Natural groups. Natural groups do not give structure at all. They are spontaneous.

2. Family groups. They have regular members who exert pressure and influence on the behaviour of members.

3. Organised groups. In one way they are formal in nature with consistent structure and having acknowledged leaders.

Sayles has classified informal groups into four types:

1. Apathetic
2. Erratic
3. Strategic
4. Conservative

Functions of informal groups

Informal groups go beyond formal groups and do things

what is not possible for formal groups. These informal groups do the following functions according to Dublin:

1. Informal groups do things naturally without being told.
2. If new methods are to be experimented, informal groups enable in making trials with new methods.
3. The informal groups advise norms of behaviour for members.
4. Personal image and integrity can be maintained through informal groups.

According to Chester I. Bernard:

1. Informal groups help in establishing norms of conduct between superiors and subordinates.
2. Informal groups are useful to maintain cohesiveness in organisations.
3. Informal groups enable to regulate people to work willingly.
4. Self-respect and independence can be bargained through informal groups.

Philip Selznick emphasises that informal groups undertake modifying functions of making goods acceptable to people.

The following are the functions of informal groups:

1. Cultural values. Informal groups help in perpetuating cultural values of people associated with the group.

2. Social satisfaction. People are social beings and they cannot work in isolation. As such informal groups would provide necessary social satisfaction to employees.

3. Solving problems at work. Groups of informal nature would help people to discuss and arrive solutions acceptable to all. Thus problems can be solved easily with the help of informal groups.

4. Sharing of knowledge. Informal groups give opportunity to interact closely with others and share knowledge.

5. Elimination of red-tapism. Due to pressure of heavy work and uncertainties officials adopt red-tapism which is inenviable. This red-tapism would be minimised with the help of informal relations and groups.

6. Group thinking. Two brains are better than one. Group thinking would offer viable solutions to problems.

7. Group decision-making. By way of informal groups intelligent and efficient ideas can be pooled and decision-making will be effective in organisations.

8. Jobs interesting. The jobs which are routine and dull can become interesting with the involvement of social attachment.

9. Instant coordination. Due to complexity of modern technology, interdependency is highly required among the individuals. This interdependency can be increased with group effort and instant coordination will be possible if the issues are taken up by groups.

10. Differentiation. To differentiate between good and bad, legitimate and illegitimate group involvement is necessary.

11. Abstract concepts. Abstract concepts such as honesty, loyalty, cooperation and self-sacrifice cannot be observed in work situations without the involvement of informal groups in organisations.

12. Uniform standards. Larger groups often maintain ethical standards designed to further the organisational groups. However, group standards are not consistent with organisational objectives. In these situations, groups (informal) enable to maintain uniform standards throughout the organisation.

13. Protection from pressures. Management often comes with proposals of change of technology and method of production by which employees are put to heavy strain and pressure. In these situations informal groups would be helpful in altering the proposals acceptable to both employers and employees.

14. Barriers of communication. Due to vastness in size and complexity in operations barriers of communication are common. Informal groups would enable to minimise the communication gap between employees and management.

Dangers from informal groups

Informal groups benefit the organisation and also cause disadvantages if not properly controlled. The difficulties with informal groups in an organisation are as follows:

1. Inhabit changes. Because business is expanding to market forces which are often changing, management has to change production methods and office procedures. Informal groups have this tendency to follow customs, conventions often resist change. They fail to see the growth and development of the organisation which in turn benefit them.

2. Role conflict. Individual goals, and organisations goals do not concur unless handled orderly. The existence of groups will cause further role conflict to the existing incompatibility.

3. Gossips. People misbehave and pass rumours in the absence of clarity in communication. When ambiguity prevails people speak casually something not relevant which stands for no proof. Existence of informal groups propel rumours and gossips in organisation causing barriers to smooth functioning.

Steps to handle informal groups

Informal groups occur in organisations without effort. They are automatic and natural. Members when fail to get satisfaction in a formal group try to affiliate with others and derive satisfaction through mutual interaction. Management should realise the existence of groups particularly 'informal' in nature. Often management treats these 'cliques' as destructive to organisations. Members try to be identified with informal groups which share time and effort when individuals are ill-treated by management. Individuals will be more loyal to groups than to an organisation, a larger entity. Management should make use of informal groups as means to develop the organisation.

Davis, Keith has recommended the following steps for smooth functioning of an organisation:

1. Management should recognise the existence of informal groups.
2. Management should integrate the group goals and organisational goals.
3. Management should not threaten the members affiliated to informal groups.
4. Management should identify individual needs and try to satisfy them.
5. Management should take informal groups into confidence and take decisions.

6. Management should be positive, flexible and accommodative to groups' interests.
7. Management should not hide matters with informal groups.
8. Management should spend more time to develop support with informal groups.
9. Management should educate informal groups to subordinate their goals to organisational goals.
10. Management should be people oriented rather than production oriented as long as they do well with the organisation.

Norms of group behaviour

Norms mean what members ought and ought not to do under certain circumstances. They tell what is expected of an individual in certain situations. Norms act as means of influencing the behaviour of group members. However norms differ from group to group. And, one should know that norms are mostly unwritten and informal.

Characteristics of norms. According to Hackman

1. Applicable to groups at length.
2. Resolve impersonal differences.
3. Ensure conformity.
4. Applicable to modify behaviour.
5. Applicable not to private thoughts.
6. Detrimental if enforced too rigidly.
7. Private acceptance is not necessary.
8. Used to behavioural modification.
9. Meant for all people.
10. Norms can be developed suddenly or wiped off.
11. Not all norms apply to everyone.
12. Influential or rich persons try to deviate from the norms.
13. Facilitate group's survival.
14. Increase the predictability of group's behaviour.
15. Reduce embarrassing interpersonal problems of members.
16. Allow members to express the central values of the group.

Types of norms

1. Performance related. Work groups typically provide their members with explicit cases on how they should work and how to get the job done. These norms are powerful and decide employee performance.

2. Informal social arrangements. These norms come from informal work groups and primarily regulate social interactions within the group. These norms affect and influence the members with whom group members eat lunch, friendships on and of the job, social games, etc.

3. Allocation of Resources. These norms can originate in the group or in the organisation and cover things like pay, providing equipment etc. These resources allocation norms have direct impact on employee satisfaction and indirect effect on group performance.

Ways of norms

1. Explicit statement made by a group member. Group leader is powerful in influencing group members by his clear statement of norm. *Ex*: No personal calls are allowed during working hours.

2. Critical events in the group history. These set important precedents. *Ex*: A bystander is injured while standing too close to a machine and from that time onwards, members of the work group regularly monitor each other to ensure that no one other than the operator gets within five feet of any machine.

3. Primary. The first behaviour pattern that emerges in a group frequently sets group's expectations.

4. Carry over behaviour from historical situations. Group members bring expectations with them from other groups of which they have been members. This is likely to increase the probability that the expectations they bring are consistent with those already held by the group.

Conformity. The group members should conform to the group norms, beliefs, etc. Conformity means adjusting one's own behaviour to align with the norms of the group. People belong to several groups and norms vary from group to group. So they conform to the important group norms and leave others.

Members *Vs.* Group norms

Normally people conforms to norms of groups. Not every member conforms every norm. People whose relations are disturbed will probably be a conformist. People may continue and oblige all the norms. Sometimes he may accept important norms but reject some other norms. Thus conformity to norms is not automatic and conformity depends upon the following factors:

1. Personality factors. More intelligent people less likely to conform to norms. Authoritarian conform to norms than non-authoritarian. Under conditions of crisis only conformity is observed more. In unusual situations and when things are not clear decision-makers confirm to the norms.

2. Situational factors. Higher the body or group more the conformity to norms. Decentralised patterns enhance conformity of behaviour.

3. Inter-group relationship. If groups have sound relationship conformity to norms is more.

4. Compatible goals. When group goals and organisational goals are not compatible, they adhere to norms.

Steps to enforce group norms

Enforcement of 'norm' in organisations is achieved through the following steps:

1. Orientation. Through orientation group norms will be successfully implementated.

2. Admonish. At times members should be admonished for not behaving appropriately with group norms.

3. Detection. Members should adhere to group norms for its survival. Some methods be developed to detect whether members are up to group's estimation or not.

4. Caution. Members may be cautioned that they will be eliminated for not following the norms of group.

5. Supportive. Group should be friendly and supportive to the members who follow norms and criticise the deviants group norms.

6. Flexible. Management should study the compatibility of norms in practice. If the norms are to be altered, management should not hesitate to do so.

7. Punishment. Management should punish the members who are behaving against the norms.

• Definition of group cohesiveness

Cohesiveness is defined as the degree to which members are attracted to one another and are motivated to stay together. Effective group cohesiveness is a group characteristic. Hence management should try to enhance cohesiveness. Cohesiveness tells how group influences its members. It is like a 'glue' that holds people together. It indicates how individuals share thoughts and subordinate their goals to group goals. It establishes more harmonious behaviour in members.

Features of group cohesiveness

1. Members have common interest.
2. Members are mutually cooperative.
3. Members have access to others.
4. Interaction between members is high.
5. Inter-personal communication is high.
6. Members are dedicated to the group and its purposes.
7. Members are active in participation of group meetings.
8. People have group loyalty.
9. Members release energies.
10. Group has sound history and track record.

Determinants of group cohesiveness. Group cohesiveness depends upon several factors some of which are as follows:

1. Time. Cohesiveness of group depends upon time available for the members to talk, work, interact etc. The amount of time members spend together influences the cohesiveness. More the time members spend one for the other, more friendly they become. The interaction leads to common interests and team work.

2. Proximity. The proximity refers to physical closeness of members in office. People who sits nearer to each other often meet and spend more time together. This need not be always true in all cases.

3. Relationship. Sound relationship among members result in high cohesiveness.

4. Severity of initiation. The more difficult it is to get entry into a group make people to be together. Heavy competition to get admission into a good medical college results in cohesiveness in class work.

5. Group size. Larger the size of the group less the group cohesiveness. Smaller the size more the cohesiveness. In bigger groups small cliques form again groups and create internal differences. And people fail to interact and understand each other.

6. Gender nature of members. Women exhibit greater cohesion than men. The fact is that women are less competitive and are more cooperative with people.

7. External threats. Group cohesiveness will be more if members are under threat from outside forces. Threat from management brings unity among employees (say).

8. Previous successor. If a group has long track record of successes, it attracts more people into its fold. They have the sole drive in their mind to maintain the same dignity. Member takes pride to join them. Once they join they tend to live upto the group expectations.

9. Goal compatibility. All the members should have common goal compatible to group goals.

10. Like-minded. The members should be like-minded in tastes, feelings and views towards organisation.

11. Status. A group with high aims and success in making strides to achieve goals will have more cohesiveness. Membership in a group is difficult.

12. Attractive leader. The group should have dynamic leader who can keep the interest of the members going together.

13. Collective power. A well-knit group will be more collective in their attempts to achieve organisational performance.

14. Homogeneity. Group having people with common interests will be highly cohesiveness.

15. Stable relationship. Members if know each other for a long time will have stable relationship as they understand each other very well.

16. Competition. Inter-group competition increases cohesion. Success resulting from inter-group competition increases cohesiveness further.

17. Dependency. Member joins group to satisfy his goals (personal). As long as group offers satisfaction the individuals depend upon group and get attracted to the organisation.

Disruptive forces. Following are the forces disrupting group cohesion:

1. Cohesion declines as sub-groups arise in an organisation.
2. If members have different views, attitudes, beliefs, they lead to group destruction.
3. Intra-group conflicts lead to less cohesion.
4. Differences in approaches to accomplish goals will cause disruption.

Group cohesion *Vs.* Productivity

Group cohesion is always desirable as long as it does increase productivity and organisational performance. Cohesive groups are more effective. Cohesiveness reduces tensions and provides supportive environment for the successful attainment of group goals. Members belonging to successful unit have high commitment. Popular slogan reminds that, 'together we win' and 'there are no individuals on the team'.

The relationship of cohesiveness and productivity depends upon the performance related norms. These norms ensure higher productivity and higher cohesiveness.

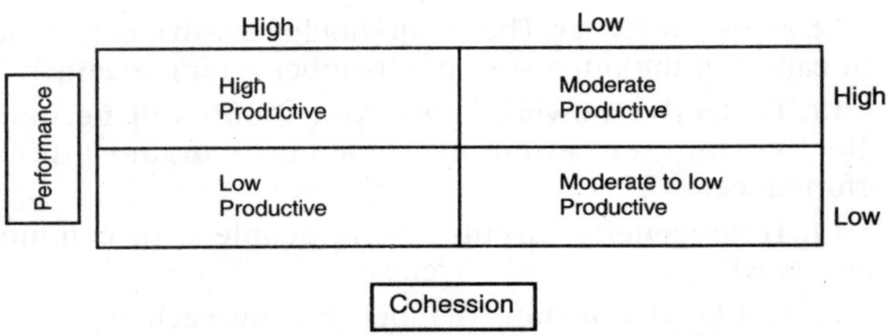

Adopted from Stephen & Robbins, *Organisational Behaviour*, Prentice Hall of India Private Ltd., New Delhi, p. 313.

The graph shows 4 quarters which indicate that if cohesiveness is low and performance norms are high productivity increases. When cohesiveness and performance related norms are both low, productivity will tend to fall into the moderate to low range.

Group decision-making *Vs.* Individual decision-making

Group decision-making means decision taken by all the concerned people and viewing the problem from different viewpoints. Two brains are better than one. Hence, a decision taken by an individual is less desirable. Group decision develops creative alternatives leading to effective performance. The following are the aspects, which differentiate group decision-making from individual decision-making.

1. Superiority. Group decision is superior to individual decision. A group refers to different intellectuals drawn from various faculties. People with characteristics can pool valuable information and expertise, to generate creative alternatives from which more practicable, valuable, acceptable and understandable solution can be arrived. Group detects mistakes quicker and judges more accurately.

2. Risk-shift. If a decision taken by a group has failed no individual is held wholly responsible. Group shares information in an open environment and members become more familiar with the problem. Once problem is familiarised then they take even risky decision. In case of individuals risk taking offers an opportunity. Hence group decision assumes more value and is highly rated. Thus risk is shared by many. So group decisions dilute responsibility and risk is shifted to many.

3. Conformity. Norms are time tested. The norms are established over a period of time unknown. The norms become standards for measuring conduct. A group enforces the norms while taking decisions since violators are liable for punishment. Thus group decisions conforms to norms of society and organisation. As such every member adheres to norms of the society.

4. Greater knowledge and information. A group is highly informative than an individual, since two brains are better than one. The group members having been exposed to various situations bring abundant information whereby plenty of alternatives can be developed from which members can take more acceptable and viable decision.

5. More alternatives. Thorough diagnosing the situation is possible in case of group. In case of individual it is difficult to imagine the problem in depth. Hence more alternatives will be available in group decision-making from which choice can be made easy.

6. Acceptability. The solution carried by group will be taken as their own idea. It is not so in the case of decision taken by an individual. Decision by participation of all the concerned increases its acceptability.

7. Better comprehension. People if participate and take a decision they understand very well. It is easy to implement since communication failure is minimised in group decision-making. All people have clear idea of the solution why it is taken and under what circumstances. Thus group thinking enhances the comprehension of the decision.

8. Consensus. Decision arrived on consensus basis is more effective than decision based on majority opinions. Consensus decision-making is possible when members have compatible interests and extend cooperation. Consensus method of decision-making is desirable when members:

(a) Present their views logically.
(b) Listen to the comments of others carefully.
(c) Don't have conflicting interests.
(d) Don't yield to the views of others.
(e) Engage views of all concerned.
(f) Encourage win position to reach.
(g) Entertain solution taking all the viewpoints completely.
(h) Do not suppress any single opinion.

9. Nature of problem. If policy decisions are to be taken, group decision is required since it requires expertise of knowledge persons. Policy decisions go a long way so individual approach is to be discouraged.

10. Qualitative. When problems are critical and crucial, solutions will not be qualitative if taken individually. Hence group decision is desirable since it adds quality to the solution.

11. Climate. When supportive climate prevails in the situation manager should adopt group decision-making.

12. Participate. When people concerned show interest and wish to participate in decision-making, management should encourage group decision-making.

13. Time. Manager should prefer and encourage group decision-making if time available for him is sufficient and permits to take decision in consultation with group member.

Problems confronted in group decision-making

Group decision-making is necessary in policy matters. The problems in group decision-making are as follows:

1. Time consuming. Members in a group with different interests do not come together and not concur in opinions for various reasons. Manager should communicate and make them to meet for thorough discussion on policy matters, which takes lot of time.

2. Conformation. Group norms are existing in society from times unknown and organisation. These norms to be upheld for satisfaction to all concerned. Yet it is difficult and decision-making in conformity to the 'norms' will be an exercise on razor's edge, because various selfish elements compel the decision-making process in their favour.

3. Domination. In group decisions individuals try to dominate and influence to fulfil their benefit. Sometimes subgroups also form and dominate the process of decision-making. Thus decisions are becoming biased many times.

4. Conflicting alternatives. People without objective look, always create win-loose situations. Thus best alternative arrived will not be accepted by all.

5. Irresponsibility. Since everyone's responsibility is no one's responsibility, no individual keeps mind and heart to take effective decision, and conclusions will not be effective.

6. Lack of compatibility. Since individuals have conflicting interests, solutions cannot be arrived satisfactorily.

7. Lack of comprehension. Decision lacks comprehension since the decisions are taken not on technical grounds but on political and social.

8. Lacks logic. Members lack presentation of views logically and cause decision-making a complicated process.

9. Fail to hear. Members always try to inform others and demand others to hear them. It is the fundamental principle on the part of participants to hear carefully and patiently to others.

10. Yield to pressures. Members yield to pressures from others on grounds such as political interest, regional feeling and the decision taken will become less viable.

Measures to improve group decision-making

Following are the techniques suggested to improve group decision-making. Manager has to select suitable technique depending upon the situation to take decision.

1. Brain storming. This technique is applied to generate ideas for decision-making. Osborn has defined it as 'using brain to storm the problem'. The technique is widely used in all institutions and groups.

(a) The problem is presented to the group.
(b) Problem is stated clearly and precisely.
(c) Members' attention is drawn to the problem.
(d) Each member is asked to give ideas.
(e) Maximum number of ideas are solicited without quality relevance.
(f) Factors inhibiting idea generation is pushed back.
(g) Session is meant for free and frank opinions.
(h) The members should not feel institutions of legal or financial nature.
(i) The chairman should not impose any restrictions.
(j) Idea evaluation is deferred to a later stage.
(k) Comment or criticism should be strictly prohibited during discussion.
(l) Anyone violating this should be gently cautioned.
(m) The technique is applied to small gathering and specific or well-defined problem.
(n) Manager should adopt and create supportive climate.

(o) During discussion manager is expected to record the feelings and opinions of participants.

(p) The manager has to choose best course of action at the end of the session.

2. Consensus technique. This technique is used to pool the ideas generated by several task groups to arrive at a decision. The task groups or sub-groups develop clarity and evaluate a list of ideas. The facilitator encourages participants for 'clusters' of ideas. Then alternative clusters of ideas are discussed and the facilitators consolidate different schemes developed by sub-groups into a representative scheme. Group members then work to revise it to reach out more mutually acceptable solution. This exercise is repeated till group as a whole reaches a single consolidated solution and final decision is based on that.

This technique is best suited for problems of multi-dimensional that have inter-connected elements and many sequential steps.

3. 'Delphi' technique. The name 'Delphi' indicates a shrine at which the ancient Greeks prayed for information about the future. The participants are widely dispersed and do not have the opportunity to have face to face discussion for decision-making. Then decision is taken without their meeting. Here communication between participants take place through mail.

Process of 'Delphi' technique

(a) Problem is defined.

(b) Structured questionnaire is prepared regarding problems.

(c) Questionnaires are mailed to participants.

(d) Every member is expected to answer independently and mail back the questionnaires.

(e) Summing up the suggestions a report is prepared for arriving solution.

(f) The report is sent along with advanced questionnaire to each member.

(g) Each member evaluates the feedback report, generate new ideas and returns.

(h) Now a final decision is taken using the suggestions given in second round.

(i) Thus the process continues until (using the suggestions given second time).

Thus anonymous inputs by mail acts as inputs. These anonymous inputs tend to eliminate the counter productive effects such as status, intimidation, emotion, face saving, etc., which play vital role in traditional group discussions. This technique takes more time than other methods. It has hidden advantage to avoid the problems in face-to-face discussion, interference and undue influence of others.

4. Nominal group technique (NGT). Though members meet, verbal communication is avoided in this technique. The management chooses members on selective basis, and the group is called 'paper group'. The number is optimum but not very large. The idea is to avoid or restrict the inter-personal communication and encourage real contribution of individual members. The nominal group follows strict procedure:

(a) Members of the select group are made to meet.

(b) Group leader outlines the problem.

(c) Members are asked to write down their ideas without any discussion with others.

(d) The best ideas are written on black board for others to see.

(e) A discussion is held to clarify the ideas.

(f) Voting is conducted on ranking the ideas.

(g) On the basis of votes polled decision is arrived.

The technique is equally superior to interacting groups. This NGT is employed in social service organisations largely to get effective decisions.

QUESTIONS FOR DISCUSSION

1. What is group and narrate the types of groups in an organisation?
2. Why do people join groups? Discuss factors influencing group formation.
3. What groups do for organisations?
4. Explain the functions of groups in modern organisation.
5. How would you use the five stage group development model to better understand group behaviour?

6. What is relationship between a work group and the organisation of which it is a part?
7. What group members resources influence the group?
8. How formal groups differ from informal groups?
9. Discuss the nature and types of informal groups in an organisation.
10. What are the functions of informal groups?
11. How does the informal groups hamper organisational development?
12. Explain, how management should handle informal groups?
13. Explain the role of norms in group behaviour.
14. Why members conform to group norms?
15. Suggest steps to enforce group norms.
16. Define cohesiveness. Explain features and determinants of group cohesiveness.
17. High cohesion in a group leads to higher productivity. Explain.
18. Discuss the situation under which group decision-making is better than individual decision-making.
19. Discuss the problems confronted in group decision-making.
20. Suggest some measures to improve group decision-making.

7

JOB SATISFACTION

- **Definition of attitude**

Job satisfaction is the result of various attitudes the employee holds towards his job and life in general.

An employee's attitude may be considered as a readiness to act on one way rather than another in the context of specific factors related to a job.

Attitude is the way an individual tends to interpret, understand or define a situation or his relationship with others.

An attitude is a set to action with an emotional overtone.

It is a tendency to regard things with approval or disapproval.

Job satisfaction. Job satisfaction refers to a general attitude resulting from various specific attitudes relating to (1) Job factors, (2) Group relationships outside the job.

Job factors. Job factors effect the attitudes of an employee. *Ex.*: Steadiness of employment, supervision, wages, working conditions, work, evaluation, treatment, etc.

Group relationships. Group relationships outside the job develop some attitudes in the minds of employee. *Ex.*: Family relationship, social status, relationship with labour, relationship with social or political organisations, etc.

Thus job satisfaction is the sum of various attitudes the employee holds towards his job, towards job related factors and towards life in general. An employee's attitude may contribute to job satisfaction. Yet the two terms are not interchangeable.

Job satisfaction is the extent of favourableness with which employees view their work.

Job satisfaction is a generalised attitude resulting from many specific attitudes in the areas of (i) specific job factor (ii) individual adjustment, (iii) Group relationship.

Importance. Job satisfaction takes place when there is concurrence between job requirements, wants and expectations of employees. Thus the job satisfaction occurs when job requirements and rewards it provides to employee matches. Job satisfaction can be viewed in relation to employees' satisfaction with their home life and community life. The job satisfaction and life satisfaction are closely related.

An employee can try for higher satisfaction in various pursuits of life when his satisfaction is low. Sometimes job satisfaction is the gap between what an employee experiences about that particular factor in his actual condition and what he thinks should be there.

Mental health. Job satisfaction and life satisfaction are linked to each other. Dissatisfaction of job will have spillover effects and people feel bad about many other things such as family life, leisure activities and community life. Many unresolved personality problems arise due to dissatisfaction at work. Thus job satisfaction, psychological adjustment in life and mental health are highly related to one another.

Physical features. Job satisfaction is essential to maintain physical health. Chronic dissatisfaction at work represents mental and emotional stress, which results in hypertension, coronary artery disease, digestive ailments and even some kinds of cancer.

Organisation goodwill. Man with high-satisfaction will give favourable sentiments about the organisation to the community at large. When the organisation goodwill is spoken high, dynamic and talented people will join the organisation. Thus organisation will be in a position to enjoy the talents of people.

Reduces absenteeism and turnover. Satisfied persons work for more time at work and dissatisfied persons leave the place of work as early as possible. People with high dissatisfaction work less number of days in a month and tries to quit the organisation.

Attachment. Employees with high satisfaction will develop attachment with the organisation and spend more time with authorities.

Determinants of job satisfaction

Job satisfaction is caused by many interrelated factors. Some of the factors are briefly stated below:

Personal factors. These factors include the personality of an employee, age, sex, education, intelligence, time on the job etc. The existence of neurotic behaviour has been found to be a cause of job satisfaction. Also, individuals who are rated high in inter-personal desirability by their fellow employees are more satisfied by their jobs.

Factors inherent in the job. These factors include the type of work to be performed, still required for work performance, occupational status involved in the job, difference in work situation, place of work etc.

Factors under the management control. These factors include, job security, pay, fringe benefits, type of supervision, the opportunity for advancement in job, etc.

Age. Age plays crucial role in job satisfaction. As workers grow older they tend to be more satisfied with their jobs. As age passes people develop adjustment nature and expect not much unlike young people, who are often tend to be dissatisfied since they expect more and more.

Occupational level. People of high level occupations tend to be more satisfied with their jobs. They are better paid and also have better working conditions. Hence they have good reason to be more satisfied.

Organisation size. Organisation is inversely related to job satisfaction. As organisation grows in size they tend to disrupt supportive processes such as communication, coordination and participation. And employees begin to feel that they are loosing control over the events as such their job satisfaction goes down.

Communication. Communication flows in all directions. Adequate communication will enhance the job satisfaction of individuals.

Training needs. When an employee changes his department or promoted to higher position he needs orientation and adequate training so that he can better discharge his duties in a new environment. Management should arrange necessary training facilities. Thus training facilities would increase job satisfaction.

Union benefits. An employee when joins union his problems are protected by the union and union will give him necessary support in bargaining with management about his privileges and rights. Thus union support will add to job satisfaction.

Challenging job. Employees tend to prefer to job that give them opportunities to use their skills and abilities very well. Jobs that have too little challenges create boredom. Under conditions of moderate challenges most employees will experience pleasure and satisfaction.

Equitable rewards. Satisfaction is likely to result in when pay and promotion are in line with the expectations of the employees.

Promotion. Promotions provide opportunities for personal growth and increased social status. Individuals who perceive that promotions are made in fair and just manner are likely to experience satisfaction.

Supportive working conditions

Employees are concerned with personal comforts, and physical surroundings. Temperature, light, noise and other environmental factors have to be moderate. Employees prefer to work relatively close to home.

Supportive colleagues. Friendly and supportive co-workers give them increased job satisfaction.

Supervisor's treatment. Employees' satisfaction is increased when the immediate supervisor is friendly.

Personality—Job fit. Individuals' abilities and vocations should be matched. Thus when talents and demands of the job are met employees will have greater satisfaction from their work.

Work group. One strong characteristic that worker exhibits is 'association with people' at work place. Further employees try to interact with others as much as possible to perform their duties. These two will be followed by an individual as long as they serve his social needs and in turn job satisfaction.

Job contents. Job contents also influence individual satisfaction in his job. They refer to factors such as recognition, responsibility, advancement and achievement etc., the employees perform. Other aspects that go into job satisfaction are job security, supervision, social relationships. These factors determine the extent of job satisfaction of an employee.

Specialisation. The relationship between job satisfaction and specialisation is crucial. Specialisation gives satisfaction up to certain point beyond which it reduces the level of satisfaction. A worker may not enjoy the job. Hence the tasks must be unified and integrated into a meaningful 'whole' to give him satisfaction. Over specialisation too does not give him satisfaction, *i.e.*, if a worker is doing the same operation number of times a day the work will not be interesting. Hence job should be optimally specialised.

Educational level. Normally the individuals should be placed in appropriate positions depending upon their educational background. But such things take place rarely. When imbalance prevails job dissatisfaction erupts because highly educated persons will have high expectations and aspire for high positions. Management should justify the highly educated persons by placing them in high positions.

Race and sex. Sex and race affect job satisfaction if not carefully the employees are positioned on the basis of race and sex. Normally woman have less expectations than men, so women derive more satisfaction though they are paid low. In the case of men the management has to do a lot more.

Number of dependents. The job satisfaction depends upon the number of subordinates working under a supervisor (employee). More the subordinate less the satisfaction and *vice versa*.

Intelligence. Job satisfaction depends upon intelligence level of workers. Studies in U.S.A and U.K revealed that intelligent workers have poorer work attitudes. Some other studies revealed that most intelligent girls employed in a chocolate factory were found to be easily bored. However, there is no consistency between the job satisfaction and intelligence. But overall analysis appears that relation of intelligence to job satisfaction depends upon the level and range of intelligence and the challenge of the job.

Personality. Studies have suggested that personality is a major cause of job satisfaction. Anxiety, extent of neuroticism, etc., are responsible for low job satisfaction. Persons who are rated high in inter-personal desirability by their fellow employees and high on total adjustment by supervisors will have high job satisfaction.

Geography. Regional variations attributable to geography will influence the level of job satisfaction. Some studies revealed that workers in large cities are less satisfied than those in smaller cities and towns.

Fringe benefits. Fringe benefits including housing, canteen, transportation, quarters, children education, etc., are also influencing the job satisfaction of an employee. However wage and salary are primary in determining job satisfaction.

Responsibility. Responsibility goes with security and experience. In some Indian studies it is found that level of satisfaction increases with level of responsibility. Ordinary employees press for rights and benefits but not for the responsibilities. Employees are reluctant to assume responsibilities which reveals that they are not satisfied with their jobs. Hence it can be concluded that satisfied employees tend to assume more responsibilities.

Measures to increase job satisfaction

The management of an organisation should take the following measures to increase job satisfaction:

Employee placement. Management should place the employee where the employee is suitable, so that he can derive satisfaction.

Age. Senior people should be given respectable jobs.

Sex. Keeping the sex in mind manager has to allot work such that gives satisfaction to the women.

Improved working conditions. Management should identify the working conditions which are responsible for poor results and take necessary action to alter them, so that employee satisfies. Thus by understanding the root cause of job dissatisfaction the management can evolve a strategy for remedial action.

Transferring dissatisfied employees. When the jobs are not compatible to their expectations employee undergoes dissatisfaction. Hence management may transfer those to such places where they are more fit and suitable. Thus by matching the employee expectations and his capabilities job satisfaction can be improved.

Changing perceptions. Employees should have positive perceptions towards the job and activities they have to perform. If this is missing there starts dissatisfaction.

Features of job satisfaction and dissatisfaction

Job satisfaction is a crucial part of organisational climate and an important element that decides management and employees relationship. It is a positive emotional state which occurs when employee expectations are fulfilled by the job requirements. People spend more time in work environment, if they are satisfied with their jobs. The employees expect their time at work to be pleasant, agreeable, fulfilling and satisfying.

Job satisfaction is an intangible, unseen, complex assemblage of beliefs and emotional feelings and such behavioural tendencies. Job satisfaction may be viewed as the pleasurable emotional state resulting from the perception of one's job as fulfilling one's job values compatible to his needs. According to Smith, job satisfaction is the persistent feeling towards discriminable aspects of the job situation.

Indicators of higher job satisfaction. Employees who are satisfied will remain in organisation for a long time and wish to be associated with the organisation.

Attendance. An employee who has higher job satisfaction will attend and participate actively in solving the problems of the organisation.

Involvement. People involve in taking risk when job satisfaction is high. Whenever some problems occur and cause troubles employees tend to avoid their involvement to escape from criticism.

Assume responsibilities. Often sharing responsibilities by themselves does not happen. People with high job satisfaction do come forward to share responsibilities and accomplish things as desired.

Low job satisfaction. Employees dissatisfaction can be expressed in a number of ways.

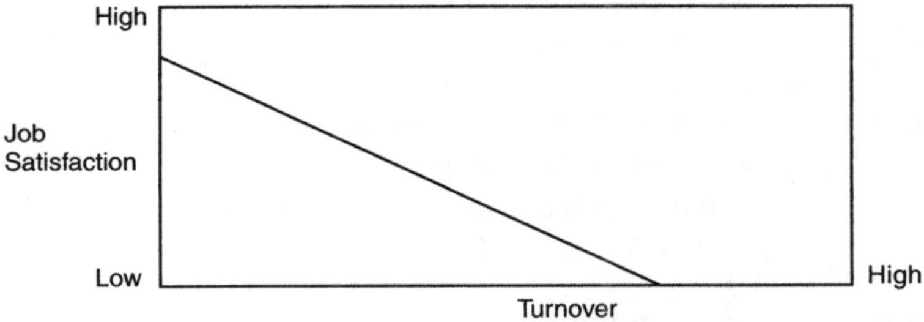

Turnover. The employees who have lower satisfaction are more likely to leave their employers.

Absenteeism. Dissatisfied employees tend to be absent more often. Employees basically do not avoid, but when some reason for absence arises the employees find it easier to respond to that reason.

Quit. Employees often dissatisfied and do not match himself with the job he will quit and search for alternative.

Complain. Dissatisfied employees often complain about things in their work place such as poor facilities and inadequate working conditions.

Insubordination. Sometimes employees disobey the orders of superior and cause strained relations for being incompatible to each other.

Shrink responsibilities. Employees not satisfied with job will fail in duties and explain inability to share responsibilities due to poor or inadequate facilities.

The employees often come with the following responses when they are not satisfied with their jobs. The four possible responses are shown in the following diagram.

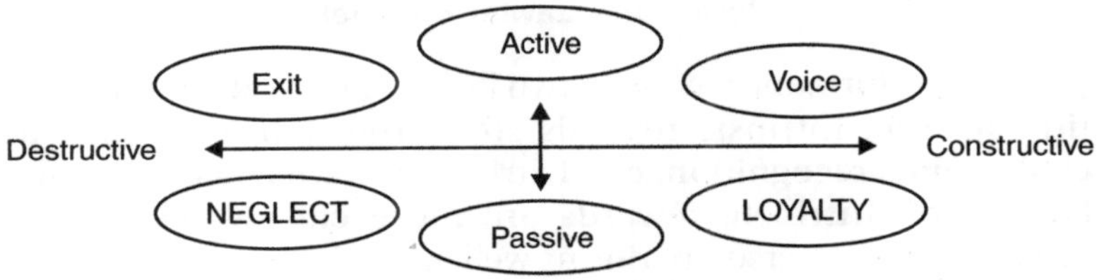

Responses of Dissatisfaction

Adapted from Stephens Robbins, *Organisational Behaviour*, Prentice Hall of India, New Delhi, p. 190.

Exit. Dissatisfied employees tend to look for a position elsewhere as well as resigning.

Voice. Dissatisfied employees entertain some form of union activities such as improving conditions, suggesting improvements and discussing problems.

Loyalty. People with less job satisfaction wait for conditions to improve. They speak up for the organisation in the wake of external threat. They trust the organisation and expect management to do the right things.

Negative publicity. People with dissatisfaction will publicly criticise the authorities and management practices also. Thus the disgruntled employee verbalises his discontentment to others in the community and make the organisation unpopular.

Relationship between productivity and job satisfaction

A satisfied employee is a productive employee and dissatisfaction in jobs result in curtailment of output. Victor Room in 1964, has studied direct link between satisfaction and productivity.

Productivity leads to satisfaction. The traditional view is that satisfied employee performs more. But Porter and Lawler holds the view that productivity leads to satisfaction (see the following figure).

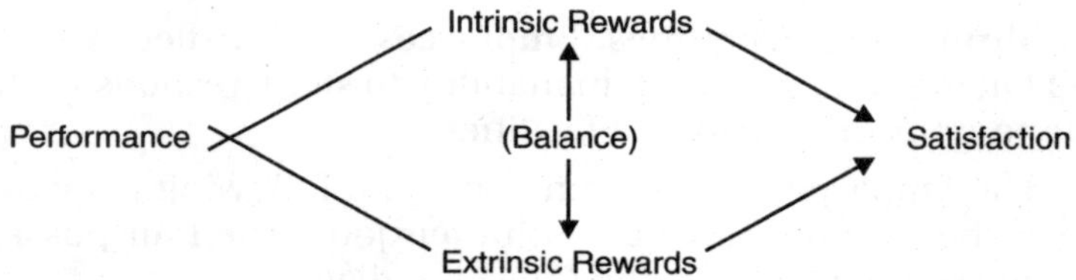

Porter and Lawler's Model

The performance leads to two kinds of rewards (i) intrinsic, (ii) extrinsic. Intrinsic rewards stem from job itself such as challenging, recognition, etc. Extrinsic rewards include salary, bonus etc. Intrinsic rewards are more closely related job satisfaction. If a person performs well on a job that is challenging he gets immediate satisfaction. To improve performance-satisfaction relationship, the management has to (1) modify the task so that it becomes capable of yielding intrinsic rewards for performance, (2) correct the extrinsic reward system so that it acts as a incentive for the high performance. When the intrinsic rewards are supported by extrinsic rewards the employee will not get dissatisfaction.

QUESTIONS FOR DISCUSSION

1. What is attitude? Explain the relationship between the employee attitudes and job satisfaction.
2. Explain the factors determining job satisfaction that need to be understood.
3. Suggest the ways and means of increasing job satisfaction.
4. Explain the features of job satisfaction and dissatisfaction.
5. Critically examine the relationship between productivity and job satisfaction.

8

Behaviour Modification

• Concept of Learning

Learning is defined as permanent change in behaviour as a result of experience. Learning means acquisition of knowledge, skills, expertise etc. It is the process of acquiring insight into a situation so that they can be recalled.

Hammer has listed the following elements essential in learning process:

(i) It involves a change in behaviour.

(ii) Change is relatively permanent.

(iii) Temporary changes do not represent.

(iv) Experience is necessary to occur learning.

(v) If the learning is not followed by reinforcement, the behaviour will disappear.

Importance. Learning is an important process of determining human behaviour. By birth man has unusual normal capacity unlike animals. He has great capacity for adapting in response to changed conditions. This is because of his learning aptitude. Hence, learning has become integral part of human talents and skills that employees need to perform effectively.

Organisational behaviour

Changing behaviour. Learning provides basis for changing behaviour. When individuals are dysfunctional in their behaviour the manager educates them.

High performance. Learning can result in higher job performance. Employees with learning can give insights into how best to develop the skills and talents that employees need to perform most effectively.

Provides guidelines. Learning provides guidelines for conditioning Organisational Behaviour. Manager should guide employees to get higher performance from individuals.

Contract the behaviour. Manager can influence the behaviour of employees by changing reward system.

Enhances morale. The positive reinforcement programme saves costs and increases morale of the employees.

Elements of learning process

Learning process includes the following elements:

(i) Drive
(ii) Cue stimuli
(iii) Response
(iv) Reinforcement and
(v) Retention.

(i) Drive. Drive arouses individuals to respond. Sometimes, it refers to strong stimulus to impel an action. Learning occurs in the presence of drive. Drives are of two types—primary and secondary. Individuals operate under many drives at the same time. To predict behaviour it is necessary to establish which drives are stimulating most.

(ii) Cue stimuli. They are objects existing in the environment. These cue stimuli will increase the probability of eliciting a specific response. Stimuli are of two types—Generalisation and discrimination.

(a) *Generalisation*: If stimuli are exactly alike, they will evoke the same response (specified). But the stimuli are not same hence responses will be different. Generalisation has important implication for learning. Because of generalisation a person need not relearn new tasks which constantly confront him. It allows members to adapt to overall changing conditions.

(b) *Discrimination*: It is different from generalisation. It is a process where an individual learns to emit a response to a stimulus but avoids making the same response to some different stimulus. Discrimination has got wide applications in Organisational Behaviour.

(iii) Responses. The stimulus results in responses. Responses may be in physical or different form, but observable in terms of attitudes, perception, etc.

(iv) Reinforcement. It is a fundamental condition of learning. Without reinforcement behavioural change does not take place. Reinforcement is related to a psychological process of motivation. But captivation is a broader term. Reinforcement may be defined as environmental events affecting the occurrence of responses with which they are associated. Individuals tend to retain a behaviour for which they are given reinforcement.

(v) Retention. The stability of learned behaviour is defined as retention and opposite is forgetting.

Extinction. It is a specific form of forgetting. It may be defined as loss of memory. Sometimes it is called the learning response.

Difference between classical conditioning and operant conditioning

Behaviour is learned. Rewarded behaviour is repeated and unrewarded behaviour is discontinued. Individuals tend to retain behaviour for which they are given reinforcement. Reinforcement is the process by which external reinforce maintains a behaviour. Reinforcement increases the strength of response and tends to induce the individual to repeat behaviour. Thus reinforcement generates, intensifies and enhances that behaviour.

People learn behaviour over a period of time. Learning process is explained by two important processes called:

1. Classical conditioning.
2. Operant conditioning.

1. Classical conditioning. Human behaviour is learned by repetitive association between a stimulus and a response (S-N association). Iran Parlor a famous psychologist has demonstrated that classical conditioning process, in an experiment he presented a piece of meat to the dog. He notified a great deal of response. Next time, he merely rang a bell the dog had not responded. In the next experiment, Parlor accompanied meat with ringing of the bell. The dog has responded. This experiment was repeated several times. After that Parlor rang the bell without presenting the meat. This time too the dog had responded to the bell.

In the new situation the dog had become classically conditioned to the sound of the bell. Thus Parlor went beyond the simple conditioning of his dog to respond to the sound of the bell, *i.e.*, second order conditioning. Most behavioural scientists agree that human beings are capable of being conditioned.

Classical conditioning has important implications for understanding human behaviour. Secondary rewards are important in organisations. Classical conditioning offers explanation for learning but fails to explain total behaviour of human beings. Therefore many psychologists do not agree with this concept. Skinner a psychologist feels that classical conditioning explains only respondent behaviour. People's behaviour is emitted rather than elicited and it is voluntary rather than reflective. The behaviour is dependent on environment. This type of behaviour is learned through operant conditioning.

2. Operant conditioning. Operant is the behaviour that produces effects. It suggests that people emit responses that are rewarded. The concept implies that behaviour is voluntary, determined, maintained and controlled by its consequences. It contends that people explore their environment and act upon it. The learning of new behaviour involves the relationship between 3 elements—(i) events in the situation, (ii) behavioural response to the situation and, (iii) consequences of the response to the person. Human beings learn and encourage those behaviours, which will be rewarding.

Differences between classical and operant conditioning

1. In classical conditioning behaviour is the result of stimulus. But in operant conditioning many behaviours are possible resulting in a particular stimulus situation. In classical conditioning there may be direct relationship between stimulus and response, while no such relationship is necessary in operant conditioning.
2. In classical conditioning a change in the stimulus will elicit a particular response. In operant conditioning one particular response occurs in a given situation. In

this case stimulus does not elicit response. Thus, response is instrumental in receiving the reward.

Classical conditioning can be shown as S/R association while operant conditioning can be expressed as R/S association. Operant conditioning has much greater impact on human learning than classical conditioning. The behaviour in organisations are learned, controlled and altered by consequences. Management can use the operant conditioning process successfully to control and influence the behaviour of employees by manipulating the reward system.

Process of reinforcement in learning

Managers can teach employees to behave in ways that will benefit the organisation. Reinforcement increases the strength of response and tends to induce such behaviour. Reinforcement is of six types:

1. Positive reinforcement
2. Negative reinforcement
3. Extrinsic reinforcement
4. Intrinsic reinforcement
5. Extinction
6. Punishment

1. Positive reinforcement. When a response is followed by something pleasant, it is called positive reinforcement. Positive reinforcement strengthens behaviour in a desired manner. Positive reinforcement is a stimulus and when added to a situation strengthens the probability of response. *For example,* a reward (reinforce) is capable of increasing frequency of that behaviour. The positive reinforcement should fulfil two conditions. (i) It should be contingent upon the rate of performance, (ii) it should match the needs of the person performing activities. There are two types of reinforcements (i) Primary and (ii) Secondary.

Primary reinforcements are innately satisfying the needs of people. *For example,* food, water, sex are of biological importance and have effects, which are independent of past experiences. Secondary reinforcements depend upon the individual and his past reinforcements history. *For example,* praise, recognition, advancement, etc., can be used to increase the performance. Management should select reinforcements that are powerful and durable.

2. Negative reinforcement. When a response is followed by something unpleasant, it is called negative reinforcement. A negative reinforcement is punishment, which may be defined as presenting an aversive consequence contingent upon a response.

3. Extrinsic reinforcement. It is a kind of positive reinforcement. It has no direct relationship with the behaviour itself. It is artificial and often arbitrary such as payment of money to the employees for new ideas.

4. Intrinsic reinforcement. It is also called positive reinforcement. They create a psychological relationship to the behaviour itself, such as assuming more responsibility, performance upto the capacity, etc. Intrinsic rewards are natural consequence of behaviour.

5. Extrinsic. It is an effective method of controlling undesirable behaviour. It means non-reinforcement. The principle behind it is that if a response is not reinforced it will eventually disappear. For example, if a student makes noise, the teacher ignores it so that the student will not try again.

6. Punishment. It is applied to control certain undesirable behaviour in organisations. Punishment reduces the frequency of responses. Managers use punishment by withdrawing the rewards or impose unpleasant consequence after a behaviour is performed. Thus punishment weakens the behaviour. Use of punishment is controversial method of modifying behaviour because it produces undesirable bi-products.

(i) Punishment reduces the frequency of undesired behaviour, but it does not promote desired behaviour.

(ii) Undesired behaviour will disappear only when the punishing agent is present and reappears, when the agent is absent.

(iii) Punishment leads antagonism towards the punishing agent as a result the effectiveness of the agent decreases over time.

Administrative reinforcement. Reinforcement is a tool to shape the behaviour. Rewards are more effective than others in bringing change in individual behaviour. Managers should recognise and administer at appropriate time.

Steps. The following steps are necessary to administer the reinforcement process successfully.

1. Selection. The manager should select appropriate rewarding system to change the behaviour of people. The reinforcement should be sufficiently powerful so that response will increase the performance. What is rewarding to one person may not be rewarding to another. Hence managers should look forward for a reward system which maximises the performance.

2. Designing. Homans accords 'Rule of distributive justice' which means that rewards enhance rewards and performance should be linked appropriately. So a manager should design reinforcement in such a way that reinforcing agents are made contingent upon the desired performance.

3. Scheduling. The effectiveness of reinforcement depends upon how it is administered, which in turn depends upon correct scheduling. If the scheduling is not made correctly it will defunct the organisation. Scheduling must be framed in such a way that reliable procedure for eliciting the desired response pattern is established. For administering a positive or negative reinforcement a separate procedures are followed.

Administering positive reinforcement. Reinforcement effectiveness depends upon timing of the reinforcement administered. There are types of scheduled *viz.*, continuous and intermittent. Under the continuous reinforcement schedule, the individual receives reward every time he performs. Thus the employee's performance increases with the reward offered. And performance declines when reward is stopped.

Under intermittent scheduling, the rewards are administered on a random basis. Here supporters of this theory said that every time it is not possible to reinforce the employee. This is also called partial reinforcement. This method, leads to slower learning but ensures stronger retention of a response than continuous reinforcement. Skinner has explained this in four ways.

1. Fixed interval schedule. Under this schedule reward is given to employees after the passage of specific time for example, hourly, daily, weekly and monthly remuneration system. In the beginning of any learning, a very short interval is introduced and as learning progresses the interval will be stretched.

2. Variable interval schedule. Variable interval schedules generate higher performance than fixed interval schedule. *Example,* supervisory visits. *Ex*: Visit by the plant manager now and then randomly instead of inspecting regularly at a fixed time 10.30 A.M. (say) the employees behave cautiously and improve performance around 10.30 A.M. subsequently the performance decreases. Whereas in variable interval schedules the performance will be higher than under fixed interval schedule.

3. Fixed ratio schedule. In this schedule reward is given only after the employee completes certain number of responses. *Example,* the worker is paid on the basis of piece rate system. The worker is paid after he completes fixed number of units. In this reinforcement practice the worker produces efficiently.

4. Variable ratio schedule. When the reward variable and relative to the behaviour of individual, the individual is said to be reinforced in a variable-ratio schedule. Here the reinforcement (reward) is given in an irregular manner *i.e.,* the reward is given after a number of responses but the exact number is randomly varied.

Administering negative reinforcement. Negative Reinforcement is used in shaping the behaviour. Negative Reinforcement may be given in the form of punishment. Punishment enables in reducing undesired behaviour of an individual. But punishment is a complex exercise. Manager should understand how to punish and administer the punishment process. The following points are to be taken care of while administering the punishment.

1. Manager should punish the undesirable behaviour not the person.
2. The employee should not take it personally.
3. The purpose of punishment is not to undermine a person's confidence.
4. The punishment should be enough.
5. Over-punishment leads to undesirable side effects.
6. Under-punishment will not deter the behaviour.
7. Punishment should be administered privately.

8. Punishment should be given at exact time to correct the behaviour.
9. The individual should be shown alternative behaviour while correcting him through punishment otherwise it will reappear.
10. The use of punishment should be coupled with the use of reinforcement.
11. Punishment should be administered carefully.

Schedule of Reinforcement

	Internal	Ratio
Fixed	Fixed Internal	Fixed Ratio
Variable	Variable Internal	Variable Ratio

Adapted from Stephen Robbins, *Organisational Behaviour*, Prentice-Hall of India Pvt. Ltd., New Delhi, 1993, p. 521.

Behaviour modification theory

Behaviour modification is an effective technique used to improve organisational effectiveness. It means according to Skinner, eliminating the undesirable behaviour and establishing more compatible behaviour and using rewards for observable behaviour.

Steps. The following steps are involved in behaviour modification process:

1. Find out critical behaviour. Employees often involve in several behaviours both productive and unproductive. The manager has to examine the behaviour of people which retards the team spirit and reduces overall performance. The manager has to hold discussion with all the concerned people and conduct behaviour audit systematically.

2. Measurement of behaviour under examination. Manager has to observe or count the responses or behaviour from time to time. If they are within allowable limits they may be ignored. Manager has to concentrate on those which are repeated and reducing organisational effectiveness. The behaviour is rated through observation or otherwise in terms of high, moderate and low.

3. Conduct functional analysis. It is a way of behaviour modification. In this stage the manager has to examine what reinforcement should be used to control such behaviour and what would be the consequences. He should also estimate to what extent the reward or punishment will correct the behaviour.

4. Intervention strategy. It means designing the reinforcement strategy to modify the critical behaviours such as absenteeism, late arrival, gossips during working hours, wandering in the hall, etc. Manager should develop appropriate strategy to reduce undesirable behaviour and promote compatible behaviour. The strategy selected should be appropriate and contribute to the overall performance of the organisation.

5. Evaluation. After adopting the suitable reinforcement method the manager has to evaluate the behaviour of people in question by comparing the response before and after the intervention. If the change is positive the manager is successful and if otherwise it calls for better intervention strategy.

Controversies surrounding the behaviour modification approach

Behaviour modification technique helps in improving job performance, profits, team spirit, etc. Yet it is not free from criticism.

Criticism. The technique is criticised on the following counts:

1. Skinner operant conditioning principles are explored after conducting experiments with rats, which cannot be taken as standard.
2. Operant conditioning constitute a threat to personal autonomy and ignores individuality of man.
3. The whole idea of rewarding or reinforcement process is based on the idea that people work solely for money.
4. Behaviour modification is underestimating the average worker.
5. Behaviour modification techniques ignore the internal rewards like job satisfaction, goodwill, etc. It always preaches that man works for money, etc., the external rewards which is always not correct.
6. The technique disregards employees' beliefs and expectations.
7. Results are expected without cognitive attention to man.

8. The technique is not applicable to people who cannot make use of full capacities.
9. The method assumes that behaviour can be measured which is not easy always.
10. The reinforcement principles are creative and not manipulative.
11. The behaviour modification technique is applied to multivariate organisation.
12. The technique is successful in laboratories but hardly applied to organisational settings.
13. The modification technique does not offer readymade solutions, but its results depend upon the way the technique is administered.

QUESTIONS FOR DISCUSSION

1. Analyse the role of learning theory for understanding Organisational Behaviour.
2. Explain various elements of learning process.
3. Discuss the difference between classical conditioning and operant conditioning.
4. What is the role and process of Reinforcement in Learning?
5. Critically examine Behaviour Modification theory.
6. What are the controversies surrounding the behaviour modification approach in practice?

9

PERCEPTION

Introduction

Perception is a cognitive factor of human being, by perception people come to know about the surroundings. There is no behaviour without perception. Perception lies at the base of every individual behaviour. A superior accurately and precisely estimates employee's perceptions and make him move. Thus perception is the process "where-by people select, organise and interpret sensory stimulation into meaningful information about their work environment".

Perception is a subjective process, different people may perceive the same environment differently. Thus the reality is perceived differently by different people. Managers should sharpen their perceptual skills to see the events as truly as they are. When misconceptions occur due to poor perceptual abilities managers are bound to take improper decisions. Thus, situation remaining the same but people see the situation differently. Hence one has to understand the perception and its different aspects.

Features of Perception

1. Perceptions is a psychological process the way one perceives the environment affecting his behaviour.
2. People's actions, thoughts, emotions, etc., are triggered by the perception of their surroundings.
3. Perception being an intellectual process, becomes subjective.
4. Different people perceive the same situation and environment differently.
5. Reality perceived by different people will be different.

Research on perception consistently reveals that individuals when look at things in a given situation perceive it quite differently. The surprising point is that most of the people do not see the reality. They call it reality that what they see. Thus most of our acts primarily depend upon our perceptions. Hence managers should develop required skill to see the things quite close to the reality.

The necessity of understanding. Perceived world is not real world. The feeling is so strong and we rarely question what we see and perceive. We all see that sun rises and sets but in reality it never rises and sets. Similarly a manager should distinguish between a perceived world and the real world. He should know that the employees develop perceptions differently.

Lawler and Rhode are of the view that experiencing an environment is an active process in which people try to make sense out of their environment. In this active process individuals selectively notice different aspects of the environment, appraise what they see in terms of their own experience and evaluate in terms of their values and needs. Hence managers should increase his perceptual accuracy. He is concerned with what others perceive about his actions. So he should know how perceptions are formed and distorted.

Sensation *Vs.* Perception

Sensation is described as the response of physical sensory organ. The physical senses are viewing, hearing, touching, tasting etc. These senses are bombarded by stimuli about external and internal to human body. Examples of sensation may be reaction of eye to colour, ear to sound and so on. Thus largely sensation deals with the behaviour determined by physiological functioning.

Perception is much more complex and broader than sensation. It is virtually a cognitive. It correlates, integrates and comprehends diverse sensations and information from many organs of the body. Perception classifies the stimuli based on past learning, feeling and motives. Thus perception is determined by both physiological and psychological characteristics of the organism. Sensation only activates the organs of the body and is not affected by such psychological factors. Dempsoy clarifies that one can see things by means of eye. It is not eye looking at the thing but the mind. He tends to see an object in its totality with a figure and forms set against a background.

Thus, in the process of looking at, both sensation and perception are involved. Eye activates to see an object and its interference is perception. For managerial action perception is required. And they have to improve the skills of perception.

Process of perception

According to Robbins perception is a process by which individuals organise and interpret their sensory impressions in order to give meaning to their environment. The perception process is explained by input and output approach.

There are three well noted mechanisms of perception *viz.*, selection, organisation and interpretation. Selection considers stimuli that are relevant. Organisation is concerned with harnessing inputs into a meaningful form. Interpretation is concerned with drawing inference from which behaviour emanates.

Perceptional process

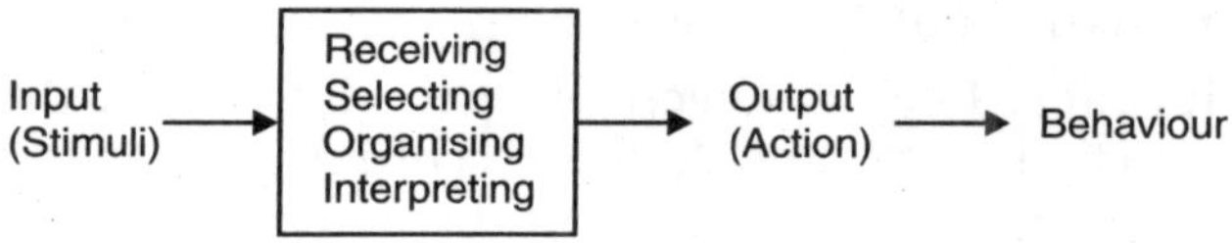

Inputs: Stimuli—objects received by the perceiver.
Process: Inputs pass through selection, organisation and interpretation.
Output: Actions, feelings, attitudes of the individual.
Behaviour: Behaviour of the individual depends upon the outcome.

1. Stimuli. Perception process cannot commence in the absence of stimuli. Stimuli is in the form of people, objects, events, etc. Events in a given situation can be termed as inputs or stimuli.

2. Receiving stimuli. Perception starts with the receipt of stimuli. Stimuli is received through the experience such as hearing, smelling, touching, seeing and tasting the things. Thus receiving stimuli is a psychological aspect of perception process.

3. Selection. Selection is the fundamental step in perception process. An individual confronts with several things, in a situation. But every thing is not necessary. Hence selectivity occurs because it is not possible for anybody to assimilate every thing. Individual then prefers to select the stimuli that are relevant to him. Thus the process of choosing certain stimuli for further processing is known as 'selection'.

Two types of factors affect the selection of stimuli for processing—External factors are related to stimuli and internal factors are related to the perceiver. External factors include size, colour, contrast, movement, repetition, familiarity, strangeness, etc. Internal factors are such as interest, experience, attitudes and self-acceptance of the perceiver. Normally, the individual selects the objects which is important and avoid others.

Selection process involves two important principles:

(1) Figure—ground principle, (2) Relevance principle.

Figure—Ground principle. In a situation certain factors are considered significant and others are not. The important factors constitute 'figure' and others constitute 'ground'. Normally what becomes 'figure' and ground depend upon needs and expectations of the individual in a given situation.

Relevancy. People selectively perceive things that are relevant to their needs and desires. According to Leavitt people perceive things that are pleasing or threatening them. When a sportsman reads news he will perceive the cricket score and hardly pays any attention to war news. An unemployee searching for employment news does not care political news to see there in that situation.

4. Organisation. Organisation means putting the 'inputs' to form into a meaningful whole. This process is also called as 'gestalt process'. Gestalt is a German word which means 'to organise'. There are many ways the people organise inputs or objects/events *i.e.*, grouping, simplification and closure.

Grouping. The information (inputs) are grouped on the basis of similarity or proximity. The inputs are grouped into one category on the basis of common characteristics. When a function is celebrated a separate row is arranged for ladies irrespective of their categories. There may be students, staff, guests etc. Thus special arrangement is made separately for ladies irrespective of their differences, since they have common factor *i.e.*, woman.

Closure. Managers when face inadequate information they will proceed on the basis of past records, history, experience, etc. *For example,* manager has to promote some of his office employees higher grade. He calls for information but complete particulars are not available. In this situation the manager is understood that all the employees are not doing well in past five years and finalised the matter by differing the issue. This brings the perceptual organisation to some kind of a rational order and closure forming the basis for managerial decisions.

Simplification. The perception ability depends upon the skills of the manager to see the reality. In that process he collects so much information. But all the information are not important. To arrive reality he gives up less-important information and concentrates on vital information which are relevant and understandable. Thus manager reduces the complexity of situation by eliminating less important things. This is called simplification.

5. Interpretation. The perceiver has to interpret the inputs (information) which have been organised using the above methods. Without interpreting information the situation will be confusing. Manager interprets the situation in terms of his assumptions. While interpreting the manager tends to be judgmental and distorts information. Yet times people use subjective feelings, opinions, emotions and tend to be biased. Manager should know the physical, social, economical, psychological and organisational settings in which an object is perceived and also affect the interpretation. The interpretation is affected by the characteristics of stimuli, situations under which perception takes place.

Perceivers sometimes use notions such as good/bad, right/wrong, wise/useless, etc., which describe the stimuli. They ignore things that are unpleasant. Because of subjectivity, judgmental attitudes, distortions, selectivity, cognitive preferences, etc., managers are failing to perceive the reality. Hence manager should aware of the possible factors that would adversely influence the perceptions and learn how to overcome them.

- **Impact of selectivity on perception**

People selectively interpret what they see basing on their interests, background, experience and attitudes. Thus perception tends to be influenced by an individual's base of interpretation than by the stimulus itself. Since one cannot assimilate all that one can see and he takes in bits and pieces. These bits and pieces are choosen according to one's interest. There are number of factors which affect this selectively.

1. Self-concept. The way a person views others depends on himself. Knowing oneself makes it easier to see others accurately. People's own characteristics affect which they are likely to see in others. They select only that aspect which they find match with their characteristics.

2. Beliefs. An individual's belief has profound influence on his perception. He conceives not what he sees but what he believes in.

3. Expectations. Expectations affect the perceptions of individuals. Expectations refer to participation of a particular behaviour from a person. These expectations may be lasting and difficult to change.

4. Inner needs. Perception is determined by the inner needs of people. Need is a state or condition of lacking something. People with different needs usually experience different stimuli. Similarly people with different needs tend to select different stimuli to respond to. When people are not able to satisfy their needs they are engaged in wishful thinking or daydreaming. Thus people will perceive only those items which are in accordance with their wishful thinking.

5. Response disposition. It refers to the tendency of an individual to perceive familiar information rather than unfamiliar ones. Thus an individual will perceive those things with which he is familiar.

6. Response salience. People look at the problem from one's own point of view not from other's points of view. Thus a problem in an organisation is viewed by marketing personnel from marketing viewpoint, personnel people from HRD viewpoint, etc. The reason for this phenomenon lies in the background of the people for which they are trained.

7. Perceptual difference. It refers to screening out those elements which are threatening an individual. In a situation the perceiver does not perceive the stimuli which are in conflict with him. He may even perceive other factors of the situation sometimes.

8. External factors. They are not connected with the perceiver. Other factors such as intensity, size, contrast, repetition, motion, novelty and familiarity affect the selectivity.

Factors influencing perception

Individuals may look at the same thing. Yet perceive it differently? Number of factors operate to distort perception. These factors can reside in the perceiver, the target and in the situation.

The perceiver. When individuals look at targets and attempt to interpret what they see is influenced by personal characteristics such as attitudes, likes, dislikes, tastes, interests, preferences, motives, experiences, expectations, threat, etc.

Target. Characteristics of the target can affect what is perceived. Motion, sounds, size and other attributes of a target shape the way we see it. Targets cannot be looked at in isolation. The relationship of a target to its background influences perception. Human tendency is to group similar things together. Objects that are close to each other will tend to be perceived together rather than separately. Persons, objects, events that are similar to each other also tend to be grouped together. The greater the similarity the greater the probability that we will tend to perceive them as a common group. Women, blacks with distinguishable characteristics tend to be perceived as a like.

Situation. The context of an object is important. Elements in the surrounding environment influence his perceptions. Thus time, location, height, heat and other factors influence the perception. Following figure summarises the factors influencing the perception.

Perceiver	**Situation**	**Target**
- Attitudes	Time	- Novelty
- Beliefs	Social Setting	- Movements
- Motives	Work Setting	- Motion
- Interests		- Sounds
- Experience		- Size
- Expectations		- Proximity
		- Background

Factors influencing perception

• **Attribution theory**

Perceptions of people are different from perceptions of inanimate objects like machines, benches and buildings. Non-living items do not have beliefs, motives or intentions. When one observes people, he develops explanations of why people behave in certain ways. Thus perceptions will be influenced by the assumptions of the perceiver. Attribution refers to how a person tries to understand other's behaviour by interpreting them as caused by certain factors. In other words the person tries to attach cause-and-effect explanation to their behaviour. Thus attribution is a distinct factor creating a tendency to visualise identical behaviour differently. Perception is distorted by the efforts of the perceiver to attribute a casual explanation to an outcome. According to attribution theory perceiver himself attributes causes for the behaviour of others.

The attributes are of two kinds: (i) internal, (ii) external.

Internal attributes. Internal attributes refer to abilities, motives, traits, intentions, etc., of others. The perceiver believes them to be under the control of the individual.

External attributes. The perceiver attributes causes for the behaviour of others. External attributes refer to social, technical, economical and religious factors which are not controllable. The perceiver believes them to be not controllable.

The manager has to decide the behaviour of others whether caused externally or internally. And the manager should realise that the behaviour depends upon three factors: (1) distinctiveness, (2) consensus and (3) consistency.

1. Distinctiveness. It refers to whether an individual displays different behaviours in different situations.

2. Consensus. If everyone of the group members in the given situation responds in the same way, then the behaviour is said to be consensus behaviour.

3. Consistency. If an individual behaves the same way over time and again, he is said to be consistent.

Figure shows the key elements in attribution theory.

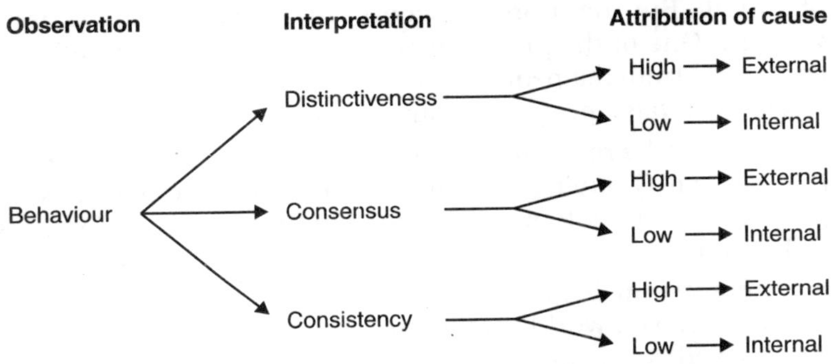

Attribution Theory

Adapted from Stephen P. Robbins, *Organisational Behaviour*, Prentice Hall of India Pvt. Ltd., New Delhi, p. 140.

Limitations

1. Fundamental attribution error. The tendency of observer to underestimate the influence of external factors and overestimate the influence of internal factors while judging the behaviour of others is called fundamental attribution error.

2. Self-servicing bias. The tendency of individuals to attribute their success to internal factors and blame external factors for his failure is known as self-servicing bias.

- **Stereotyping**

Stereotyping is the tendency to perceive an individual belonging to a group and attributing favourable or unfavourable characteristics to the individual basing upon a widely held opinion about the group.

Following are some of the examples:

'Aged persons are traditional and conservative'

'Very rich persons are different'

'Union people expect something for nothing'

'Managers do not give a damn about their people only getting the work done'

'Aged workers have higher absentee rate as they are often sick'

'Women employees show less initiative than men.'

Generalisation helps in clearing with unmanageable number of stimuli. But the problem occurs when stereotyping is used wrongly. One of the problems is that they are widespread and contain no truth but people are making the inaccurate perception based on a false premise about a group.

It should be remembered that valid or accurate stereotyping is functional. Grouping is useful for educational decision-making purposes to stereotyping students coming from rich families to be more able to pay higher college fees.

Stereotyping helps the perceiver to simplify the complexity of the perceived world. But the trouble is when the people are generalised. It is difficult to see unique characteristics and problems. Stereotyping greatly influences perceptions in organisations. Haire found that individuals will both perceive and be perceived.

Stereotyping is a source of social and racial bias. According to Braner businessmen are stereotyped internationally. There is a consensus about the traits which members of these categories possess. Though they are perceived to have certain traits, actually they may not have those traits.

Biases contributing to distortions or misperceptions

There are many more factors which cause perceptual distortions. Perceptual distortion is a situation where a person cannot perceive something as it is. This may happen due to the factors associated with person, target group and situation.

1. Personality. Personality of the perceiver influences greatly. There are two types of personalities—(1) secure people and self-accepting people. Secure people perceive others as warm individuals rather than cold and indifferent. (2) self-accepting people will defensively perceive the situations.

2. Mental set. In a given situation an individual reacts in one way or the other. This depends upon his mental condition. In organisational setting people tend to perceive others on the basis of this mental condition.

3. Attributes. Perception of people is different from inanimate things like trees, buildings, machines, tables etc. Thus non-living things (such as building, tables, etc.) do not have feelings and beliefs. When manager observes people he develops explanation of why people behave in certain manner, since people behave with beliefs and feelings. Thus the behaviour of people is influenced by their feelings, attitudes and beliefs. Hence manager attributes reasons for the behaviour of others by causal and effect relationship.

First impression. People try to create first impression in the looks of others. Many times the first impression principle works when persons meet on first occasion. Being carried by first impression is not always good. This can be corrected by frequent interaction.

'Halo' effect. The halo effect is similar to stereotyping. Under halo effect the person is judged by his trait or an event. In this model the observer rates the individual on the basis of one or two events good or bad and evaluates the entire personality. Burner and Tagiuri have explained that "Halo effect" occurs when the traits to be perceived are not clear in behavioural expressions.

Stereotype. It is a personal bias while perceiving the behaviour of others. Here the observer (manager) perceives on the basis of group to which the individual belongs to. In this, favourable or unfavourable characteristics will be attributed to the individual based on widely field generalisation about the group he belongs to. It helps the manager in dealing with unmanageable number of stimuli. But the problem occurs when stereotyping is used wrongly.

Person/object perceived. The perception is influenced by the qualities of both perceiver and person being perceived. The first factor is status of the person. Many a time the person is perceived by the 'status' not by his actual traits. Because the person of high status is believed to have desirable qualities.

Contextual factors. The context one sees an object is also important. Elements in the surrounding environment will influence one's perceptions. Thus time, location, heat and other situational factors influence the perception.

Defense mechanism. People might use some defense mechanism and distort what they see or totally avoid seeing what actually exists when he is threatened. Defensive mechanism occurs when people receive information which is incongruent with their self-concept. The greater the degree of perceived threat to a person's self-concept, the greater the likelihood of a defensive response to be perceived and hence distortion. The problem with defensiveness is that when perceptual errors occur, responses to problem situations are not made appropriately and bad judgment and incorrect decisions result. If the defenses are not broken manager continues to be ineffective.

Projection. It means attributing one's own characteristics to other people. People who engage in projection tend to perceive others as they imagine. Managers tend to see people as more homogeneous than they really are.

Lending evidence to self-fulfilling tendencies. It is the process by which one tries to fit his attitudes, beliefs and expectations to reality. What one perceives could then be governed by what we expect to find. Thus when the manager is not aware of the adverse influence, he may make errors of judgment.

Lack of experience. Experience and knowledge have a constant bearing on perception. Successful experiences enhance and boost the perceptive ability and lead to accuracy in perception of a person whereas failure erodes self-confidence.

Size. Size is also influencing the perception process. The bigger the size of the perceived stimulus, the higher is the probability that is perceived. Size overrides other things and thereby enhances perceptual selection.

Intensity. The greater the intensity of a stimulus, the more likely it will be noticed. An intense stimulus has more power to push itself than does a weaker stimulus. The essence of intensity principle is that a loud noise, strong odour, bright light will be noticed very easily. It is not always valid but the intensity factor has to be considered in the light of the situation, sometimes.

Frequency. Frequency principle states that repeated external stimulus are more likely to draw attention. Repetition is one of the most frequently used technique in advertising.

Contrast. Stimuli that contrast with the surrounding factors are more likely to draw attention. A contrast can be caused by colour, size etc. The contrast principle states that external stimuli that stand out against the background will receive their attention.

Measures for improving perceptual skills

There are no set of norms to develop the perceptual abilities, but some guidelines can definitely help and promote the skills of the perceiver.

1. Knowing and perceiving himself accurately. The reason why people misperceive others is that basically they do not know accurately about themselves. Therefore the observer (manager) should understand himself, the more accurate he can perceive others. The best way of knowing himself is collecting information about himself from others such as superiors, peers, subordinates and other colleagues.

2. High self-concept. Self-concept or self-image is a function of how successful one accomplishes. Competent and successful managers will develop a sense of self-regard and self-confidence. Those who do not have enough skills will not enjoy 'regard'. If and when managers are over-qualified they should go for better jobs to utilise their skills. And if they do not have enough skills, they should enhance their skills through training. Persons with self-regard will perceive others accurately and be perceived.

3. Positive attitudes. There is relationship between attitudes and perceptions. Managers having positive attitudes about the events will correctly perceive. If managers have biased attitudes, their perceptions are likely to be distorted. So managers should always get rid of any negative feelings. This will keep them to enhance perceptual skills.

4. Be emphatic. Before making final decisions managers should look at the problem from others point of view. This means going into the shoes of others. This is possible only when he is sensitive to the needs of others.

5. Open and effective communication. To dispel the misconceptions managers should communicate openly and pass on adequate information at right time and a right place. Employees at work places act according to their own perceptions. Therefore managers should encourage two-way communications with employees. This will help the managers to perceive the situation much better.

6. Avoid attributions. Managers may make inappropriate attributions that cause dysfunctional consequences. Hence managers should try to avoid making attributions. They can make possible if they put continuous efforts and make the decisions only after careful analysis of the situation.

7. Avoid common distortions. There are many distortions such as effect, stereotyping, first impression hallo, etc., causing misperceptions. In order to have better perception of the situation managers should guard themselves against these common biases.

Johari window concept of self-understanding

One of the major reasons why people misperceive others is that they fail to perceive themselves accurately. Therefore, the important thing which a person must do is that he should understand him more accurately. The more accurate he understands himself, the more accurate he can perceive others. The best way of knowing himself is to obtain information on how others perceive him from as many sources as possible superiors, peers, subordinates and friends. Johari window model is explained below.

Harry Ingharm has developed the Johari window. According to this model there are four parts in everyone—the Public Area, the Blind Area, the Private Area and the Dark Area. They are referred to as the open-self, blind-self, hidden-self and undiscovered self. Thus one can be compartmentalised into 2 × 2 matrix. What is known to himself and others is called "public area". Yet times an individual does not know about him which others know is called 'blind area'. Sometimes individual knows himself but others do not know, this is called 'private area'. Sometimes it so happens that he does not know about himself which others too do not know. This is called 'dark area'.

It is possible to become aware of himself and remove blind spots by obtaining feedback from others how he is perceived by a superior, friends, subordinates, and colleagues, etc. By removing blind spots one gives himself a chance to see how he is really perceived by others instead of perceiving himself 'ideal'. Thus by enlarging 'public area' and narrowing 'dark area' through feedback help him to understand others by limiting his personal biases in perception.

QUESTIONS FOR DISCUSSION

1. What is perception? Why is it important?
2. Demonstrate how sensation is different from perception.
3. Explain briefly the process of perception.

4. How does selectivity affect the perception?
5. What factors influence the perception?
6. What is Attribution theory? How it explains OB?
7. What is Stereotyping? Give some examples of how stereotyping can create perceptional distortion.
8. What are the biases often contributing to distortions or misperceptions? Explain.
9. Discuss the measures for improving perceptual skills.
10. What is Johari window concept of self-understanding?

10

ORGANISATIONAL CLIMATE

Introduction

Organisational climate is the human environment in which employees do their work. One cannot see it but one can feel and experience it. It is effected by everything and everyone in the organisation. Like fingerprints, organisations are different from one another. Each organisation has its own culture, traditions and methods of action. Some organisations are easy going and others are efficient. Some are quite human and others are hard. Just as people choose to move to certain geographical climate of sea, mountains or desert, they also choose organisations by their climate. Organisational climate refers to the environment. It refers to the attitudes of top management, company policies and other matters.

Definition of Organisational Climate

According to Bowditch and Buono it refers to the beliefs and expectations of people and the extent to which they are fulfilled. It refers to the set of characteristics and factors such as job description, organisational structural format, performance and evaluation standards, leadership style, challenges and innovations, organisational values and culture which influence the behaviour of people.

Richard M. Hodgetts has divided organisational climate into two parts. He has given an analogy with an iceberg which has two parts. One is visible and the other part is under the water which is not visible. It refers to hierarchy, goals and objectives of the organisation, performance invisible part includes organisational factors such as supportiveness, superiors and a sense of satisfaction with the job. Both these parts are assumed in the form of an iceberg.

Overt factors:	Hierarchy
	Financial resources
	Goals
	Skills
	Technology
	Performance
	Attitudes
	Feelings
Covert factor:	Values
	Supportiveness
	Satisfaction
	Interaction

Source: Richard M. Hodgetts, *Organisational Behaviour*, Macmillan Publishing, 1991, p. 430.

Organisational climate refers to enduring quality of the internal environment that is experienced by the members of an organisation. Organisational climate is the manifestation of the attitudes of people towards organisation itself. Campbell *et al.*, defines organisational climate as a set of attributes specific to a particular organisation that may be induced from the way the organisation deals with its members and its environment. Climate consists of a set of characteristics that describe an organisation to distinguish it from other organisations.

Importance. Organisational climate influences motivation, performance and job satisfaction. It is a long run proposition. Just as an asset contributes to production, it is incremental in nature. A sound organisational climate enhances the job satisfaction, morale, participation, involvement, team spirit and contribution of employees. A sound climate extremely understood as the stability, creativity and effectiveness of an organisation. It tends to attract people and keep them fit. Climate may be different in different departments. So one should integrate to have a whole view of an organisation. Hellreigal and Slocum viewed an effective climate in dynamic and complex environment. Hence one should not take fragmented view of climate in a single department but the overall climate in the whole organisation to be meaningful.

Benefits

1. Employees like to perform the job with pleasure and satisfaction.
2. Employees like to be in association with others.
3. Managers experience that employees follow their orders with respect.
4. Managers' instructions will be pleasantly obliged by the subordinates.
5. Subordinates will work hard and show confidence in their superiors.
6. Management and employees will have ultimate gains through low cost of production and better incentives respectively.
7. The society will be benefited by the regular supply of goods at lower prices from an effective organisation.
8. Employees work happily and associate with the company for a long time.
9. Employee turnover, absenteeism will be lowered when morale is high.
10. Employees develop a sense of attachment with the organisation.
11. High morale attracts and holds good employees.
12. It results in increased job performance.
13. It improves cooperation and brings unity.
14. It creates favourable atmosphere among customers, public, suppliers and organisational particulars.
15. It keeps organisation healthy.

Factors affecting the organisational climate

Employee morale is a very complex phenomenon and is influenced by many factors. These factors are explained in the following paragraphs.

1. Organisation structure. This includes centralisation of powers, balance between authority and responsibility, span of control, etc. These factors influence the organisational climate to a greater extent.

2. Individual responsibility. It refers to the feelings of individuals towards freedom, autonomy, discretion and responsibility.

3. Rewards. The rewards should be appropriate and compensate the risk undertaken by the employees.

4. Risk and risk taking. Employees' perceptions towards risk in the work situations will affect the organisational climate.

5. Warmth and support. Employees' attitude of supporting the organisational policies would decide the soundness of organisational climate. Their positive feelings and involvement will speak high of organisational climate.

6. Tolerance and conflict. The employees tolerance towards the changing conditions of technology, sociol and economic will affect organisational climate. Any change should be in limits and should take the acceptance of employees.

7. Managerial support and philosophy. Sound organisational climate depends upon 'support' factor from management. Managerial support is necessary to enforce rules, policies, traditions and norms which indirectly influence climate. Management should match the goals of organisation with the goals of individuals to create sound organisational climate.

8. Concern for new employees. Employees with long experience in a company do adjust to the situations in different times. But new employees will form feelings on the basis of temporary events that take place. So a 'concern' for new employees is necessary to keep interest going.

9. General satisfaction. Employees' satisfaction varies from time to time. It is difficult for management to satisfy all people all times. But general satisfaction on an average gives feeling of association and indicates sound climate.

10. Sense of direction. People work comfortably if objective setting is clear, planning and feedback are proper. It is a continuous process. And everyone should feel sense of direction and purpose of job.

11. Opportunities to exercise individual initiative. Every individual tries to do something innovative and looks for opportunities to prove his capacity. An organisation must give such opportunities to deserving persons and establish a climate where individuals come forward to take initiative.

12. Working competitive. Employees work in a competitive manner to reach higher goals and share the fruits. If competitive environment is absent and merit is not encouraged the growth is not ensured to both organisation and individuals. So sound organisational climate depends upon competitive nature at work.

13. Co-operative and pleasant people. Climate also goes by the way people work. If people are pleasant and co-operative in nature, it leads to team spirit and ensures sound climate.

14. Result oriented. Every activity and individual should be result oriented in an organisation. One should know what he is expected to do why he is expected to do and how it helps the organisation and himself. Such atmosphere is an indication for sound organisational climate.

15. Rules orientation. In every field of activity rules are framed by the management. If rules are violated confusion is the outcome and targets will not be achieved. So a sound organisational climate is built on rules impartially framed.

16. Closeness of supervision. Supervisors should closely look at the things and judge the matters impartially. Without close watching at people one should not conclude and take decisions. People will be alert and active only if the supervision is fact finding in nature. Thus nature of supervision differentiates organisations.

17. Universalism. Management principles are universally applicable in any organisation, wherever it may be. The functions of management such as organising, staffing, directing and controlling are common whatsoever the organisation is. Sound climate of organisation depends upon the principle of universalism.

18. Achievement orientation. The employee should get his benefit of promotion which is due. And the employee should work with a orientation to achieve it, for which he should be encouraged. And it depends upon the atmosphere prevailing in the organisation. Hence organisation climate is greatly affected by the way people orient themselves.

19. Process. In every organisation certain processes are vital to function on sound lines. Some among those are communication, decision-making, motivation and leadership. These things enable management to carry out its objectives. The success of an organisation depends upon how leader maintains his relations with subordinates, how employees are informed of their work, how workers are motivated and how decisions are taken.

20. Physical environment. The employees' perception towards physical environment influences the organisational climate. Physical environment includes space, ventilation, lighting, furniture, weather noise, etc. Better physical conditions encourage workers to contribute.

21. Systems, values and norms. Every organisation has its own norms, values which are unique by themselves. These things are communicated to employees through rules, regulations and policies so that they can adapt themselves and modify their behaviour. These values and norms play important role in deciding the climate of an organisation.

22. Mutual trust. Employer and employees should trust each other at work. Absence of such trust will lead to misconceptions and misunderstandings which will spoil the team spirit and unity. Thus mutual trust influences organisational climate.

23. Feeling of useful work. Employees feel that organisational climate is favourable when they are doing something useful that provides a sense of personal worth. Employees frequently accept challenging work that is intrinsically satisfying. An organisation should give them feeling that their work is useful to them.

24. Employee participation. Manager's decision-making makes so much difference in creating or running the organisational climate. The employees should know what they are expected to do. This gives them satisfaction and will be motivated. This is possible if manager invites employee participation in decision-making.

Measuring the climate

Several instruments have been developed to measure organisation climate. The instruments typically measure number of elements of climate, assign the numerical scores and then interpret those scores.

Climate profile charts

These charts are used to measure climate. Elements under consideration are shown on charts. Elements refer to the factors influencing the organisation climate. The views are collected on a scale varying from 1 to 10.

Climate elements	Range									
	1	2	3	4	5	6	7	8	9	10
Leadership										
Motivation										
Communication										
Interaction										
Decision-making										
Goal setting										
Control										

Climate Profile Chart

———————— Present ============= Planned

Generally, the questionnaires are closely related. The elements studied are conformity, responsibility standards, rewards, organisational clarity, warmth, support, leadership, etc. Litwin and Stringer have developed a survey that covered 9 elements such as structure, responsibility, reward, risk, warmth, support, standards, conflict and identity. They concluded that different management approaches lead to different climates. Likert a management specialist has developed a survey covering 7 elements such as leadership, motivational forces, communication, decision-making, goal setting, control and interaction and influence process. He concluded that human oriented climate produces both a higher level of performance and greater job satisfaction. Some researchers have concluded that climate influences productivity, performance, motivation and satisfaction. It is reported that climate depends upon what is perceived by the employees. Thus climate varies from group to group and cadre to cadre. Climate also depends upon environmental uncertainty.

Models of organisational climate

Sound organisational climate is set through an organisational behaviour system. Organisational behaviour philosophy depends upon fact and value premises. Further organisational climate is contingent upon the type of people, type of technology, level of education and expectations of people in it.

Man is three types such as economic, social and self-fulfilling. Each class of man has different set of thinking, motivation and hence requires a particular organisational climate. In order to build a sound organisational climate managers must understand their people in the organisation. Individual differences suggest that there cannot be all-purpose organisational climate. Keith Davis has summarised three models of organisational climate—automatic, custodial and supportive.

Models of organisational climate

Depends upon	Autocratic power	Custodial economic sources	Supportive leadership
Managerial Orientation	authority	money	support
Employee Orientation	obedience	security	performance
Employee Needs met	subsistence	maintenance	higher order

Source: Keith Davis, *Human Behaviour at Work*, New Delhi, Tata McGraw Hill, 1985, p. 30.

Autocratic climate/model. In this model of organisational climate, managers use authority to complete the work. Employees live on the subsistence level and depend upon boss. This model is based on theory-x, where man is inherently distasteful to work and try to avoid responsibility. Likert's management system is comparable with this mode, wherein better performance is ensured through fear, threats, punishment and occasional rewards. There is little interaction between managers and employees.

Custodial climate/model. This approach is common in many business organisations in India. And this phenomenon is most predominant in family practices to the organisational settings. Just as parents decide what is necessary for children, management decides what is good for the employees. This model of climate is not well recommended for matured employees.

In this climate employees depend on organisation for pay. Security also influences the employees to depend on the organisation. Thus in this climate employees maintain very well but lack motivation. Employees in the custodial model feel happy but do not enjoy freedom and autonomy. Management does not give required authority to take decisions. Management feels it is their prerogative to decide what to be or not to be provided to employees.

Supportive model. The employees expect management support for salary and incentives. The employees to achieve their personal goals need the encouragement of managers. Also employees are primarily interested to participate in decision-making and interact with supervisors in organisational matters. Matured employees prefer autonomy and freedom in decision-making. So management should support the decisions which are taken by the employees in the interests of the organisations. This climate is quite similar to the assumptions of McGregor's theory—This model believes that people are self-motivated and have self-direction and control. Organisational processes like communication, leadership, freedom, autonomy, authority, discretion, interaction help employees to fulfil their higher order needs such as esteem and self-actualisation.

This model of climate can be applied in organisations where technology is sophisticated and professionals are involved. And it cannot be applied in all circumstances and at all levels. In advanced countries where basic needs are fulfilled this model is suitable. In less developed and in less structured organisations, social conditions are different. Supportive model creates conducive environment and best can be extracted from people of self-motivation in nature.

Management has to match the model with the human environment existing. All models are not suitable in all cases. And no single model exists in any organisation. The models are based on need hierarchy. Needs of people change with education, maturity, age, social background, personality and work environment. Considering these factors management should build suitable model.

QUESTIONS FOR DISCUSSION

1. What is meant by organisational climate and explain its importance and benefits?
2. Explain factors affecting the organisational climate.
3. Explain how to measure the climate.
4. Explain the models of climate in organisations.

11

MORALE

Morale is a widely used term. It refers to *esprit de corps*, a feeling of enthusiasm, zeal, hope and confidence of an employee that he will be able to cope with the job. A person's zeal for his job reflects his attitude of mind to work, employer and environment in which he is employed. Feelings, emotions, sentiments, attitudes and motives—all these combine and lead to a particular type of behaviour of an employee which is known as morale.

Definition. According to Dale Yoder, morale is a feeling and related to *esprit de corps*, enthusiasm or zeal.

Flippo has described morale as mental condition or attitude of individual and group which determines their willingness to cooperate. Mooney has viewed morale as the sum of several psychic qualities which include courage, fortitude, resolution and above all confidence. Haimann says, "It is a state of mind and emotions affecting the attitude and willingness to work which in turn affect the individual and organisational objectives."

Davis observes, "Morale is basically a mental condition of groups which determine their attitudes." Lighton describes that, "Morale is the capacity of people to pull together persistently and consistently in the pursuit of a common purpose."

Morale. It refers to overall tone, climate or atmosphere of work sensed by the members. It is a mental process which permeates the entire group and creates a mood which results in the formation of a common purpose. It is manifestation of worker's strength, dependability, pride and confidence in and devotion to his work. In a general way it is readiness to cooperate warmly in the tasks and purposes of a given organisation.

Morale includes:

(i) Faith in organisation.

(ii) Attitude of mind that results in mobilisation of energy.

(iii) Feelings, hopes and sentiments which affect the willingness of people to cooperate.

(iv) Courage, confidence in the performance of a job.

(v) Job satisfaction.

Characteristics of morale

1. It is a psychological concept. It is the sum of several psychic qualities that include, courage, fortitude, resolution and above all confidence.

2. Morale is multi-dimensional concept. It is a mix of several elements such as feelings, attitudes, devotion, confidence etc. It recognises the influence of job situation on attitudes and also includes human needs as motivational forces.

3. Morale is a group phenomenon. It consists of pattern of attitudes of members of the group. It refers to the spirit of the organisation and managerial climate.

4. Morale is also a form of teamwork. Morale is the state of attitude of the member in a group where teamwork is a condition. Good morale is helpful in achieving teamwork. Sometimes teamwork is not possible when morale of group is low.

5. Morale is a long term condition. It refers to the rate of balance and health within an organisation. It must be viewed from long-term point. Raising morale among persons or groups is possible in the long-run and cannot be achieved in the short-run by one short action.

6. Morale will be high or low. Like health morale varies and is expressed in terms of degree, say high or low. High morale is a hallmark of sound climate. Low morale is indicated by inefficiency, waste, indiscipline, disputes, confrontations, etc.

7. Morale is different from motivation. The effects are similar. Morale and motivation are different conceptually. Morale describes a state of complex attitudes and feelings about work situations whereas motivation is a function of wants and needs. Motivation refers to mobilisation of energy and morale is treated as "mobilisation of sentiments".

8. Morale is contagious. It spreads among people. It is difficult to build up morale among people. But when morale is low, it can deteriorate rapidly when unfavourable events occur.

Factors affecting the morale of employees

Employee morale is the resultant of employee's belief that organisation serves his personal interests. Favourable attitude reflecting high morale will be exhibited through a feeling of teamwork and job satisfaction. Conversely, low morale will be exhibited through jealousies, conflicts and non-cooperation. The level of morale becomes higher and higher as the feelings shift from a state of indifference towards satisfaction. Morale develops out of mutual satisfaction and through the process of integration of individual and organisational interests.

According to human relations approach high morale leads to higher productivity and *vice versa*. Modern managers are taking care than ever before in the area of 'morale' of employee. Today employee morale is a challenge to leadership. It is also recognised that continued low morale increases absenteeism and turnover.

Factors affecting morale. The factors that affect employee morale are grouped as follows:

1. Employee factors

(a) The status, role and type of employees influence their morale in an organisation. The level of understanding of employees about rewards, pay and standards of performance also influence their morale.

(b) Employees form into groups invariably for social and economic reasons. The feelings of togetherness of employees is an important determinant of morale. Group feeling gives to employees satisfaction and enhances the group morale.

(c) A sense of participation in decision-making by groups and employees develops morale. Length of service of an employee in an organisation influences the morale of employee.

(d) Morale is also affected by the employees' relations with their superiors and fellow workers.

(e) *Fellow workers*: Attitudes of fellow workers will certainly enhances the morale of employees. Co-workers will share responsibilities and share the risks by which employee grievances will be reduced and automatically morale is increased.

(f) *Personal needs*: Personal needs of people do effect worker's morale. Increase in pay, incentives, transportation, training, housing facilities do encourage the morale.

(g) *Self*: A person, who is generally not clever and physically handicapped or poor in health will have low morale as they cannot compete with others.

2. Management practices

(a) *Information*: Employees need to work comfortably, need timely and adequate information. Management has to provide necessary information required by the employees. In the absence of such information they will not be able to work effectively. Hence information enhances the morale of employees at work.

(b) *Goal setting*: Management has to set goals keeping the abilities of employees. Hence management has to invite employees to participate in setting goals and targets to enhance the morale of employees.

(c) *Recognition and praise*: Employees loose morale and feel frustration in the absence of recognition and praise by management for their hard work and dedication. So management has to recognise and promote employees to boost their morale.

(d) *Organisation structure*: The structure refers to the relationships among people and authority sharing between superiors and subordinates. In this process the structure should be flexible and if the structure is made rigid it will adversely affect the employees' morale.

(e) *Equipment and maintenance*: Type and quality of equipment given to employees would decide the performance of employees. And performance is closely linked to the equipment, discomfort to handle them will lower production.

(f) *Leadership*: The style of leadership exhibited by managers has considerable impact on the confidence of employees to their boss and organisation. Autocratic or authoritarian boss cannot impress the employees as employee centred or paternalistic style of leadership.

(g) *Attitudes of managers*: Attitudes of supervisors and

managers towards the subordinates will affect the feelings of employees.

(h) *Working conditions*: Better and congenial working conditions influence the employee morale.

(i) *Size of organisation*: Bigger the size of organisation people become impersonal to each other. And people are managed by rules, policies and procedures. It is difficult to maintain personal touch with all. Absence of personal touch will reduce morale of people.

(j) *Sense of participation*: Management gives chance to people to participate in decision-making. This encourages people to take risk and involve in performing tasks.

(k) *Need satisfaction*: Management should identify needs of people and satisfy them. This will increase morale of people.

3. Outside forces

(a) *Union*: Union feeling will have its influence on the attitudes of employees. Union provides protection to employees and enhances their bargaining capacity with management. Union membership increases the morale of employees.

(b) *Environmental factors*: Pollution causes ill health to workers. Better colonies and housing facilities encourages to work happily.

(c) *Friends*: The way employees work depends upon the 'friendship' they enjoy with others at work and outside the factory.

(d) *Personal health*: Employees with better health work happily and interact with colleagues productively. Illness causes troubles like absenteeism, late going to work place and applying for sick leaves, etc. These will not allow employees to develop and in turn reduce their morale.

(e) *Food and physical welfare*: To develop morale some companies give subsidy on food. This will encourage attendance. Just as a chair depends on four legs, morale also depends on four factors. If any of the four factors are disturbed the situation looks like a chair with broken leg. Dr. Lighton has expressed them as follows:

(i) Confidence of individuals in (the purpose of) their group.

(ii) Confidence of employees in their leader.

(iii) Confidence of members in their co-workers.

(iv) Confidence of the people in the environment where they work.

Morale and productivity

In general, morale enhances productivity of employees. But they are not absolutely related. It is possible to increase morale with favourable shifts in productivity. Keith Davis demonstrates that high productivity does not imply high morale among employees, because manager can increase productivity through close supervision, time sense, scientific methods, etc. And also an employee with high morale need not show more productivity.

Attitudes are the individuals' likes and dislikes directed towards persons, things or situations. Since all expressed attitudes are not to be put into practice, it is expected that morale will not be reflected in productivity.

Another interesting point that is revealed by empirical research is that different combinations of productivity and morale are possible. For instance, Likert and his associates have found that organisations with different possibilities such as high morale and low productivity, high morale and high productivity, low morale and high productivity and low morale and low productivity. These can be seen in the table given below:

	HIGH	
Low Productivity & High Morale		High Productivity & High Morale
	MORALE	
Low Morale & Low Productivity		High Productivity & Low Morale

Morale and Productivity

Figure shows that productivity is a function of four factors such as organisational factors, individual factors, attitudes and morale which are interdependent. Low morale sometimes happen even when productivity is high. This position will not continue for a long time since low morale creates resistance, dissatisfaction and restriction which eventually lead to low productivity.

Individual factors	**Organisational factors**
- Satisfaction	- Morale
	- Attitudes
	- Productivity

Morale and productivity model

Morale and performance. Prior to Hawthorne studies it is assumed that satisfaction leads to performance. Happy workers are better workers though the research findings failed to support it. Thus, sometimes satisfied workers perform better and sometimes they do not. Hence taking actions to boost morale will not necessarily lead to better performance.

Research studies also support the view that morale and productivity are not perfectly related, according to Bray Field. According to Crocket there is little evidence that employee morale has any relationship to performance on the job. Herzberg presents more optimistic view that morale improves workers' output even though relationship between productivity and morale is not absolute.

Causes and indications of low morale

Signs of low morale are generally not noticed till something has gone wrong. By the time management recognises the fact that the morale is deteriorated, worst would have happened already.

The warning signals of morale are as follows:

1. High rate of absenteeism.
2. Tardiness.
3. High labour turnover.
4. Strikes and sabotage.
5. Lack of pride in work.
6. Low quality of work.
7. High wasteland scrap.
8. Grievances.
9. Need for discipline.
10. Fatigue and monotony.
11. Low productivity.

Suggestions to boost the morale

Morale building is a continuous process. Management should collect periodic information on the morale levels of every employee. The information indicates the measures to be taken to improve morale.

1. **Sound manpower management.** Manpower management is concerned with grievance handling, safety measures, discipline rules and welfare activities. Such measures help in improving employee morale which is reflected by better attendance and low turnover.

2. **Human relations approach.** Management should treat the people not as machines but as human beings. No one is more important than others and contribution of each should be recognised. Management should create an environment that increases interpersonal competence, inter-group cooperation, flexibility and the like. In this environment employees are given an opportunity to develop to the fullest potential and there is an attempt to make work challenging consequently leading to more job satisfaction.

3. **Management of attitudes.** Management should change the attitudes of people working in an organisation. They can use persuasion, effective communication, leadership, etc., to encourage them for performing adequately. Sometimes, management can use coercion, threat, punishment for non-compliance of behaviour. The former course of action goes a long way in raising the level of morale.

4. **Organisation design.** Organisation structure influences the morale of employees. Upward communication will be difficult in 'tall' structured organisations than 'flat' structured ones. Hence more the levels less the morale among employees. Reans has proved that absenteeism, accidents, and strikes will be more in big organisations. Flat structures shorten the time taken to communicate vertically and offers scope for self-actualisation.

5. **Participation.** Employee participation in decision-making enhances the morale of employees. Unless employees participate, it is difficult to implement the decisions taken at higher level. McGregor defines participation as a natural means of integration of self-interests with the organisation. However effective

participation depends upon factors such as managers' philosophy, employees' attitudes, situation, etc.

6. Job enrichment. When an employee feels monotony, boredom, fatigue in his job, management enriches and enlarges his job by adding some more duties to him. The job enlargement satisfies some higher order needs of employees and in turn improves morale.

7. Building responsibility factor into a job. Employees should be encouraged to take risky decisions. This can be ensured by delegating authority to them and making them responsible for results.

8. Changing work environment. This involves changing work groups, use of committees and teams.

9. Flexible working hours. If working hours are made flexible, the employees can have enough time to look after their children, family and other personal affairs. This can be ensured by providing freedom to them.

10. Job sharing splitting. Two workers will share the full-time job between themselves. Old persons (retired), mothers, handicapped prefer part time jobs on hourly basis. This way employees will be happy and need not spend the whole time at factory and they can earn elsewhere. This is not true in all jobs.

11. Job rotation. At times employees are shifted to different works. When an employee is associated with the same work for a long time, he will experience monotonous and boredom. Job rotation helps in relaxing one's own tensions on job and increases satisfaction.

12. Fair and equitable remuneration. The employees should feel that their job is worth doing. The payment should be according to capabilities and contributions. Whenever management finds employees' morale is 'low' then management should first of all check its wage structure and then make necessary modifications to build high morale.

13. Job security. Employees are always worried about future when better today is available. The selection policy should ensure job security and stability of income to motivate the employees.

14. Grievance redressed. Grievances are responsible for low morale among employees. A sound procedure to settle grievances and disputes would enhance the morale of the employees. The employees should be given opportunity to present their problems before management. A sound procedure itself ensures better and fruitful solutions.

15. Transfer. When employees (some) are not doing well in a given situation, management can transfer them to a place where they can better discharge their duties with little disturbance to their morale.

16. Other measures. (1) Morale can be improved by taking appropriate measures that may be indicated through analysis of records and good supervision.

(2) To prevent turnover of employees, management should study the reasons and take corrective steps.

(3) To reduce monotony and fatigue, management can study each job and redefines the jobs such that the components causing fatigueness are removed.

Sources of information on employees' morale

I. Organisations measure morale by collecting necessary information. A typical method is opinion-attitude-survey. It tells how employees feel about their jobs. Surveys are conducted through questionnaires such as objective, descriptive and projective.

(a) *Objective questionnaire*: It contains both questions and answers. The worker merely has to mark the answer of his choice.

(b) *Descriptive questionnaire*: The employees are asked to answer the questions in their own words. It encourages employees to express their own feelings on a topic directly or indirectly.

(c) *Projective questionnaire*: It presents abstract situations totally correlated to the organisations or the job and requires the worker to pass comments to them.

II. Observation. Managers observe the feelings and behaviour of employees and interpret.

III. Company records. Company records maintained by personnel department will provide information on 'employee turnover' and 'absenteeism', grievances, disputes, accidents, wastage, spoilage, disciplinary actions taken, inquiries conducted, punishments given, number of workers dismissed, quit, man-days lost, warnings, medical expenses, etc. Such information will help to assess the morale.

IV. Counselling. This method aims at identifying broadly the causes of employee problems or dissatisfaction with a view to offer help and remain effective in his job. This can at times be a source of discovering the symptoms of low morale among employees.

V. Informal enquiry. Managers can often involve in discussion of informal nature with subordinates. Sometimes the employees reveal their inner and real feelings consciously or unconsciously.

A comparative view of different methods of measuring morale is presented in the following table:

Comparative Position of Different Methods of Measuring Morale

Method	Advantages	Problems
Interviews	1. Allows Data Collection on a range of possible subjects 2. Source of 'Rich' Data 3. Build Report	1. Expensive 2. Interpretation difficult 3. Self-report bias
Questionnaire	1. Responses can be easily summarised 2. Easy to use with large samples 3. Relatively inexpensive 4. Can obtain large volume of data	1. Predetermined questions may miss issues 2. Response bias
Observations	1. Collects data on behaviour 2. Real time not retrospective 3. Adaptive	1. Coding problems 2. Sampling is a problem 3. Observer bias 4. Costly
Personnel Records	1. No Response bias 2. High face validity 3. Easily quantified	1. Validity problems 2. Coding problems

QUESTIONS FOR DISCUSSION

1. What are the main characteristics of employee morale and how can management build high morale in an organisation?
2. Enumerate factors affecting the morale of employees.
3. What is the relationship between morale and productivity?
4. Explain the causes and indications of low morale. Give suggestions to improve it.
5. How can morale information collected? And explain the ways of measuring morale.

12

ORGANISATION CULTURE

Introduction

Organisational culture provides employees with a clear understanding of the way things are done. It influences attitudes and behaviour of organisation members. Culture can be traced back to the notion of 'institutionalisation'. An organisation is said to be institutionalised when it takes on a life of its own. It produces common understanding among members about what is appropriate and fundamentally meaningful behaviour.

Meaning and definition

Culture can be considered as a constellation of factors that are learned through interaction with the environment. Just as a growing baby learns basic set of values through family and cultural socialisation so with the organisational member in an organisation. Sechein says that organisational culture is a system of shared beliefs and attitudes that develop in an organisation and guides its members. According to Senn Larry corporate culture consists of norms, values, unwritten laws of conduct as well as management styles, priorities, beliefs which together create a climate that influences how well people communicate. Culture means a complex 'whole' which includes knowledge, belief, art, morale, law, custom, capabilities and habits acquired by man in a society. Cultural moves are passed on from generation to generation, cultural ethos are shared among members of a society. Ralph M. Kilmann has defined organisation culture as philosophies, ideologies, values, assumptions, beliefs, expectations, attitudes and norms that knit an organisation together and are shared by its employees.

The word culture is derived from the idea of cultivation. Culture refers to the pattern of development reflected in a society's system. Since development differs from society to society, the culture also varies according to a given society's stage of development. Accordingly, culture varies from one society to another. For example, American work culture is different from Japanese work culture.

Characteristics

Organisational culture refers to a system of 'Shared meaning' held by members that distinguishes the organisations.

According to Mosfstede *et al.*, the following characteristics reflect the essence of an organisation culture.

1. **Member of identity.** The degree to which employees identify with the origination as a whole rather than with their type of job or field of professional expertise.

2. **Group emphasis.** The degree to which work activities are organised around groups rather than individuals.

3. **People focus.** The degree to which management decision is taken into consideration effect of outcomes on people within the organisation.

4. **Unit integration.** The degree to which units within the organisation are encouraged to operate in an interdependent manner speak about culture.

5. **Control.** The degree to which rules are used.

6. **Risk tolerance.** The degree to which employees are encouraged to take risk.

7. **Reward system.** The degree to which rewards such as promotions remuneration, salary are given to employees as per rules.

8. **Conflict tolerance.** The degree to which employees are encouraged to air criticism openly.

9. **Means-ends orientation**. The degree to which management focuses on results processes to achieve goals.

10. **Open-system focus.** The degree to which the organisation responds to changes in the external environment.

Origin of organisational culture

Founders of organisations. Organisational culture is a continuous process of development of values and attitudes over many generations. The culture can be traced back to the values held by the founders of the organisations. Founders are dynamic personalities with strong values.

Environment. Culture of organisation is a product of environment. An organisation continuously interacts with environment which includes market, technology, demand, etc.

Organisation mission. Culture is the end of organisational goals and mission for which the organisation is established.

Levels of organisation culture

According to Sechein organisation culture has 3 levels—such as—Observable anti-facts, Shared values and Common assumptions. To understand the organisation culture three levels should be studied.

1. Observable anti-facts. These are the symbols of culture in the physical and social work environment.

(a) *Heroes*: The behaviour of top management reflects the philosophy of organisation. The leaders become the role models and they represent what the company stands for.

(b) *Functions*: Members of the organisation who have achieved success are recognised on special occasions. Special occasions are celebrated like ceremonies. These ceremonies bond the members of organisation. Picnics, retirement dinners, annual conventions are celebrated. These activities bring people to come together.

(c) *Stories*: Stories of key persons of the organisation reinforces cultural values. The new employees are oriented through the illustrations.

(d) *Cultural symbols*: Symbols communicate culture of organisations and people wear specific dress with company logo. These symbols make a statement about the company. These symbols include—spacious offices, specially decorated chambers, exclusive parking space for automobiles, etc.

2. Shared values. Values shape the thinking and behaviour of people. Values are reflected in the way individuals behave. These values are of two types—(1) Instrumental and (2) Terminal. Instrumental values refer to enduring beliefs that certain behaviours are appropriate at all times irrespective of objectives. Terminal values are beliefs and objectives which become more important than the appropriateness of the behaviour in achieving such objectives.

Values are emotionally changed priorities. These values are learned during socialisation, in family environment and religious influences. A sound management develops dominant and coherent set of shared values.

3. Common assumptions. Assumptions are the most fundamental level of culture diagnosis. These are deeply held beliefs violation of which would be unthinkable. For example, in Japan, the stockholders are considered less important than the employees because shareholders are only interested in profits whereas the employees are interested in the survival of the company as they stand with the company for their entire lives.

Impact of culture on organisational effectiveness

Culture has both functional and dysfunctional effects on organisation. Employees' perception of objective factors become the organisational culture. These perceptions affect performance and satisfaction of employees on job.

Objective Factors

Member identity
Group emphasis
People focus
Integration
Control
Risk tolerance
Reward criteria
Conflict tolerance
Means-ends orientation
Open-system focus

Impact of organisational culture

Source: Robbins, *Organisational Behaviour*, Prentice Hall of India, p. 621.

1. Satisfaction and performance. If there is congruence between individual needs and culture, the employees derive satisfaction out of it. Job satisfaction depends upon the employee's perception of the organisation's culture. An organisation with a culture of free supervision will give job satisfaction to employees only if they have high achievement need.

Regarding performance, it will be higher if the culture suits the technology. If the culture is informal and technology is non-routine the performance will be higher. The formally structured organisations will achieve higher performance when routine technology is utilised.

2. Socialisation. Socialisation has influence on performance. If an individual is properly indoctrinated into the organisation, his performance tends to be higher.

3. Direction. It refers to the path indicated by the organisation's culture. Direction may or may not be progressive. It depends upon goal attainment.

4. Pervasiveness. The organisation will have divisions. At times, the culture of divisions may vary. If divisions have different cultures, they reduce the overall effectiveness of the organisation.

5. Commitment. Culture facilitates the generation of commitment to something larger than one's individual self-interest. Dedication, sacrifice, commitment are the qualities that an individual nurtures from the last generations or the offenders of organisations. In some organisations people work with dedication and develop service mind. For example, Satya Sai Institutes.

6. Social system stability. Culture is the social glue that helps and holds the employees together by providing appropriate standards. Social system will be stable and it depends upon culture of an organisation. National interest, gratitude, service, dedication, complacency are the basics for any social system to be stable and successful.

7. Strength. The strength of the culture depends upon the life of an organisation. Strength also depends upon the experience of each member. If the employee turnover is high the culture of an organisation will not have much impact on organisational effectiveness.

8. Distinction. Culture has a boundary defining role. It creates distinction between one organisation and others. An organisation is identified by its traditions, norms, policies which constitute a culture of its own.

9. Sense of identity. Culture of an organisation carries a sense of identity. Identity of an organisation comes from its practices in market and trade. If an organisation is known for quality, someone else is known for innovativeness. Thus culture is instrumental for an organisation to be successful or effective.

10. Sense making. Indian companies are built on Hindu culture. The word HINDU stands for Humanity (H), Individuality (I), Nationality (N), Divinity (D), and Unity (U). The corporate people are always reminded by the "sense making" questions—What for they are? Why they have taken birth? What is their contribution to society at large? Thus the culture is imbibed by the founders of the organisations will continue 'making sense' and encourage people to contribute more and more.

11. Automatic control mechanism. Culture acts as an automatic control mechanism and builds the organisation. Culture guides and shapes the behaviour of employees. Every organisation develops a core set of assumptions, understanding and implicit rules that govern day-to-day behaviour in work place. Such understanding automatically controls the misbehaviour of employees.

12. Uniform thinking. Culture of an organisation will streamline different thinking of people. In any organisation it is not desirable for people to think differently and act away from organisation's philosophy. Culture guides the people to think in the same stream as others and what all think.

13. Consistency of employee behaviour. Employee behaviour should be consistent. An employee with inconsistent behaviour will not do well and live in the organisation. Culture gives orientation to newcomers to learn rules and makes them fit.

14. Reduces ambiguity. Employees feel ambiguity in times of change they do not know what to do and what not to do. This ambiguity is cleared by the culture which educates people to become perfect and acceptable.

Evolution of sub-cultures and counter-cultures

Organisational culture refers to a common perception on shared values held by the organisation's members. Though members belong to different levels in the same organisation or departments, they describe the organisation's culture in similar terms.

Dominant culture. It expresses core values that are shared by majority people in the organisation. Organisation culture means culture in domination by and large in the entire organisation. It is the macro view of majority.

Sub-cultures. They tend to develop in large organisations with many divisions or departments. These sub-cultures take place when organisations are identified with geographical separations. Sub-cultures include core values of the dominant group plus additional values unique to members of the division. The unit physically separated will retain core values but reflect modified values with distinction. Yet times sub-cultures too influence the behaviour of members of entire organisation. These sub-cultures co-exist and enhance the value of overall organisation culture.

Counter-cultures. Counter-cultures hold beliefs, values that contradict the dominant social norms, values and behaviour of people. Counter-culture erupts when individuals or groups feel that the existing organisational culture (dominant culture) is too rigid to recognise their creativity. In relation to the dominant organisational culture, the counter-cultures usually engage in three types of dissent:

(1) direct opposition to organisation's dominant values.

(2) opposition to the dominant culture's power structure.

(3) opposition to the methods of interaction with the dominant culture making.

Different dimensions of organisation culture

Organisation culture is concerned with the characteristics of an organisation. It is descriptive in nature.

1. Mechanistic culture. It exhibits the values of bureaucracy. In this culture people are seen as machines and not as human beings. There is a great deal of departmental loyalty and interdepartmental animosity.

2. Organic culture. This is incontrast to the mechanistic culture. Formal authority, values, channels of communication are frowned upon. There is great deal of emphasis on task accomplishment, team work. The staff do have better understanding of problems and willingness to solve them.

3. Authoritarian culture. In the authoritarian culture power and authority are in the hands of leader who only knows what is good and what is bad. He issues orders and seeks obedience from others.

4. Participating culture. In a participation culture all the members see themselves as 'equals'. The people are committed more because the decisions are not imposed but taken on a participation basis. Since the solutions to problems and consequences are thoroughly shared by them, implementation is made easy.

5. Dominant culture. It expresses that core values are shared by the majority of the organisation's members. Organisation's overall culture is nothing but dominant culture. It is the macro view of all.

6. Sub-culture. It occurs in divisions of a big organisation. When divisions are physically away, sub-cultures emerge. The people in divisions will exhibit core values of the dominant culture plus additional values. Sub-culture influences the behaviour of whole organisation sometimes.

7. Strong culture. In a strong culture, core values are so much held by many members for quite a long time. They intensely hold such shared ideas and have greater commitment to those values. The employees who have continued for a long time in an organisation will have strong culture. A strong culture demonstrates high agreement among members, loyalty, cohesiveness and encourages to live together.

8. Weak culture. Members of organisation will have less commitment and less propensity to work together. They do not have much shared opinions and core values. In this culture employees would like to go away frequently and turnover will be high.

Culture *Vs.* Institutionalisation

Culture provides employees with a clear understanding of 'the way things are done'. Culture influences attitudes, behaviour of organisation members. The origin of culture can be traced back to the notion of institutionalisation. When an organisation becomes institutionalised, it takes a life of its own apart from any of its members. When an organisation becomes institutionalised, it becomes valued for itself not merely for the goods it produces. It acquires immortality, when its long term goals are irrelevant, it does not go out of business. It redefines itself. For example, when the demand for Timex watches declined, the company merely redirected itself into the consumer electronics business. Institutionalisation operates to produce common understanding among members about meaningful behaviour.

Culture *Vs.* Formalisation

An organisation's culture increases behavioural consistency. The term refers to the degree to which jobs within the organisation are standardised. If job is standardised, the employee will have minimum amount of discretion. Where formalisation is less and jobs are relatively non-programmed, the employees will have more freedom in their work. Standardisation eliminates the possibility of employees engaging alternative behaviours. The degree of formalisation varies from organisation to organisation. Certain jobs are not far known to have formalisation. Thus formalisation enables to regulate employee behaviour. High formalisation creates predictability, orderliness and consistency. Strong organisation culture achieves the same without the written rules and regulations. Therefore, formalisation and culture are two roads leading to a common destination. Stronger the culture less the need for formalisation of jobs to guide employees' behaviour. These guides will be internalised in employees when they accept the organisation's culture.

Culture creation. Culture is acquired through learning. Organisation's current customs, traditions and general way of doing things form basis for organisation's culture. They have a vision of what the organisation should be. They are not constrained by previous customs or ideologies. The organisation's culture begins with the interaction between (1) founder's biases and (2) initial members employed by founders.

Sustenance of culture. The culture once initiated will continue and it depends upon three aspects such as selection process, top management actions and socialisation, formalisation and institutionalisation.

Selection. The aim of any selection process is to identify individuals who have the knowledge, skills and abilities to perform the jobs within the organisation successfully. Final decision of management is influenced by the candidate's 'fitness' into the organisation. This attempt is to ensure proper 'match' of skills required and skills possessed. Selection process provides information to applicants about the organisation. This is to enable him to avoid conflict after selection. Thus selection is a two-way process, allowing both employer and employee to match one another. In this way, the selection process sustains an organisation's culture by selecting those individuals to perpetuate the core values of this organisation.

Creation and sustenance of organisation culture

Top management actions. The actions of top management also decide the extent of sustenance of an organisation's culture. What the top management says and does go a long way in surviving an organisation. The ideas and norms established by top executives will filter down through the organisation.

Socialisation. Socialisation is a process of adaptation. It takes place when employees pass from outside the organisation to the role of an inside member. It conveys to the employee how the things are done and what matters. New employees, not fully indoctrinated in the organisation's culture, are likely to disturb the beliefs and customs that are in place. Therefore, organisation wants to help new employees to adapt to its culture. This adaptation is called socialisation. This socialisation process is made up of three stages: Pre-arrival, encounter and metamorphosis. This first stage encompasses all the leaving that occurs before a new member joins the organisation. In the second stage the new employee sees what the organisation is really like. In the third stage, the relatively long lasting changes take place. The new employee masters the skills required for his job, successfully performs his new roles and makes the adjustments to his group's norms. The three stage process influences the new employee's productivity and eventual decision to stay with the organisation.

Institutionalisation. The origin of culture can be traced back to the notion of institutionalisation when an organisation becomes institutionalised, it takes a life of its own apart from any of its members. When an organisation becomes institutionalised, it becomes value for itself not merely for the goods it produces. It acquires immorality. When its long term goals are irrelevant it redefines itself and does not go of business. Thus institutionalisation operates to produce common understanding among members about meaningful behaviour.

Formalisation. It refers to the extent the jobs in an organisation are standardised. If the jobs are standardised employees will use minimum discretion in their jobs. Employees will have more freedom if the jobs are non-programmed. And in organisations with more formalisation of jobs, it is easy to achieve the goals which takes long time through culture orientation. Thus formalisation supplements the culture process.

Integration of diverse cultures into single global culture

Culture is institutional in character. A person and his culture are interwoven and they cannot be separated. But the attitudes of people differ on subjects such as technology, acceptance of change, work habits, risk taking, etc. Management should respect the differences in attitudes towards issues to bring harmony among workers. Lack of understanding of these attitudes could cause an undesirable conflict. Respect for diversity in the work environment has further gained momentum in the wake of multinational companies with different cultural characteristics. The organisation culture should support global view because the expanding industrial horizons would necessarily incorporate diversity in the global culture.

Rhinesmith has suggested six ways to integrate the various diverse cultures into a simple global culture.

1. Create a clear global culture.
2. Build up a system to ensure mission statement.
3. Broaden managers' minds to think globally.
4. Establish global career paths. Executives working in home country will go and serve branches elsewhere and executives working abroad will go to home country.

5. Use culture differences as a major asset and adopt overseas management styles in home country sometimes.
6. Encourage unified training efforts that emphasise corporate values.

The world is becoming a global village and hence these guidelines assist organisations to create global culture.

Functionality and dysfunctionality aspects of organisational culture

Functional and dysfunctional aspects of culture are discussed under different dimensions of culture. In most cases the same aspect can be functional in one way and can be dysfunctional in another way.

Dimension	Functionality	Dysfunctionalities
1. Fatalism	Fatalism as a mode of surrendering to circumstances is dysfunctional for managing change. In this a person or a group has high external locus of control. However, this orientation makes a group more realistic and helps it to survive. In some societies an absence of this mode of externality may lead to frustration and dysfunctional conflicts. It help persons to perceive constraints about which nothing can be done.	Fatalism is obviously dysfunctional, making individuals and groups passive, and reactive. It lowers self-confidence and reduces exploratory tendencies to search for solutions.

(*Contd.*)

Dimension	Functionality	Dysfunctionalities
2. Ambiguity	Ambiguity tolerance helps a culture to develop several rich traditions which are not seen as necessarily conflicting. It develops tolerance for differences. Also there is much higher role flexibility in such cultures.	In a culture with a high tolerance of ambiguity there is lower importance for strucure and time. Many organisations in which structuring is necessary culture is left unattended causing confusion, delays and anxiety.
3. Contextualism	High context cultures develop much more insight into social complexities and have higher empathy for others who may differ in their behaviour from the known norms. Persons in such a culture are more sensitive to other persons and groups. They are able to understand the contextual factors faster.	In high context societies and organisations common norms and procedures take time to develop. There may be confusion in interpreting the events or behaviour.
4. Temporalness	Emphasis on the present results in high involvement of individuals in the current actives.	Present cultures are likely to develop competencies of working with and using temporary system.

(*Contd.*)

Dimension	Functionality	Dysfunctionalities
5. Collectivism	The following are the strengths of this orientation contributing to individual and organisational strengths.	Collectivism produces several handicaps for the indviduals and society.
	(a) Good relations are maintained and the affiliation needs are satisfied.	(a) People find it difficult to confront their seniors in matters requiring confrontation and exploration.
	(b) There is high trust amongst the members of the collectivity with collaboration.	(b) There is lack of initiative by individuals and groups.
	(c) Consensus is attempted more frequently.	(c) There is lack of self-confidence and lack of efforts for individuals living under the shade of their collectivity. They do not develop autonomy and individual identity.
	(d) There is sharing of work and reward.	
	(e) Members have a high sense of belonging and collectivity.	

(*Contd.*)

Dimension	Functionality	Dysfunctionalities
6. Particularism	Persons have a very high sense of identity with their groups.	On the other hand in-group/out-group feelings reduce objectivity of the members who are generally prejudiced in favour of their in-groups and against the out-groups. Favouritism and clique formations are encouraged taking attention away from the achievement results.
7. Other directions	Norms laid down by the society may help and reduce improper behaviour of individual members. The concern to save face may also contribute to behave well for the collectivity.	Lack of internalisation of values and criteria which are internally consistent to oneself cause people afraid of taking risks.
8. Androgyny	Androgyny contributes to the values of the future society. It helps groups to value (and develop) interpersonal trust, caring, harmony, concern for the weak and collaboration.	However over-emphasis on such values may reduce the effectiveness of competition.
9. Tolerance for power distance	There are some strengths in societies with high tolerance of power distance. Respect for seniority	However, high tolerance for power distance may result in stress. There may be centralisation with

(*Contd.*)

Dimension	Functionality	Dysfunctionalities
	and aged may help persons to learn from experienced people. Conformity may be high and is needed for effective functioning of the groups.	little autonomy for lower level units and individuals.

QUESTIONS FOR DISCUSSION

1. Explain the meaning of organisation culture and its characteristics.
2. There are three levels of culture from the most visible to abstract. Describe.
3. What is the impact of culture on organisational effectiveness?
4. How sub-cultures and counter-cultures develop within the dominant organisational culture?
5. Explain different dimensions of organisation culture. What forces might contribute towards making a culture strong or weak?
6. What is the relationship between institutionalisation, formalisation and organisational cultures?
7. How is an organization's culture maintained?
8. How does the managers integrate various diverse cultures into a single global culture?
9. Discuss functionality and dysfunctionality aspects of organisational culture.

13

PERSONALITY

Introduction

Behaviour of man is a function of person and environment. From organisational perspective, manager has viewed employees as rational beings who are motivated by money. Thus man is treated both as economic man and also rational man to predict his behaviour. The scientific management has viewed man as basically motivated by incentives. As days passed human relations thought is developed and manager has viewed human being as social man. That is, man is a social being who wants to belong to a group and then depends upon social needs emerging at work place. Latter, Hathorne studies indicated that economic motives alone do not govern human behaviour and treated man as a 'social being'. Subsequently organisational behaviourists treated man as a 'complex unit' because man is composed by traits, characteristics, predispositions and needs. Functional behaviour will emerge if there is a match between them and the work environment. Understanding the concept of personality enables manager to function most effectively by predicting their behaviour at work.

Thus behaviour is the function of personality and environmental factors.

B = f [personality × environmental factors]

Personality is a composition of several components just as concrete work is made up of components such as cement, chips, sand and steel plus water, personality too is an organised whole without which a individual has no meaning.

Personality is derived from Latin word 'Per Sonnave', which means 'to speak through'. The Latin word denotes 'the marks' to wear in ancient Rome. Thus personality is referred to external appearances (actions).

According to Gordon Allport, "Personality is the dynamic organisation within the individual that determines his unique adjustments to his environment."

Personality is the sum total of ways in which an individual reacts and interacts with others.

Maddi defines personality thus:

> "Personality is a stable set of characteristics and tendencies that determine those commonalties and differences in the psychological behaviour, thoughts, feelings and actions of people that have continuity in time and that may not be easily understood as the sole result of the social biological pressures of the moment."

Laymen tend to equate Personality with social success or dominant characteristics of a person such as height, weight, etc. Kluckohan and Murray have beautifully concluded "To some extent a person's Personality is like all other people, like some other people, like no other people".

Bonner provides six propositions to classify the nature of Personality within the context of change and development:

(1) human behaviour is composed of acts,

(2) personality visualised as a whole actualises itself in a particular environment,

(3) distinguished by self-consistency,

(4) it forms a time integrating structure,

(5) it is goal directed, and

(6) it is process of becoming.

It means a general sum of traits or characteristics of the person. It is a unitary mode of response to life situations. Personality is a pattern characteristics traits of an individual, relationship between these traits and the way in which a person adjusts to other people and situations. Personality is a pattern of characteristics of a person that influences his or her behaviour towards goal achievement. Personality is something like outgoing, invigorating interpersonal abilities.

Thus there are few thousand words that describe personality. Gordon Allport categorised them into five major areas labelled as follows:

(a) *Omnibus*: Personality as the 'sum total aggregate of properties'.

(b) *Integrative and configuration*: Personality is the organisation of personal attributes.

(c) *Hierarchical*: In one sense the hierarchical character of a person to the environment is treated as Personality.

(d) *Adjustment*: In a sense the adjustment character of a person to the environment is treated as Personality.

(e) *Distinctiveness*: Supporters of this category stresses the uniqueness of each Personality.

Determinants of personality

Several factors influence in shaping the personality. The important factors in the development of Personality are discussed below:

Biological factors

Heredity. It is an accepted fact that heredity plays an important role in shaping personality. Human values, temperament and ideas are transmitted through heredity. The physical characteristics are also inherited from parents and forefathers.

Brain. Another biological factor that contributes to personality is brain. Studies on electrical stimulation of brain (ESB) revealed that structure of brain determines the formation of personality.

Physical features

External and physical characteristics are important ingredients of personality. They will also influence personality. Similarly rate of maturation also affect personality. Persons in different age groups are exposed to different physical and social situations differently.

Family and social factors

Family and social groups have most significant impact on personality development.

(i) Socialisation process. It is a process by which an individual is exposed to environment and acquires behaviour potentialities that are open to him. Firstly the man at birth is exposed to family members, later on social groups. Thus socialisation process starts with interaction between child and mother subsequently family members.

(ii) Identification process. An individual identities himself with one of his family members, father (say) whom he feels ideal in the family. An individual normally identifies with one of his family members due to similarity of behaviour and motives between him and the model.

(iii) Home environment. The environment where a man is brought up in his childhood has bearing on the personality development. There is difference in his emotions and adjustment nature between a child brought in an institution and a child grow under parents care.

(iv) Family members. There is high co-relation between attitudes of parents and children. Parents and family members influence the personality development of an individual. Next to parents come brothers and sisters followed by teacher who influences personality building.

(v) Social groups. Personality is shaped by the school environment, friends and other work groups.

Cultural factors

Culture too influences the personality of an individual. Culture guides the life and traits to be acceptable to the social groups. Culture determines one's attitudes towards independence, aggression, competition and co-operation.

Situational factors

Actions are determined by situation and personality is determined by circumstances which exert pressure and constraints. Thus situational factors have a very big influence on the personality. A worker who is in need of power and achievement may become frustrated and react aggressively if he is put in a bureaucratised work situation. Thus personality composition changes because of changed situation.

Experiences in life. Whether one trusts or mistrusts others depends upon the past experiences of the individual. Personality characteristics are moulded by frequent access to positive or negative experiences in life.

People interacting with. "A person is known by the company he keeps" is a common adage. People who have common interests come together. That is, like minded people interact and influence each other. From childhood onwards people are interacting with various persons such as parents, brothers, sisters, friends, colleagues etc., and thus personality is shaped by the persons they are interacting with.

Personality attributes influencing organisational behaviour

Need patterns. According to Steers and Braunstein people in work setting manifest four personality needs such as achievement, affiliation, autonomy and dominance. Achievement oriented personalities engage themselves pro-actively to feel proud about their achievement and success. Affiliation oriented people would like to work cooperatively with others. Autonomy willing persons function best when they are not closely supervised. And persons of dominating nature are very effective in work environment.

Locus of control. Some people believe that they control and shape the course of events in their lives. They are called internals. Some people believe that they are controlled by events that occur by chance. They are called externals. Internals seek job related information, influence others at work, rely on their own abilities and seek opportunities for advancement.

Introversion and extroversion. According to Hellriegel, Slocum and Woodman personalities are of two types— (1) Introverts and (2) Extroverts. Introverts turn inward and experience feelings, thoughts and ideas within themselves. Extroverts turn outward looking for external stimuli with which they can interact. Extroverts are preferring to interact with a small intimate circle of friends. Introverts are more likely successful when they work on highly abstract ideas in a relatively quite atmosphere.

Tolerance for ambiguity. Lorsch and Morse opined that Tolerance for Ambiguity is a personality dimension. Managers should possess it for success in rapidly changing conditions.

This characteristic indicates the ability to work effectively in times of uncertainty and rapidly changing conditions of external environment. Managers having high tolerance for ambiguity can cope well under changing conditions. Managers having low tolerance for ambiguity may be effective in structured work settings but find it difficult to operate when things are changing rapidly and information about future events is not available.

Self-esteem and self-concept. In the opinion of Cooper Smith 'self-esteem' denotes the extent to which individuals regard themselves as capable in an organisation. High self-esteem provides a sense of high self-concept which in turn reinforces high self-esteem. Thus these two are mutually reinforcing. Individuals of high self-esteem will try to take more challenging assignment and are successful. They define themselves as highly valued individuals.

Authoritarianism and dogmatism. Individuals with authoritarian dimension deal with subordinates high handedly. Dogmatism refers to a person's rigidity to others viewpoints. These two personalities do not ensure creativity and effectiveness since new ideas at lower levels will neither be listened to nor implemented. Selective organisations accept authoritarianism where members lack administrative know-how.

Machiavellianism. "Manipulation of others, as primary way of achieving one's goals is all about Machiavellianism." Individuals of machiavellianism tend to be logical assessing the system around them. They twist the facts and influence others by manipulating the system to their advantage. Such personalities do not continue for a long time and hence may become infective, in the long run.

Type A and Type B personalities. Type A personalities feel a chronic sense of time urgency and they are achievement oriented. They exhibit a competitive drive and feel impatient when their work is slowed down. They help the organisation to move ahead in a relatively short period of time. Type B personalities are easy going and will not be competitive. Type A personalities may suffer from setbacks in health and also detrimental to the organisation in the long run.

Work ethic. Some personalities are highly work oriented and known as workaholics. They are greatly involved in the job and have little outside interests. This type of personalities do achieve organisational goals quickly and effectively. But such personalities often get health problems and cause estrangement to immediate family members.

Risk taking. People are risk avoiders. High-risk-taking managers take rapid decisions and use less information than low-risk-taking managers. High risk taking may lead to effective performance and *vice versa*.

Self-monitoring. It refers to a personality trait that measures an individual ability to adjust his or her behaviour to external situational factors. Individuals of self-monitoring show considerable adaptability in adjusting their behaviour to external factors. They are highly sensitive to external ones and behave differently in different situations. High self-motivators are more successful in managerial positions. High self-monitors are capable of showing different faces for different audiences.

'n Ach'. It refers to the need to achieve or strive continually to do things better. People with high 'n Ach' can be described striving to do things better. They want to overcome bottlenecks and feel that their success depends upon their actions. They also invite challenging tasks.

Theories of personality

There are innumerable concepts and views on personality. Many psychologists and behaviouralists have carried out research to reach consensus on personality perspectives. Grouping of theories relating to personality are categorised on various themes.

Psychoanalytic theory. The theory is based on the notion that unseen forces motivate man. Freud concluded that unconscious framework motivates a man. This framework contains three aspects such as Id, ego and super ego. They are so interrelated and cannot be separated for individual study.

(i) *The Id*: Id refers to instinctual needs. They are two types—(1) life instincts and (2) death instincts. Life instincts are hungry, thirsty and sex. The Id would go unchecked to satisfy needs such as sexual relations and pleasures. As individual matures, he learns to control the Id. Yet, it will remain as a driving force throughout life. Id is an important source of thinking and behaving.

(ii) *The ego*: It is the logical and conscious part of the human personality. If Id represents unconscious part, ego represents conscious part. Thus ego keeps Id under check. Id wants immediate action and ego wants to postpone it to appropriate time.

(iii) *Superego*: It represents noble thoughts acquired by a person from parents, teachers, friends, colleges, organisation, religion, etc. From childhood, he absorbs cultural values and develops a superego. It determines whether the idea proposed by 'ego' is right or wrong. Thus superego acts as a sensor on the individuals. Freud says that ego mediates between Id and superego. A Personality becomes disorderly developed when either Id or superego becomes dominant.

Defense mechanism. The Id, ego and superego are often in conflict. The conflicts among Id, ego and superego result in the following defensive mechanisms to reduce tension caused by the conflicts:

(i) *Aggression*: People become aggressive and attack a person when conflict arises. Sometimes the aggression may be directed towards some innocent object.

(ii) *Repression*: It refers to postponing or avoiding the conflicting situation. The problem cannot be solved by this method of defense mechanism.

(iii) *Rationalisation*: Here the individual resorts to redefining the situation. Ego tries to find excuses for the problem and therefore not conducive to problem-solving and personal development of the individual.

Reaction and interjection. Projection is a safety valve where ego blames something else without admitting the feelings and actions. Under projection are a person, his feelings, and actions to someone else. Interjection is one when ego takes in something from outside and sees it as a part of himself. Sociologists label this process, internalisation, which occurs when people start growing.

According to Likert and Spiegler this theory is unique and influences the people psychologically and philosophically. Four important characteristics are given here:

1. Deterministic. Behaviour is caused, even unconscious slips reveal a certain meaning.

2. Dynamic. It assumes that human action results from psychic energy called libido, which means life maintaining and pleasure seeking energy that may be attached or detached from various goals and objects.

3. Developmental. Human development begins at birth and progresses through life.

4. Structural. It establishes structural relationship among three structures of personality which are Id, ego and superego.

The theory is also known as metapsychology as it extends human behaviour beyond conscious elements. The theory is criticised on methodological grounds and largely unstable.

Sheldon's physiognomy theory. Sheldon established relationship between body type and characteristics of human behaviour. He identifies 3 types of bodies—(1) endomorphic, (2) mesomorphic and (3) ectomorphic. Their typical behavioural patterns are described in the table on next page.

1. Endomorph. He is bulky and beloved. Sheldon says, that person is fatty and also which in proportion to his height. The person seeks, comfort, loves fine food, eats much, jovial, affectionate and liked by all persons. The personality temperament is viscertonic.

2. Mesomorph. The individual is basically strong, athletic and tough. His physical and body condition is appreciated by all. According to Sheldon such individual tend to be somatotonic temperament, *i.e.*, he tends to be aggressive, self-assertive and fond of muscular activity.

3. Ectomorph. He is thin, long and physically not developed well. His temperament is 'cerebrotonic' *i.e.*, he suffers from excessive inhibition, restraint and avoids social contacts. He is labelled as absent-minded and shy.

Carl Jung's theory. Carl Jung has explained the important dimensions of personality—Thinking, feeling, sensation and initiation.

(a) Thinking - Logical reasoning

(b) Feeling - Interpretation on a subjective scale

(c) Sensation - Perception in general sense

(d) Initiation - Unconscious inner perception

TABLE: Relationship between Body type and Behavioural temperament

Body Type	Behavioural Temperament Features
1. **Endomorph** (Bulk and spherical appearance)	likes comfort, eats heavily, likes people even tempered prefers relaxed posture reads slowly tolerant of others prefers to be lead easy to get along with others
2. **Mesomorph** (Strong, athletic and tough)	likes physical adventure risk taking needs physical activity aggressive and intensive to others courageous desires action, power seeks outdoor activity
3. **Ectomorph** (Delicate body, thin and light muscled)	displays restraint desire for concealment distrustful of others works in closed areas reacts quickly prefers solitude anxious dedicated

Adapted and abridged from David Laeless, *Effective Management Special Psychological Approach*, Prentice Hall of India, Englewood Cliffs, nj, 1972.

According to Carl Jung, sensation and intuition are important for gathering information and the other two functions *i.e.*, thinking and feeling for evaluating and judging the situation. Individuals are strong in sensation/intuition while gathering information and strong in thinking/feeling while evaluating it.

Sensation and intuition. Individuals gather information either through processing facts or through visualisation of what the scene depicts. Sensation type persons depend on a lot of information and concentrate on the present time. The intuitive type persons are very imaginative and futuristic.

Thinking and feeling. People evaluate and make judgments in objective and subjective fashions. Thinking type persons make systematic enquiry and they are unemotional in making judgments. They are not sensitive to the feelings of others. Feeling type persons are sentimental and rely on human feelings. They try to please others and emphasise the human aspects of dealing with organisational matters.

Hence managers fall into one of the following categories—Sensation thinkers, intuitive thinkers, sensation-feelers and intuitive feelers.

1. Sensation thinkers. They create effective structures for organisations which ensure stability. They are factual and dependable. They do not act quickly.

2. Intuitive thinkers. They give much thought to new ideas and build new systems on operating effectiveness. They are the pro-active change masters. They may be not sensitive to the feeling of others and are likely to experience setbacks in their interpersonal relationships.

3. Sensation feelers. They are pragmatic in their approach and deal with problems in a systematic fashion. They effectively use the resources and have the co-operation of the people working with them. They cannot conceptualise, recreate ideas, hence *status quo* may prevail in the system.

4. Intuitive feelers. They are effective in group setting. Managers are good inventors, developing their subordinates professionally. They normally have a bias and take decisions on likes and dislikes rather than objective criteria.

Socio-psychological theory. This theory emphasises the relationship between man and society. The individual serves society which in turn fulfils his needs. Popular sociologists namely Adler, Horney, Fromm and Sullivan support this theory. They have accepted that socio-psychological factors determine personality. Horney suggests that human behaviour results from three predominant interpersonal orientations such as complaint, aggressive and detachment. Complaint people are dependent on others and move towards others. Aggressive persons are motivated by the need for power and move against others. Detached people are self sufficient and move away from others. This theory offers solutions to the problems that emerge from psychology in shaping personality.

Major traits theories

Another dimension to understand human personality is 'Trait' that one possesses. A trait is defined as 'an endure attribute of a person that appears constantly in different situations.' It is a distinguishable characteristic in which one individual differs from another. Popular characteristics include, shy, aggressiveness, lazy, ambitious, loyal and timid. These characteristics when exhibited in a large number of situations are called 'Personality Traits'. A trait is said to be important if consistently and frequently seen in diversified situations. Supporters of this theory have made assumptions to consider characteristics as traits:

1. Traits are common in many individuals but vary in absolute amounts between individuals.
2. Traits are seen consistently and frequently in diversified situations.
3. Traits are relatively stable and exert fairly universal effects on behaviour.
4. Traits can be inferred from the behavioural indicators.
5. Traits distinguish one personality from another.
6. Traits can be quantified and do not defy measurement.

Trait theory is an extension of type theory. The theory assumes that individual's personality can be described in terms of traits. One frequently uses the following terms friendly, continuously, excitable, aggressive, kind hearted, anxious, etc. People abstract these things from their behaviours.

Cattel isolated 171 traits and identified 16 traits which have been found to be general and constant source of behaviour.

TABLE: Sixteen Primary Traits

1. Reserved	*Vs.*	Outgoing
2. Less intelligent	*Vs.*	More intelligent
3. Affected by feelings	*Vs.*	Emotionally stable
4. Submissive	*Vs.*	Dominant
5. Serious	*Vs.*	Happy-go-lucky
6. Expedient	*Vs.*	Conscientious
7. Timid	*Vs.*	Venturesome
8. Tough-minded	*Vs.*	Sensitive
9. Trusting	*Vs.*	Suspicious
10. Practical	*Vs.*	Imaginative
11. Forthright	*Vs.*	Shrewd
12. Self-assured	*Vs.*	Apprehensive
13. Conservative	*Vs.*	Experimenting
14. Group dependent	*Vs.*	Self-sufficient
15. Uncontrolled	*Vs.*	Controlled
16. Relaxed	*Vs.*	Tense

Norman has provided different descriptive objective pairs of words for the same kind of trait.

Trait dimension	Descriptive objective pairs
Extroversion	Talkative - silent
	Open - secretive
	Adventurous - cautious
Agreeableness	Good natured - irritable
	Gentle - headstrong
	Co-operative - negativist
Conscientiousness	Tidy - careless
	Responsible - undependable
	Preserving - quitting
Emotional Ability	Calm - anxious
Culture	Sensitive - insensitive
	Intellectual - unreflective

Allport's theory. Gordon Allport has provided most exciting version. He mentioned common traits that are comparable.

He has indexed six categories such as social, political, religious, theoretical, economic and aesthetic. He has mentioned some unique traits which the individual possesses. They are cardinal (most pervasive), central (unique) and secondary (periphery)

Allport emphasises that all individuals possess all the six orientations (common traits). But some may be high in economic and low in others. Thus the proportions vary from person to person. It is the profile of an individual's values that is useful in defining his personality.

Cattel's trait theory. Cattel has identified two categories of traits namely 'Surface traits' and 'Source traits'. A surface trait is something like a medical cause of diverse symptoms. An example of surface trait is affectionate-cold, wise-foolish, sociable-reclusive, honest-dishonest, etc. He identified source traits such as good nature-critical, trustfulness-suspicious, maturity-immaturity, realism-evasiveness, dominance-submissiveness, cheerfulness-depressed and energetic-subdivided feelings.

Maddi has reduced them to four personality types such as extrovert and high anxiety, introvert and high anxiety, extrovert and low anxiety and introvert and low anxiety.

	High Anxiety	**Low Anxiety**
Extrovert	Tense Excitable Unstable Warm Sociable Dependent	Composed Confident Trustful Adaptable Warm Sociable dependent
Introvert	Tense Excitable Unstable Cold Shy	Composed Confident Trustful Adaptable Calm Cold Shy

Adapted from Stephen P. Robbins, *Organisational Behaviour*, Prentice Hall of India Ltd., New Delhi, p. 103.

- Traits ignore situational contexts.
- Traits ignore the dynamic interchange that occurs between an individual's personality and environment.
- Traits may be too extract.
- Without knowledge how they are related and important it is not possible to describe an individual's personality.
- Traits are descriptive rather than analytical.

Self-concept

Self-theory of personality is very relevant in OB. According to Carl Rogers self-theory is composed of perceptions of the 'I' or 'Me' and the perceptions of the relationships of the 'I' to 'Me' to others. There are four factors in self-concept.

(i) Self-image. It is the way an individual sees himself. Every person has certain beliefs about himself that what he can and he will. These beliefs put together refer to self-image or identity.

(ii) Ideal self. It refers to the way one would like to be. It is different from self-image. Self-image indicates the reality of a person as perceived by others, while the ideal self indicates the ideal position as perceived by him. Thus there is gap between these two characteristics.

(iii) Looking glass self. It refers to the perception of a person about how others are perceiving him. It is not the way people actually see him. But it is what one thinks people perceive him.

(iv) Real self. It is what one really is. Self-image is confirmed the responses of others with whom he corresponds. In the light of feedback from the friends and environment he reevaluates himself and adjusts his self-image to be more consistent.

A person's self-concept gives him a sense of meaning and consistency. According to Gellerman, the average man is not well acquainted with himself. In analysing OB self-concept plays very important role. A person perceives a situation depending upon his self-concept. This has a direct influence on his behaviour.

Maddi's models of personality

Maddi's personality theory explains three models of individual behaviour in organisations. He proposes them as

Conflicting model, Self-fulfilment model and Consistency model. These three models explain individual behaviour to reduce tension, attain psychological rewards and achieving cognitive consonance respectively.

I. Conflicting model. According to this model of personality, individuals confront with two opposing desires. They operate well within himself. Fulfilment of one desire affects the other. When such two forces the individual is put to tension as to what do. And finally he will do something to reduce his tension.

II. Self-fulfilment model. This model depicts being driven by a positive force to self-actualise. According to this model, man always sets something goal and achieve it using best of his potential. Self-actualisation is never completed. Human potentials are unlimited and one is constantly in the process of self-actualisation. Thus, throughout life man is motivated to reach goals one after the other and keeps himself striving throughout life.

This model also explains that if an individual is deficient in one area, he will try to reach perfection in another sphere to compensate it. A polio victim who cannot walk may be a singer. He strives to become great singer and compensate himself. Thus fulfilment model explains the behaviour in terms of one's search himself. Thus fulfilment model explains the behaviour in terms of one's search for self-fulfilment and perfection.

III. Consistency model. Every individual knows about his strengths and weaknesses. Individuals seek feedback from friends and others, about how he is perceived by them. If the feedback is same as what he perceives himself then he is said to be in a state of equilibrium or internal consistency. If the feedback is different it creates cognitive dissonance. Then he strives to correct himself or change the perceptions of others about him. Thus consistency model explains the behaviour as driven by the need to seek equilibrium.

The three models of personality make sense. Everybody belongs to one of the models at a given point of time. Everybody sometimes operates in the conflicting model to reduce tension or engage in self-motivation to reach perfection or seeking feedback to attain cognitive consistency thus all the three models help in explaining behaviours. Manager should identify in which state he is to handle effectively.

Erikson's developmental model

Developmental model of personality is useful in understanding the human behaviour. Man grows from childhood and faces various problems at various stages. These problems carry over to the place of work and influence the behaviour in organisations. Erikson described 8 models as follows:

Stage 1: Thrust *Vs.* **Mistrust:** Just as children depend upon parents in their initial stage; employees also when they have joined organisation depend upon some people around them. Whether they like or not others, here the employee (newly joined) trust some people to find place in the system. When others do not respond to him he develops a sense of mistrust.

Stage 2: Autonomy *Vs.* **Shame:** When employee completes his training period he would like to do job independently without much dependency on others. In doing so he has to take several decisions independently. And success or failure is a matter of time and luck. In the absence of success the employee has to feel ashamed of.

Stage 3: Initiative *Vs.* **Guilt:** An employee has to attend several activities by his own initiative. But the activities may be successful or failed. When things go wrong the employees feel sorry for taking initiative and feel guilty of wasting time and efforts.

Stage 4: Industry *Vs.* **Inferiority:** In an organisation manager openly learns and manages the activities. If he is successful he feels good about himself and if goes wrong he feels inferior and maintains low self-concept.

Stage 5: Identity and role diffusion: An individual in a society during his adolescence will experience conflict due to the socially imposed requirement of becoming an independent and effective adult. This at times becomes difficult in the organisational context also. An individual is expected to establish himself as high performing member, but it is not easy.

Stage 6: Intimacy *Vs.* **Isolation:** During adulthood individual wants to develop contacts and establish relationships with important persons in the society. Similarly in organisations also individuals at their adulthood try to establish relationships with others, which is difficult. Then they remain in isolation in the system.

Stage 7: Generatively *Vs.* **Stagnation:** Just as in society, an individual in his middle adulthood age is expected to meet others and help them to develop. But it is difficult to get followers and he does not do this effectively. This results in a feeling of stagnation in the system.

Stage 8: Ego integrity *Vs.* **Despair:** As age passes and nearing death one's social and biological role gets diminished. Similarly in organisations also individuals experience the same thing. The employee experiences happiness by consolidating his lifelong achievements, before retirement or leave the organisation with a sense of purposelessness and despair.

Many a time conflicts are not resolved. The unresolved issues are carried forward to the subsequent developmental stage. Managers can play a role in identifying the unresolved conflicts and try to help the employees and deal with them.

QUESTIONS FOR DISCUSSION

1. What is the nature of Human beings and define the term Personality?

   Or

   "Personalities, an organised whole without which an individual would have no meaning." Comment on this statement.

   Or

   "Personality essentially deals with variations in thought and behaviour that differentiates one person from another." Elucidate this statement.

   Or

   "People are similar yet they are different." Comment.

2. What are major determinants of Personality?

   Or

   How does heredity influence Personality? Environment? Situation?

3. What behavioural predictions an employee had?

   (a) Low self-esteem.

(b) High 'n Ach'

(c) An external locus of control.

Or

What are the advantages and disadvantages of employing type a personalities and workaholics in organisations?

Or

Describe major Personality attributes influencing O.B.

Or

Describe various personality dimensions in modern organisations.

4. What are the various theories of personality? How will you integrate them to get a satisfactory theory of personality?
5. Do personality traits inconsistent from day-to-day?

Or

Can you identify major personality traits of employees in an organisation?

Or

What constraints the ability of personality trait to precisely predict behaviour?

6. What do you mean by self-concept? Elaborately explain the Carl Rogers theory of personality and its applicability in organisations.
7. Describe Maddi's models of personality.
8. How does understanding 'Eriskson's developmental model' help managers in organisations?

14

ATTITUDES

Attitude is an internal condition of a person that is focused on objects as it exists in the person's psychological world. Human behaviour is a function of attitudes. In organisations employees have attitudes related to work environment. The individual's attitudes and apathy towards his work environment:

- An attitude is the predisposition of an individual to evaluate some object.
- Attitude is a predisposition to respond to certain set of facts.
- Attitudes are evaluative statements concerning the objects.
- An attitude is a mental state of readiness organised through experience exerting a specific influence upon a person's response to objects with which it is related.
- An attitude as the way one feels about something.
- An attitude is 'a set of actions with emotional overtone'.
- Attitude is a tendency or readiness to respond to some social effect.
- According to Allport, attitude is a 'mental and neural state of readiness, organised through experience, exerting a directive or dynamic influence upon the individual's response to objects and situations with which it is related.'
- Attitude is a heightened responsiveness to certain stimuli.
- Krech and Crutchfield define attitude as an enduring organisation of motivational, emotional, perceptual, and cognitive processes with respect to some aspect of individual's world.

- Kartz and Scotland define attitude 'a tendency or predisposition to evaluate an object in a certain way'.

Characteristics of attitudes

Attitudes can be distinguished in terms of characteristics:

1. Valence. It refers to the magnitude or degree of favourableness or unfavourableness towards the object.

2. Multiplicity. It refers to the number of elements constituting the attitude.

3. Relation to needs. Attitudes can also vary in relation to needs they serve.

4. Centrality. It refers to the importance of the object.

Components

Person's attitude comprises of three components such as, cognitive, affective and behavioural.

Cognitive component. It refers to the opinion, belief, segment of an attitude. It sometimes referred to as opinion. The cognitive component is very important and consists of the individual's perceptions like beliefs and ideas. According to Krech *et al.*, the cognition include 'evaluative beliefs' such as old or bad, desirable or undesirable, favourable or unfavourable qualities of an object. If affective component refers to feelings, this cognitive component refers to beliefs.

Affective component. It refers to the emotions associated with an attitude object. Basically, it consists of the feelings a person has towards an object. It is often expressed as like or dislike, good or bad, pleasing or displeasing, favourable or unfavourable. The expression of love, hate, etc. are treated as affective component.

Behavioural component. It refers to the way one intends to behave towards an object. Both the cognitive and affective components influence the way a person intends to behave towards an object.

Behaviour. Attitudes play an important role in influencing the behaviour of people. Attitudes are serving four functions and thereby affecting the behaviour. (1) utilitarian, (2) ego-defensive, (3) value orientation, and (4) knowledge.

1. Utilitarian. Attitudes enable a person and act as means to achieve desired goal. Attitudes are the 'sum' of sentiments based on experiences in attaining the motive satisfaction.

2. Ego-defensive. People expend their energies in the process of learning to live in doing so one's attitudes serve the function of defending one's self-image.

3. Value orientation. Many attitudes serve the function of value orientation. According to Katz, attitudes not only give clarity to the self-image but also mould that self-image closer to the heart's desire.

4. Knowledge. This function is based on a person's need to maintain a stable, organised and meaningful structure of the world. Attitudes provide a standard against which a person evaluates various aspects of his world assumes the knowledge function too.

Attitude formation

Attitudes are basically learned, people are not born with specific attitudes. Individuals learn about environment with which they interact. Thus all the elements of environment should be taken into account.

Group factors. Group factors play vital role in the attitude formation in the minds of an individual.

Family members. Father, mother and brothers or sisters are the basic sources from where an individual learns. All the family members have influence on the attitudes of individuals. In the process of socialisation man learns and forms attitudes. As man grows he comes into contact with persons outside the family.

Family members have two important roles to play. Family members have certain values and attitudes which they share among themselves. Family mediates the influence of larger social systems on the individual's attitudes. An individual interacts with other family members and simultaneously influences other's attitudes and being influenced by others.

Reference groups. The people coming in touch with the individual in his day-to-day life are called reference groups. They influence the individual's attitudes and behaviour. They provide necessary inputs to an individual while learning attitudes. This learning takes place in the process of socialisation. Socialisation is a process where individuals learn value system and norms of society where they live.

Social factors. Social classes possess certain culture and attitudes. They transmit these attitudes to some groups and families. These families in turn transmit to the individuals. Thus attitudes are formed in the minds of individuals.

Experience. People through job experience learn attitudes. They develop attitudes about work environment such as pay, job, working conditions supervisor, company, etc. when they go to new job, they form and develop different attitudes about the job, supervisor, pay and company. Previous experience is responsible to develop difference in their attitudes. Managers used to have differences in attitudes and they attach importance to the job content in order to form positive attitude in the new job.

Association. People are influenced by the associations they belong to. The region, religion, education system, race, sex, age and income—all these influence attitudes of individuals. The influence depends upon the distance between the groups and individuals.

Peer groups. As man grows, he relies on peer groups for approval of his ideas. People often seek out others who share attitudes similar to his attitudes to conform himself.

Personality factors. They are important in attitude formation. There is positive relationship between different personality factors and attitudes. Adrone *et al.* express that there is a coherent pattern of ethnocentric attitudes among authoritarian personalities. McClosky has found a relationship between personality factors of conservatism and liberalism.

Methods of attitude development

Attitudes are subjective attributes of people. Attitude measurement is developed by sociologists. Managers have to tap these attitudes of people to function effectively. In the ideal situation, management can know the attitudes of employees through first line supervisors at all levels. When communication in an organisation is two-way at all levels and interpersonal contacts are fairly frequent, open and congenial, attitudes are easily known to the management. There are indicators such as grievances, labour turnover, go-slow, gheraos, pen-down and sit-down strikes, material wastage bad house-keeping, lowering of production fall of productivity, etc., which reflect the poor attitudes of people at work. Important methods used in measuring employee attitudes are given below.

1. Questionnaires/attitude survey method. It is a process by which responses are elicited from employees using questionnaire about how they are feeling about their work, supervisors, organisation and work groups.

2. Following table illustrates what an attitude survey might look like. Here employees are issued a questionnaire wherein a set of questions are posed. The items are tailored to obtain the specific information that management desires. An attitude score is achieved by summing up the responses. These scores are averaged for job groups, divisions or departments and organisation as a whole.

TABLE: Sample attitude survey

Rating Scale	A = strongly agree
	B = agree
	C = undecided
	D = disagree
	E = strongly disagree

Statement	
1. Company is pretty good place to work	( )
2. Company is prosperous	( )
3. Salaries/wages are competitive with other companies	( )
4. Employe promotions are made fairly	( )
5. My job takes best use of me	( )
6. Work load is challenging	( )
7. My boss is open-minded	( )
8. I know my boss very well	( )

Advantages

1. The answers can be made definite and are easy to tabulate.
2. It is cheaper than interview.
3. It avoids errors of memory.
4. Well structured questionnaires will clearly indicate the administrative action.
5. It can elicit facts on a secret basis.
6. Employees can give critical opinions without any fear.

Disadvantages

1. It bypasses supervisors.
2. It gives impression that supervisors are not taken into confidence.
3. It will reflect that management could not get reliable information from supervisors.
4. Supervisors do not have opportunity to know about the attitudes of his subordinates face to face.
5. Face to face explanation is not possible in this method.
6. It is not possible to get elaborate and detailed information.
7. Employees will be victimised if confidentiality is not maintained.
8. Unless management evolves follow up action for mutual benefit, questionnaire based surveys will be mistaken.
9. Without management and its favourable attitude surveys will not be effective.

Attitude surveys with the help of questionnaires are commonly used where different questions are posed to the employees to evaluate and rate the attitudes towards the objectives. Different scales are used to measure the employees' attitudes. The popular scales are namely—Thurstone's scale, Likert's scale, Bogardens's social distance scale and Guttman's scale.

Thurstone's scale. Thurstone has developed large number of statements in which attitudes are to be measured. The statements may be on any object—for example, religion, education, war, peace, etc. The statements both favourable and unfavourable are placed into eleven piles. 1. represents favourableness and 2. represents unfavourableness. Individuals will be asked to check those statements with which they have agreed. The average of the scale values of the items which they have accepted will give an indication of the place of a person along the attitude continuum. For example if the average happens to be low, this would indicate high degree of favourableness in attitudes in this particular area of field and if the average happens to be high, it indicates low degree of favourableness in attitudes in the areas.

Likert's scale. It consists of fire boxes ranging from strongly agree to strongly disagree. Under each statement of attitude, the respondent will be given a change to check one of five boxes and finally all the ratings will be summed up. The Likert's scale is also called a summed-rating measure, because several statements are collected in an attitude area, such as one's attitude about a job and the scales are added up or summed to obtain a person's attitude toward his job. The summed rating scale provides a means of measuring the intensity of one's attitude towards a particular object in addition to the direction.

Interview technique. Interviewing the employees is one of the techniques. Supervisors can ask questions face to face on various aspects of the environment that affect greatly their attitudes and feelings. The main purpose of interview is to seek more information from the employees, to give them accurate picture of the situation, to convince them with facts and impress them by persuasion and also to clearly examine with personal attention in order to give them opportunity of two-way communication. Interview system will give opportunity to both supervisors and subordinates to interact with each other. It develops team spirit as they thoroughly understand each other. Interview method gives opportunity to avoid 'hiding' of facts. Both the parties understand each other very well and sort out the differences. Physical arrangement is of great importance as it enhances the goodwill of the supervisors for holding direct talks with subordinates. The supervisor and subordinates can see each other clearly without any ambiguity. The interview if held in a confidential manner both parties feel free to talk and arrive acceptable solution on the matter. Interviews arranged in a privacy and comfort manner, the employees will show readiness to respond positively and openly.

Manager should conduct interviews in a free atmosphere to extract more insight of people.

Group discussion. Management conducts group discussions by inviting all concerned employees on the matters such as policies, procedures, norms, etc., of the company. Here management creates free atmosphere and allows all to discuss the matters at length and in all directions. Supervisors should see all union people attend the discussion and participate. The outcome of the discussion depends upon the extent of participation and involvement in discussion. The participants may be encouraged by giving gifts to best points raised at the time of discussion. Tea and snacks served at the time of group discussion will encourage better participation. Supervisors should ensure members that recording of discussion will not be there. This kind of assurance will encourage the employees to actively present their views and come with true insights. The superiors should hold the discussion in a more friendly and informal method so that employees will not have barriers.

Cognitive dissonance theory

People seek consistency between attitudes and behaviour. That is to say individuals seek to reconcile divergent attitudes and align their attitudes and behaviour so that they appear to be consistent. Cognitive dissonance theory explains the linkage between attitudes and behaviour of employees.

The theory was proposed by Leon Festinger in 1950s and has become more popular. It has greatest impact on the study of attitudes. This theory deals with idea relationship of a person with one another. It states that there are three types of relationships between all cognitions such as dissonance, consonance and irrelevance. Cognitions are dissonant when they are incompatible. That is, they are opposed to one's experience about the relationship of events. Cognitions are consonants where one follows the other. And cognition are irrelevant when two events are not interrelated.

Dissonance refers to psychological inconsistency among different cognitions associated with attitudes and behaviour. Two cognitions are said to be in a dissonant relation if one implies the opposite of the other. Festinger argues that any kind of inconsistency is not comfortable and individual attempts to reduce it. Thus dissonance is a state of condition of an individual where he attempts to reduce the inconsistency. Festinger has suggested the following steps to reduce the dissonance:

1. Reduce the importance of dissonant elements
2. Add more consonant elements
3. Change the dissonant elements altogether.

He further states that dissonance is a function of the proportion of relevant elements that are dissonant with one another relative to the total number of consonant and dissonant elements. Higher the degree of dissonance, higher would be the effort to reduce it.

The theory is applied to several situations affecting behaviour of persons. A person experiences dissonance when he engages in behaviour contrary to his attitudes. For example, a male individual, while marrying, he has to choose between two girls—one is beautiful and the other is employed. He experiences conflict before the decision but after the decision he experiences dissonance because of positive features of rejected alternative and negative features of selected alternative *i.e.*, dissonant with the choice. Attempts can be made to reduce the dissonance by increasing the value of chosen alternative and decreasing the value of rejected alternative.

Factors affecting attitudinal change

In this world of changing situations, people should change their attitudes. From organisation point of view attitudinal change is necessary so as to shape the behaviour in tune with the changes taking place from time to time. Managers are often put to the problem of changing attitudes of themselves and their employees. When existing attitudes are hindering the growth and performance, managers should attempt to change the attitude of people concerned. And the 'change' techniques can be more effective if the following basic factors are taken care of:

1. Characteristics of the attitudes.
2. Personality of the attitude holder.
3. Group affiliation of the attitude holder.
4. Characteristics of the communicator.

5. Methods of communication.
6. Situational factors.

Characteristics

Before changing attitudes analysis of attitude characteristics is important and scanning of attitudes suggests the following characteristics:

- Extremeness of attitude
- Multiplicity
- Consistency
- Incorrectness
- Centrality of related values
- Simplicity

Keeping these characteristics one should attempt to change the attitudes accordingly.

1. Personality of attitude holder. Attitudes are subjective. Change of attitude may be possible or may not be fully or partly. This depends upon the character of the attitude holder. Manager should act differently with different personalities to bring change in their attitudes. The manager should adopt different techniques to pursue the employees.

2. Group affiliation. Individuals often express their attitudes in the name of groups to which they associate with. In such a case people in a group think alike and it is difficult to change attitude. Manager should pursue the individual keeping the attitudes of group in mind by and large.

3. Characteristics of the communicator. Managers who attempt to bring change in the attitudes of employees should know that his character plays an important role. The features of manager such as status, prestige, attractive, likeness, trust-worthiness, would decide the extent of change in the attitude of target person.

4. Method of communication. Manager should communicate effectively to bring change in the attitudes of others. Here manager should use appropriate media, at appropriate time depending upon the employees. Manager should use convincing manners and present clear view without any bias. If necessary manager should 'influence' the employees in order to change their attitudes.

5. Situational factors. Managers should also keep situational factors in mind before influencing the employees to change their attitudes. Attitudes, publicly expressed are more difficult to change. In a group discussion manager can bring change in the attitude of an employee since he develops that his group members are also favourable to the manager. Many a time member prefers 'easy go' to change his attitudes towards the group.

QUESTIONS FOR DISCUSSION

1. What is the concept of attitude? How do attitudes affect the behaviour?
2. What are the factors responsible for attitude formation? How can these factors be controlled?
3. What are the methods of attitude development? How does they help management?
4. What is cognitive dissonance theory and how is it related to attitude?

15

SOCIALISATION

Socialisation is a process of adaptation. It refers to the adaptation that takes place when an individual passes from outside the organisation to the role of an inside member. Organisational socialisation attempts to adapt the new employee to the organisation's culture by conveying to the employee how the things are done and what matters.

Benefits of socialisation

Following are the benefits of socialisation:

1. Comfortable. Employees after socialisation will feel comfort and able to work with all ease in his routine activities.

2. Internalisation. The work groups will have his own standards of acceptable behaviour. Norms of the organisation will tell the new employees what to do and what not. The new employees learn the behaviour, acceptable to their peer groups. An internalised employee is more acceptable to the work groups.

3. Self-confidence. The socialisation enhances the self-confidence of employees joined newly into the organisation. By socialisation, the employees adapt themselves to the culture of the organisation.

4. Trusted and valued individuals. The newly joined employees will be trusted and treated as 'valued' in their work group by the people at work. In the orientation given to the new employees the work groups will study the attitudes of new employees and encourage like minded people.

5. Competence. As the existing employees share their views and extend cooperation, this will enhance the competence of new employees.

6. Success at the job. Success of employees at work depends upon the cooperation of other employees. During socialisation process the new employees understand the work environment and the organisation system.

7. Morale. Socialisation enhances the morale of employees. The employees who understand the culture, rules, procedures of the organisation will have high morale and work encouragingly.

8. Performance. The employees who could adopt to the organisation culture will perform their tasks effectively with more ease and convenience.

9. High productivity. As time passes the employee (new) learns work and improves performance. This will automatically increase the productivity.

10. Less employee turnover. Well adjusted employees to the organisation culture will not leave the organisation. Thus effective socialisation process will reduce the employee turnover.

11. More commitment. People develop loyalty and commitment towards the organisation where socialisation is complete and adequate orientation is given to employees.

12. Organisational stability. Socialisation influences organisational stability over years and if jobs are filled and vacated with minimum of disruption the organisation will be more stable.

13. Transformation of objectives. Socialisation enables in transferring values and objectives to next generations.

14. Reduces anxiety and stress. New member undergoes severe stress and suffers from anxiety due to lack of identification. A fresher will feel new with supervisor, location, workers, etc. Loneliness and a feeling of isolation is not desirable. Socialisation reduces uncertainties and ambiguities by providing adequate information.

15. Increases motivation. Socialisation motivates employees to learn the values and norms of their newly assumed role and they become accepted members easily.

Purpose of socialisation

Socialisation refers to the process of adaptation to new environment which includes superior, subordinates, job, rules, regulations, location policies of the company, etc. And the process gets completed when the member becomes comfortable on the job. Following are the purposes of socialisation:

Overcome outer-insider passage. When an employee joins an organisation, everything will be new for him, until then he does not know the culture of the organisation. It is necessary for him to adjust to the organisation culture, activities, new boss, coworkers and different set of standards for a good performance. This process of adaptation happens when an employee shifts from one company to the other.

Learn organisation culture. Every organisation has its own culture. And no two organisations are same. It depends upon location, technology, atmosphere, people, product, etc. Culture includes traditions, customs, prejudices, standards, group relationships, individual behaviour, sharing of work, communication, etc. The employees adjust themselves to the environment will be same.

Assumes roles. Every employee will behave in a particular way. It is called the 'role'. To acquire the required skills and set of behaviour in an organisation every employee needs socialisation.

Internalise values. Values are basic convictions about what is right or wrong, good or bad, desirable or not desirable. Every individual has a value system. The existing value will significantly influence the behaviour of new members. The role of an individual is influenced by the organisational values. Hence socialisation is necessary to expose the new employee to internalise the values.

Understand norms. Norms tell members what they have to do under varying circumstances. And also what they have not to do is guided by the organisational or group norms. The new employees work group will have its own standards of acceptable behaviour. Socialisation helps the individuals in knowing about the norms of the organisation.

Confomist *Vs.* Rebel

An employee may become conformist or rebel, it depends upon his acceptance of the following:

1. How he orients himself to the organisation.
2. How he adapts to organisation culture.

3. How he plays role, desirable to the organisation.
4. How he internalises the values of the organisation.
5. How he understands the norms of the organisation.

1. Orientation. Orientation covers the activities involved in introducing a new employee to the organisation. It helps to reduce the initial anxiety. Orientation programme is to familiarise an employee with the organisation's objectives, history, philosophy, procedures, rules and policies.

2. Culture. An employee should be indoctrinated in the organisation's culture. An employee, after recruitment, will have to be inducted into the organisation with a culture so far he does not know so he should familiarise with the organisation culture and follow the beliefs and customs of the organisation. An employee should know his work environment including new boss, work, activities, co-workers, and standards.

3. Roles. An employee should behave not in his own way. His behaviour depends upon the job and the employee is expected to fulfil certain requirements. The set of such behaviour is called 'role' that one has to play. Hence the employee should play the 'role' acceptable to the superiors and in the interests of the organisation.

4. Values. Values are basic convictions of employees about what is right and wrong. Existing employees have a value system. The new employee should internalise himself the values of the organisation and follow them.

5. Norms. Norms tell the members what to do and not to do under certain circumstances. An employee should accept the norms of an organisation.

The individuals at their place of work may accept these roles, values and norms fully or not. The individuals who readily accept all of them become conformist and those who reject or not accepting are known as rebels. Rebels do not last long and will be expelled from the organisation for their inability to adapt to the way the organisation works.

Stages of socialisation

It is not possible for all the employees to accept all the organisation's standards, norms, etc. But management expects the employees to conform the norms of the organisation. And such individuals who do not conform will not be accepted as full-fledged members of the organisation. Successful socialisation means that having personnel who knows what to do and what not to do.

Assumptions of socialisation

1. Socialisation strongly influences employee performance and organisational stability.
2. New members suffer from anxiety.
3. Socialisation does not occur in vacuum.
4. People adjust in similar ways.

Socialisation is conceptualised as a process of three stages. Pre-arrival, encounter and metamorphosis (see figure below). In the first stage, all the new employees see what the organisation likes and dislikes. In the second stage, the new employees conform to company norms and those who do not conform will leave the organisation. In the third stage, long lasting change takes place. The new employee masters the skills required for his job, successfully performs his new roles and continue in the organisation. The socialisation process gives impact on the new employees' work, productivity, commitment to the organisation's objectives and eventual decision to stay with the organisation.

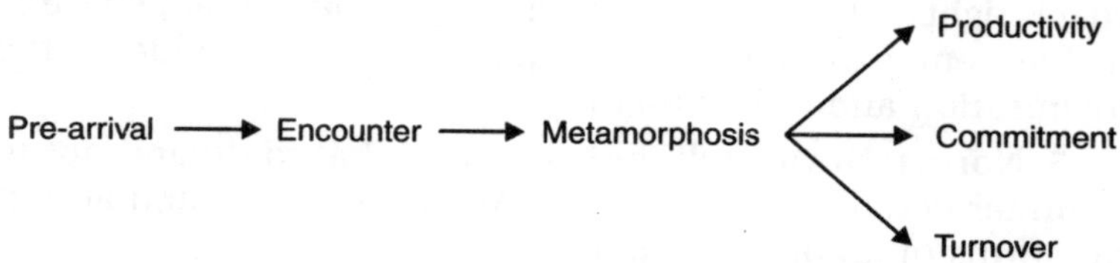

Socialisation scheme

Pre-arrival stage. It is the stage of an employee before he joins an organisation. Each individual arrives with a set of attitudes and expectations. Normally business graduates undergo training in a business school. The purpose of a business school is to socialise business students. Business executives believe that successful employees value the profit, ethic, loyal, work hard, desire to achieve and accepts directions from superiors. Executives will hire those individuals from business schools who have been moulded in the required pattern. The selection process is utilised to inform prospective employees about the organisation as a whole. Also selection process helps to identify 'right type' persons who will fit in the organisation. In pre-arrival stage company looks for an individual, whose expectations are in line with the requirements of the company

Encounter stage. In this stage an employee sees what the organisation really. After his entry into an organisation the employee sees the reality, where he compares his expectations with the reality of the organisation. If the difference is not much the employee reaffirms the perceptions gained earlier. And if his expectations and reality differ, the employee has to socialise himself and replace the previous assumptions by those with the organisational pivotal standards. Sometimes the disillusioned employees with realities may leave the organisation. Proper selection of employees will reduce such eventualities.

Metamorphosis stage. In this stage the employee adjusts himself to the actualities such as company/group values and norms. After encounter stage the employee either experiences comfort or discomfort with the company practices/procedures, policies. If he is comfortable he will continue. Otherwise, he starts adjusting himself to the realities and become internalised. The new members are self-confident that they can complete the job successfully. They could understand not only their tasks but the rules and procedures. New employees could understand how they will be evaluated besides the informal practices. The new members feel accepted by their peers as trusted and valued individuals. Successful metamorphosis will have positive impact on new employee productivity and reduces the propensity of an employee to leave the organisation.

Different ways of socialisation

Managers adopt different ways to socialise their employees. Following are the alternatives that managers forms consider use designing socialisation programmes.

Formal socialisation. The more a new employee is segregated from the ongoing work setting and differentiated in some way to make explicit his newcomer's role, the more formal socialisation is, management employs in its design and execution. In case of formal socialisation the newcomer will acquire known set of standards. In this model of socialisation, the newcomer is more likely to think high of himself.

Informal socialisation. Informal socialisation puts the new employee directly into his job without any attention. Newcomers will not be differentiated from the existing employees. The success of the employee depends upon the new employee choosing co-workers who are knowledgeable about the job. In case the newcomer selects marginally knowledgeable co-worker as his guide the socialisation process will be of less effective. Informal socialisation is better for maintaining individual differences. Novel approaches to problem-solving are the way of individual who has received informal socialisation. Transfer of knowledge from an agent is not necessary because socialisation takes place on the job. Both formal and informal socialisation programmes represent two extremes along a continuum. A common practice of a company is to use both.

Individual socialisation. New members if socialised individually, it is called individual socialisation. It is done in professional offices. This model socialisation approach develops less homogeneous views. It preserves individual differences. But it is expensive and time consuming. It fails to allow the new entrants to share their anxieties with others. Small organisations are preferring individual approach.

Collective socialisation. Newcomers could be grouped together and processed through an identical set of experiences, as in military boot camp. Here, the new entrants share problems and usually develop similar solutions. Therefore collective socialisation tends to form a common perspective on the organisation among group members. Sometimes groups deviate from standards than does individual approach to socialisation. The group is more likely than individual to resist or redefine the organisation's demands. Large organisations tend to rely on group socialisation techniques.

Fixed socialisation. This refers to time schedule in which newcomers make the transitions from outsider to insider. A fixed schedule establishes standardised stages of transition. This characterises rotational training programmes. It also includes probationery periods. Fixed schedule reduces uncertainty for the new members.

Variable socialisation. Variable schedules give no advanced notice of their transition time-table. This describes the typical promotion system, when one is not promoted until he is ready. Variability characterises the socialisation schedule for most professionals and managerial persons. It gives an administrator a powerful tool for influencing individual behaviour.

Serial socialisation. Serial socialisation is characterised by the use of role models who train and encourage the newcomers. Sometimes, experienced employee guides a newcomer, thus the experienced employee acts as a tutor. This model socialisation maintains traditions and customs and consistent application of this strategy will ensure a minimum amount of change. Newcomer sees their future by looking at the experienced colleagues. Some disadvantages too happen when a newcomer follows a frustrated employee as such the new employee may leave the organisation. If the tutor is knowledgeable the newcomer will be enthusiastic and if the tutor's morale is low the new member will leave the organisation.

Mentors. Employees looking for higher positions should acquire a mentor. The mentor vouches for the member, introduces, advises and guides for moving effectively to higher positions through the system, thus mentors look for their protégé.

Random socialisation. In random socialisation role models are deliberately withheld. The new employee is left on his own to figure out things. The newcomer does not have any experienced employee to guide him. Unlike serial socialisation, the newcomer is not burdened by traditions. It is more likely to produce more inventive and creative employees. Sometimes this model fails in socialising people successfully since the newcomer will not have guidelines and directions.

Investiture socialisation. Investiture socialisation assumes that the newcomer's quantities and qualifications are necessary ingredients for job success. The candidates are selected on the basis of what they bring to the job. Recruits may be given more freedom to take decisions that will reflect on their performance.

Divestiture socialisation. Divestiture socialisation tries to strip off some characteristics of the recruit. Fraternity 'pledges' go through divestiture socialisation to shape them into the proper role. If the management wants to produce similar employees, a divestiture approach is used. It will achieve similar results with each recruitee and the process itself will promote a strong fellowship among those who have followed the same path to membership.

Depending upon organisation newcomer management implement their socialisation programmes. The recruitment and selection do not end in itself their purpose is served only through effective socialisation. The socialisation programmes go a long way in shaping the employees. When socialisation works effectively the benefits go to organisation and to the employees. An organisation gets higher productivity, greater employee commitment and lower employee turnover. Employees achieve reduced anxiety, increased awareness acceptance from peer groups, receive self-confidence and job satisfaction.

QUESTIONS FOR DISCUSSION

1. Define socialisation in an organisation and what benefits can socialisation provide for the organisation?
2. Explain the reasons for socialising the employees.
3. Briefly explain the purpose of socialisation.
4. How roles, values and norms influence socialisation?
5. What makes an employee conformist or rebel?
6. Explain the three stages of socialisation process.
7. Discuss the major considerations in the design of socialisation programme.
8. Explain different ways of socialisation.

16

STRESS

Introduction

Current life is full of stress with rapid changes occurring in the environment, stress is caused. Urbanisation, industrialisation, unemployment, poverty, career planning, etc. are causing stress in life. In organisational life planning, participation, interaction, transaction and reputation have become key issues with its frustration attached. Stress is a part of life and it cannot be ordered. And stress is multiplied with increase in size and number of activities. Hence the modern manager should understand causes for stress and apply strategies for minimising it.

Concept definition. Hans Selye in 1936, viewed stress as the non-specifically induced changes within a biological system.

Ivancerich and Matteston have defined stress as an adaptive response mediated by individual characteristics and psychological processes which is consequence of any external action, situation or event that places specially physical and/or psychological.

Meaning. Stress is an adaptive response to an external factor that results in physical, psychological or behavioural deviations in an individual. Stress is a state of mind which reflects certain biochemical reactions in the human body and is projected by a sense of anxiety, tension and depression which is caused by the external forces or internal forces that cannot be met by the resources available to the person. The events or conditions which induce stress are known as 'stressors'. Any demand made on the body that is for natural or routine activity does not create stress. Example, walking, thinking, writing etc., are not stress producing forces. All situations requiring adaptation to new situation such as fear, pain, fatigue, humiliation, frustration, need for concentration, loss of blood, drugs, occurrence of unexpected events produce stress. Stress, strain, conflict and pressure are the terms synonymously used.

Types. Stress is of two kinds one-'enstress', two-'distress'.

Enstress. It is created by desirable and successful effects. It is a positive, healthy and developmental response. Some level of stress may lead to better performance and a more adjusted personality.

Distress. Stress created by undesirable outcomes is known as 'distress'.

Levels of stress. Stress may be at varying levels in an organisation, higher level stress and lower level stress. Some levels of stress are necessary for growth, creativeness and acquisition of new skills. Example, leaving computer and driving car, etc. But highly stressful situations weaken a person's physical and psychological capacity and such stressors have dysfunctional consequences. Low levels of stress is undesirable for they cause boredom, lack of stimulation, innovation and challenges. Thus moderate level of stress is necessary for better performance. The diagram shows the relationship between stress and performance.

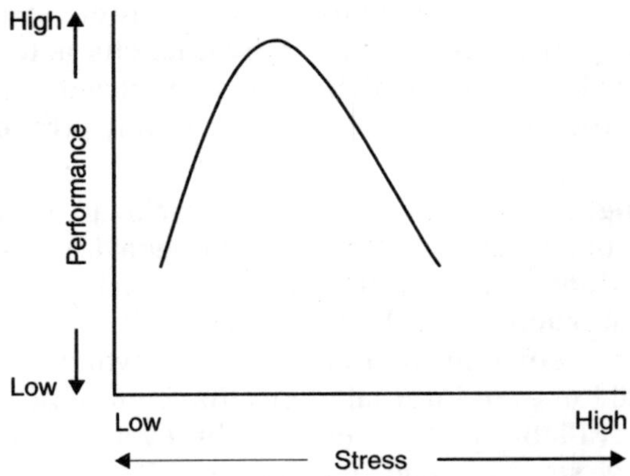

Source: Henry L. Tossi, John R. Rizzo and Stephen J. Carroll, *Managing Organisational Behaviour*, Ballinger Publishing Co., 1986, p. 296.

Features of stress. Following are the features of stress:

1. Stress is accompanied by anxiety. Stress may result in any kind of deviation—physical, psychological or behavioural. This deviation is from the usual state of affairs.
2. Stress is the resultant of stimuli *i.e.*, interpersonal interaction or event. This stimuli produces deviation in the individual.
3. Stress may be temporary or semi permanent; mild or severe. It depends upon the individual and situation. People who have strong will power can tolerate and can cope with even severe stress quickly. People with poor will power and who are not stray at will power and who are not strong at 'will' may experience stress heavily though stress caused by the situation is mild.

Sources of stress

Stress is a part of one's routine life. Both enstresses and distresses occur in one's life everyday. The stresses caused at the place of work are causes to non-work places and *vice versa*. The stresses are grouped into four categories. (1) individual, (2) group, (3) organisational, and (4) External Environmental. These stresses would put stress on individuals.

1. Individual stresses. The stresses may develop in the context of organisational life or personal life. These causes change in life and career, personality type and role characteristics.

(i) *Life and career changes*: Changes in life and career produce stress. Young people report more stresses than old people. Stress has been found more among urban population than in rural people. Like life changes, there may be changes in career, such as promotion, demotion, transfer, separation, etc. with each change man experiences some stress.

(ii) *Personality of type*: People who work with extremely high ethics are moving, walking rapidly, eating very fast and doing two or more things at a time and experience more stress. They always measure success in terms of quantity and are hard pressed for time. Some people appear to be more aggressive and competitive, they experience more stress.

(iii) *Role characteristics*: **(a) Role conflict.** Because of role conflicts some people experience stress. Role conflict occurs in different systems like family, club, work organisations and voluntary organisations, etc. They have to fulfil different obligations in different systems. They have to play different roles in different situations as such people fail to fulfil the conflicting requirements and are put to heavy stress. The incompatibility between job tasks, policies and rules cause stress.

(b) Role ambiguity. Sometimes people experience role ambiguity as are not clear about the actual expectations from a role due to lack of knowledge and information. This again causes stress.

(c) Role overload *Vs.* Role under-load. Role overload causes 'stress' to the employees. It refers to the individual being expected to do too many things within a limited time. Individuals may discharge duties few days but it is difficult for them to attend too many activities in the long run. Role under-load occurs when there is too little work and individual's potentiality is underutilised. Employees show little interest (see figure, p. 235).

(d) Ethical dilemmas. Ethical dilemmas such as whether or not one should report the observed unethical behaviours of another person can cause stress in individuals. This is true in the case of people having moral values.

2. Interpersonal and group stresses

(i) *Lack of group cohesiveness*: Members working in an organisation will have tendency to work in groups. And people tend to have group interaction when some members are desirous of group satisfaction, this will cause stress.

(ii) *Lack of social support*: Members need support to function effectively, in the absence of such support employees do not take initiative which causes stress.

(iii) *Conflict*: Conflicts arise between groups and individuals. These conflicts will become sources of stress.

(iv) *Strained relations*: Disputes and strained relations reduce openness between the individuals and result-in misunderstandings. Unpleasant interactions cause stress and to avoid this stress people remain absent to work place and look for other jobs.

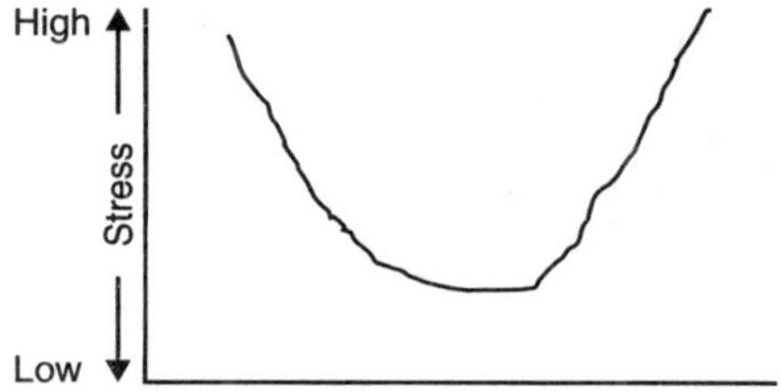

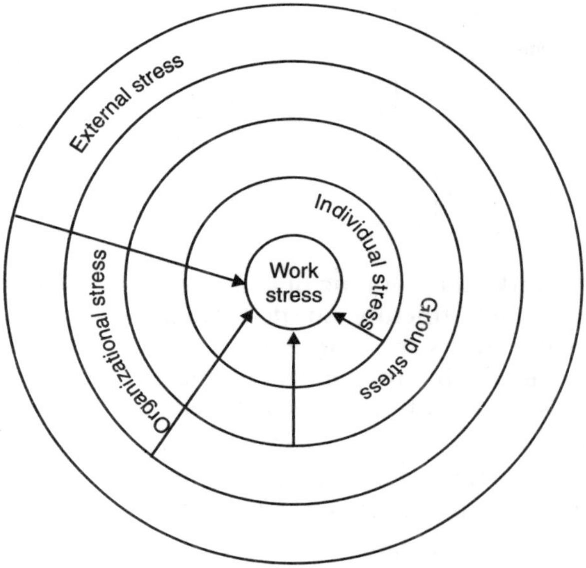

Sources of work stress

3. Organisational stresses. The factors responsible for organisational stresses are as follows:

(i) *Organisational policies*: Unrealistic and unfair corporate policies will affect the functioning of individuals and cause stress. *Example*: ambiguous procedures, inflexible rules, rotating work shifts, frequent relocation of activities, arbitrary performance evaluation, etc. are sources of stress.

(ii) *Organisation structure*: Successful functioning of an organisation depends upon sound organisation structure.

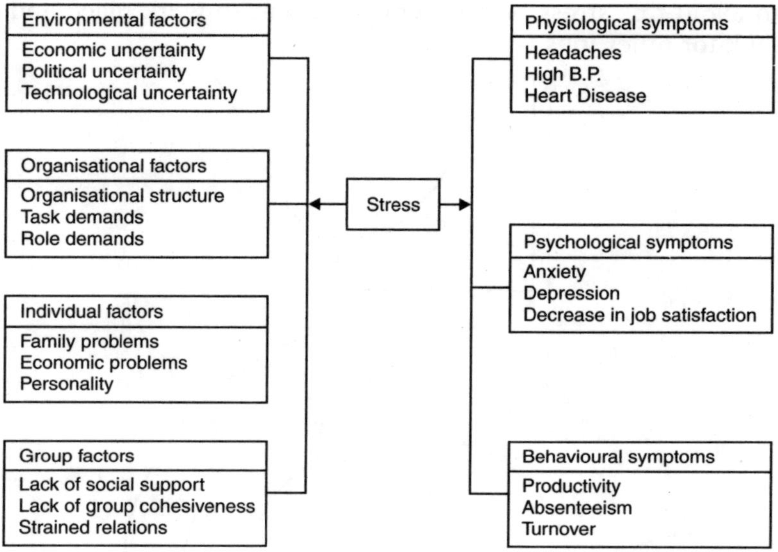

Division of work and grouping of activities form the basis of a sound organisation structure. Any defect in framing organisation structure will cause stress and employees' behaviour will be affected. Excessive interdependence, line and staff conflicts, over specialisation are the sources of stress causing disturbance.

(iii) *Organisational processes*: Communication system, poor feedback, inadequate information, unfair control system, cause stress and individuals and groups fail to work competitively.

(iv) *Work environment and physical conditions*: Lack of privacy, excessive noise, crowdy environment, pollution, poor lighting, absence of safety equipment cause stress physically and mentally to the employees.

(v) *Job characteristics*: The individual is likely to experience stress if the job is too heavy, dull and boring. Also if the job demands frequent travelling and transfers, employee is likely to undergo stress. Some duties and responsibilities such as fire-fighter, or the police squad cause stress. Thus the nature of job often induces stress.

(vi) *Structural factors*: They refer to rules, regulations and systems which are not palatable to the individuals may act as stressors.

(vii) *Lack of career progress*: Lack of career paths in organisations may be additional stressors. For aspiring managers, the lack of career progress can be a constant stressor resulting in the job burnout. Burnout is the condition where the employees see no relief or satisfaction and experience physical, emotional and mental exhaustion.

(viii) *Task demands*: The interdependence between persons and tasks of others, the more stress there is. Autonomy lessens the stress of employees.

(ix) *Organisational leadership*: Some executives establish a culture characterised by tension, fear, and anxiety. They impose unrealistic pressures to perform things in short run, impose excessive tight controls and routinely fire employees.

(x) *Organisation's life stage*: Organisations go through different stages such as establishment, growth, maturity and decline. Organisations undergo different problems in different stages but the establishment and decline stages are stressful.

(xi) *Lack of participation*: Employees participate in decision-making influences in reducing role ambiguity and role overload resulting in reduced noise.

(xii) *Responsibility for people*: Less control over subordinates for whose actions managers are responsible is a concern of stress for managers.

4. External factors. Certain forces could be the sources of stress. Sudden changes in the market place, technology, financial market, economic, and community conditions, etc., act as stressors. Innovations, political and economic uncertainties could also cause stresses.

Symptoms of stress

Stress consequences take place differently in different ways. They depend upon situation and individuals' ability to withstand. Often stress is taken negatively. Manager should learn the effects of stress on employees and himself. So that necessary steps can be thought of to bring them under check. The stress shows its effects physically, psychologically and behaviourally.

Physiological problems. Stress causes physiological ailments such as excitement, increased heart rate, blood pressure, high level of cholesterol can result in diseases such as heart, ulcer

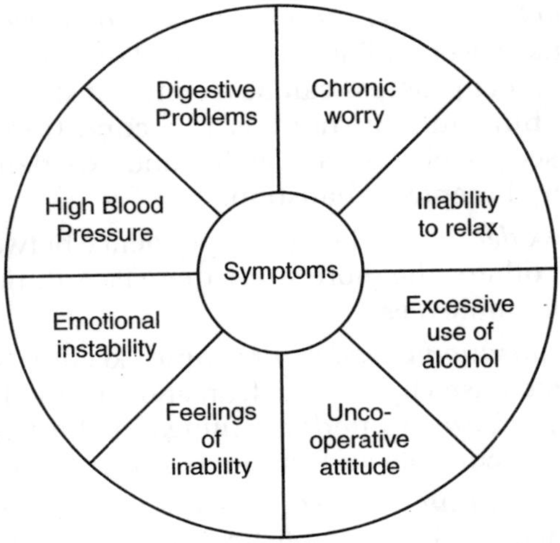

and arthritis. Cancer too takes place in certain cases of stress. These health problems not only trouble the individual families but the organisations too.

Psychological problems. Depending upon the bearing capacity of the individual psychological reactions such as anger, anxiety, depression, nervousness, irritability, tension boredom take place. These will in turn reduce job satisfaction, morale and will power of employees. At times executives will fail to concentrate on problems and find solutions which will affect productivity and cause wastage.

Behavioural problems. High levels of stress result in dysfunctional behaviour of employees. They may addict to drugs, alcoholism, smoking, sleeplessness, over- or under-eating, etc. Yet times high level of stress makes employees to suicide. Sometimes employees stay away from the work place and change the organisations. Both when stress is low or high, the performance level will be low. When the stress is very low and moderate the individuals will be stimulated and better their performance. But too high stress places unattainable demands on a person which lowers the performance.

The effects of distress on individual, family and organisation

This distress is influencing negatively and shows effects on individual, family and organisation.

Consequences for the individual. The impact of distress has subjective, cognitive, psychological, behavioural and health facets to it. The subjective effects of stress are feelings of anxiety, boredom, nervousness, depression, fatigue, anger, irritation and aggressiveness on the part of individuals experiencing stress. The cognitive effects include poor communication, inability to take decisions. The psychological effects can be observed through increased heart and pulse rate, high blood pressure, dryness, smoking, etc. The manifest health effects could be stomach disorders, asthma and other psychological disorders. The individual cannot function effectively and his performance will decline.

Consequences for the family. Distress has dysfunctional effects on family. The individual consumes food excessively and do not attend the work place. Spouse abuse and children abuse will take place in family. Stress increases heavily if both (wife and husband) are employed. Additional stress is experienced while handling the personal, social and cultural dilemmas of balancing work and family, discharging parenting responsibilities, handling competition at the work place and within the family.

Consequences to organisations. Dysfunctional effects of stress are many. The adverse consequences include low performance and productivity. The employees frequently change the organisations and resort to high rates of absenteeism. Destructive and aggressive behaviour result in strikes and sabotages. The stress experienced by employee causes inconvenience to customers and clients too. An employer, put to distress may face in accidents at work place and cause wastage of time and materials. Employee stress at work may cost the firm by way of poor reputation, loss of business, declining assets, etc.

Contrast Type A and Type B behaviour

M. Friedman and R.H. Rosunmen (1974) developed Type A behaviour. During 1980s it is used most frequently as a variable related to stress. The behaviour is characterised by a feeling of chronic sense of time urgency and excessive competitive drive. It refers to aggressive involvement in a chronic incessant struggle to achieve more and more in less and less time, if necessary against the opposing efforts of others.

Type A behaviour features

1. People of Type A behaviour are always moving, walking and eating rapidly.
2. People feel impatient with the rate at which most of the events take place.
3. They strive to think or do two or more things at a time.
4. They cannot cope with leisure time.

Type B behaviour features

It is opposite to Type A behaviour. They participate in an endlessly growing series of events.

1. They never suffer from time urgency.
2. They seem to be not impatient.
3. They do not discuss their achievements unless situation demands.
4. They relax without guiltiness.
5. They prefer to be relaxing rather than exhibiting their superiority at any cost.

Type A people are believed to be prone to heart disease. But the fact is that all behaviours of Type A could cause heart problems. A closer look at Type A reveals that only hostility and anger behaviour will lead to heart disease and not all. Also persons with suspicious mind, mistrustful nature are also at risk. A person who is competitive and impatient does not mean that they are susceptible to heart disease. Quickness to anger, hostile outlook and cynical mistrust are the harmful elements of human behaviour causing stress.

The strategies for preventing stress

Stress effects the individual, organisation and family through changed behaviour both psychologically, physiologically and hence efforts should be made to reduce high levels of stress. Following are the strategies or approaches to reduce the stress.

Individual coping strategies

1. Physical exercise. Physical exercise is advised to overcome stress. Activities like walking, playing, swimming brings change in his mental outlook. Yoga and meditation are encouraged to reduce the stress at work place. Yet times relaxation, getting mind off the work, enhanced self-esteem will reduce mental stress. Individuals who are busy with work can go away from place of work for few days to spend time with family members elsewhere, it will reduce tension, strain and stress.

2. Readjust life goals. Because of severe competition, many individuals set high goals. They are trying to do too much in too little time. They have fear of failing and they are running no-where. Thus high expectations with limited resources result in stress. Accordingly, they have to re-set the practicable goals keeping the resources in mind.

3. Relaxation. Stress can be overcome through relaxation. Some techniques applied are meditation, bio-feedback and passive attitude by which one can eliminate stress. Relation refers to state or condition where the individual is detached from both the immediate environment and body sensations. 15-20 minutes a day of deep relaxation provides a person peacefulness. Significant changes in heart race, blood pressure can be had from deep relaxation methods.

4. Advance planning. Whatever shall be, will be is the attitude of many. They do not plan the life, and effort whenever the problems occur in someway or the other. Many times people face situations which induces stress because they do not plan or do bad job of planning. Hence planning reduces the stress.

5. Work-home transition. This technique advises a person to reach home relaxedly at the end of day's work. He may review the day's work completed before he goes home. He can plan for tomorrow's work at the end of the day's work so that he can be comfortable in his next day's work.

6. Yoga. Yoga is an effective remedy for stress. It is used for centuries to control mind and heart. Its use is realised in India and abroad. Yoga is practised in several ways, but following are said to be useful to cope with the stress.

(a) *Annamaya Kosha*: Traditional voluntary internal techniques, 'yogarana' and 'sharasana'.

(b) *Pranamaya Kosha*: Five types of systematic regulated slow deep respiration with or without breath holding.

(c) *Manomaya Kosha*: Analysing and understanding the nature of one's problems.

(d) *Ananadamaya Kosha*: Practising joy under adverse circumstances.

7. Cognitive therapy. This therapy suggests to study the events at work and identify those that cause stress and replace them. Lectures and interactive discussions would help the employees to better organise themselves.

8. Networking. It suggests to develop trusted colleagues, who are good listeners to him. Such friends and co-workers build confidence and provide moral support required to push through stressful situations.

9. Time management. Tension and stress are resultant of hectic work in office. If work is sorted out and time is managed optimally, it will reduce the stress. So job demands can be better managed if time for each work is planned and utilised carefully. In doing so, an employee can adopt the time management principles such as (1) making daily list of activities to be completed, (2) prioritising activities by importance and urgency, (3) knowing daily work cycle thoroughly, etc.

10. Social support. Talking to friends, colleagues, family will provide an outlet when stress levels are excessive. One should expand social support network to reduce tension. Someone to hear the problems gives a more objective perspective of the situation.

11. Control the situation. One must avoid unrealistic deadlines. He must do his best and beware of limits. It is impossible to please everyone.

12. Open up to others. One must express to one's feelings, emotions, fears and frustration in the presence of others who care for him. This process reduces the stress and individuals feel relaxed.

Organisational coping strategies

Organisational stressors are controlled by management. Through the following strategies stress can be moderated.

1. Supportive climate. Stressors happen due to faulty organisational processes and practices. They can be controlled by establishing supportive climate. This depends upon leadership mainly. Employees support or no support depends upon their involvement in decision-making and policy framework. Such climate develops team-work and reduces stress.

2. Job enrichment. Monotonous jobs cause stress, so manager can design jobs by improving content factors such as responsibility, recognition, opportunity to grow, etc., and make the jobs interesting. The jobs should be enriched to use the existing skills of employees maximum and such phenomenon helps in reducing the stress.

3. Role clarity. Managers by conducting role analysis can ensure role clarity by avoiding role ambiguity and role conflicts. Sometimes stress occurs due to overloading or under-loading of job. Hence, by breaking down the job into various components one would give rise to understand the job expectations well by the employees, consequently reducing job stress.

4. Selection and placement. Stress varies from job to job, and certain jobs are associated with mental stress. Similarly experienced persons have more stress bearing capacity. So management should keep both job factors and individual characteristics into consideration and select such people to match the situation.

5. Goal setting. People perform jobs better if feedback is timely given on their performance. This goal feedback reduces uncertainties and minimise employee frustration, stress and role ambiguity.

6. Career planning and counselling. Career planning and counselling helps employees in reducing the stress. It makes them to know what additional qualifications they should acquire for career advancement. Career planning programmes are designed to counsel the employees. For example (1) Workshops will assist the individuals in goal setting and action plan for change. (2) Educational programmes will help in making new careers. (3) Programmes will educate the individuals to know about new opportunities. (4) Devices designed to aid the employees in self-assessment and self-understanding. (5) Career counselling through interviews by managers, professional specialists, etc., would provide much scope to employees in changing their attitudes whereby 'stress' can be reduced.

7. Job redesign. Employee should have greater control over the job he is doing and should have feedback timely to perform very well. So management should design the jobs from time to time keeping the employee abilities in mind. Employees who aspire for growth may be entrusted the challenging jobs.

8. Stress control workshops. Managers can give counselling on social, personal and organisational problems. Seniors of organisation can touch upon personal finance, health, children education and marriage aspects to orient them better so that stress can be minimised.

9. Participation in decision-making. Employees feeling uncertain about goals, expectations, performance evaluation and a like will undergo stress. So employees should be given opportunity to know about what affects him. Hence managers should encourage employee participation in decision-making to avoid after effects such as tension and stress.

10. Communication system. To some extent stress and confusion are the effects of interpretation by employees on organisational matters. Employee perceptions should be altered meaningfully by proper and timely communication of rules, procedures etc. So management by formal communication can reduce the role ambiguity and role conflict among employees.

11. Wellness programmes. Organisations should organise wellness programmes and focus employees attention on health. Management should organise programmes to increase health awareness among employees. The employees are personally responsible for their mental health and physical wellness. Management only should help and educate them.

12. Team work. Management should create a work environment in which the members of the work group consider themselves as members of the same family. There should be no room for interpersonal conflict or between group and individuals. Such conflicts cause stress hence they should be eliminated. Hence members should work with team spirit.

13. Equitable performance appraisal and reward system. It is necessary that appraisal be impartial and rewards be justifiable to performance. The employee should know what is expected of time and for what he is accountable. Employees performance and work should be recognised, appreciated and rewarded. This will reduce stress and tension and develop enthusiasm and a sense of dedication, which is a stress fighting phenomenon.

Relationship between potential stresses and experienced stresses

1. **Perception.** Employees react to the problem depending upon their perception towards the problem. Hence perception will moderate the relationship between a potential stress condition and an employee reaction to it. So what an employee perceives a challenging work may be viewed by others as threatening job. Thus the stress does not lie in the objective condition but in employee's interpretation of the job.

2. **Job experience.** Experience makes man perfect and one's own experience is once own 'Guru'. It is a stress reducer. Generally newness of the situation and uncertainty creates stress but as one gains experience the stress disappears. Thus in general stress and experience are inversely related to each other. People who experience stress in an organisation tend to leave as they lack stress-resistant traits. And people who remain in an organisation for long time are considered to have more resistance to stressors. Eventually, people develop stress bearing capacity over a period of time.

3. **Social support.** People with high social need involve with family, friends and community. The same characteristics helps an employee to involve himself in an organisation with colleagues and work associates at work. This kind of social support both in society and work place enhances the stress bearing capacity.

4. **Belief in locus of control.** Locus of control is a personality attribute. People with internal locus of control believe that things are under control and believers in external control. Locus are controlled by outside forces. Internals perceive their jobs to be less painful and externals. So externals who are helpless in stressful situations do experience stress.

5. **Hostility.** According to Friedman 'type A' behaviour is used most frequently as moderation variable related to stress. The behaviour is characterised by a feeling of chronic sense of time urgency and excessive competition drive. It refers to aggressive involvement in a chronic incessant struggle to achieve

more and more in less and less time if necessary against the opposing efforts of others.

Type B behaviour is opposite to Type A. They are rarely carried out by the desire to obtain a widely increasing number of things or to participate in an endlessly growing series of events in an ever-decreasing amount of time.

Meaning of burnout

Burnout is a chronic emotional stress as a result of physical exhaustion, lowered job productivity and over depersonalisation.

Emotional/physical exhaustion. It is an inner condition caused by various personal and organisational factors such as marital, legal, financial problems. As a result of these problems the employee will be helpless and changes his behaviour. This will affect the performance and lowers production and productivity. This in turn impinges on the workers' welfare, making them less productive and less happy and ultimately less motivated. Depersonalisation refers to dehumanisation owing to technology advancement through mechanisation and computerisation. Thus automation reduces human interactions and causes burnout.

Causes of burnout. Generally, factors contributing to burnout can be identified as organisation characteristics, organisation perceptions, role perceptions and individual characteristics. These factors lead to burnout, but they never guarantee that burnout will occur once stress reaches second phase of continuum, seven changes begin to appear in the individual. These changes can occur in workers' health, attitude, emotions, etc.

(A) Organisational characteristics

(i) Caseload
(ii) Formalisation
(iii) Turnover rate
(iv) Staff size

(B) Perceptions of organisation

(i) Leadership
(ii) Communication
(iii) Staff support

(iv) Peers
(v) Clarity
(vi) Rules and procedures
(vii) Innovation
(viii) Administrative support

(C) Role perceptions

(i) Autonomy
(ii) Job involvement
(iii) Supervision
(iv) Work pressure
(v) Feedback
(vi) Accomplishment
(vii) Meaningfulness

(D) Individual characteristics

(i) Family support
(ii) Friends support
(iii) Sex
(iv) Age
(v) Tenure
(vi) Ego level

Indicators of burnout

I. Health indicators

(i) Fatigue and chronic exhaustion
(ii) Frequent and prolonged colds
(iii) Headaches
(iv) Sleep disturbances: night-mares, excessive sleeping
(v) Ulcers
(vi) Gastrointestinal disorders
(vii) Sudden losses or gains in weight
(viii) Flare-ups of pre-existing medical disorders, diabetes, high blood pressure, asthma etc.
(ix) Injuries from high risk behaviour
(x) Muscular pain
(xi) Menstrual disorders

II. Excessive behavioural indicators

(i) Heavy use of caffeine, to backer, alcohol
(ii) Use of medicines, drugs
(iii) Auto/cycle accidents
(iv) High risk hobbies
(v) Gambling
(vi) Violent and aggressive behaviour
(vii) Over/under eating
(viii) Hyperactivity

III. Emotional adjustment indicators

(i) Emotional distancing
(ii) Paranoia
(iii) Depression
(iv) Decreased emotional control
(v) Fear of going crazy
(vi) Daydreaming
(vii) Feeling of going crazy
(viii) Nervous 'ticks'
(ix) Undefined fears
(x) Inability to concentrate
(xi) Intellectualisation
(xii) Angry
(xiii) Tension

IV. Relationship indicators

(i) Isolation from or over-bonding with other staff
(ii) Responding to clients mechanically
(iii) Isolation from clients
(iv) Expression of anger and mistrust
(v) Interpersonal conflicts
(vi) Away from work

V. Attitude indicators

(i) Grandiosity
(ii) Boredom
(iii) Cynicism
(iv) Sick humour
(v) Distrust of management

(vi) Air of righteousness
(vii) Expressions of hopelessness

VI. Value indicators

(i) Sudden and often dramatic changes in values and beliefs.

VII. Socialisation

(i) Over-involvement with clients using clients to meet personal needs.

The process of reducing burnout

Following are the techniques used to reduce the burnout.

1. Identification. Techniques for the analysis of the incidence, prevalence and characteristics of burnout in individuals or work groups.

2. Prevention. An attempt to prevent the burnout process before it begins.

3. Mediation. Procedures for slowing, halting or reversing the burnout process.

4. Remediation. Techniques for individuals who already burned out are rapidly approaching the end stages of this process.

These techniques are then coupled with the four specific areas (sites) of intervention such as individual, interpersonal relations, the work place and the organisation. Table below shows matrix of the burnout interventions. The key point here is that accurate identification is made and then programme is tailored to meet that need.

TABLE: Burnout interventions

Site	Identification	Prevention	Mediation	Remediation
Personal	• Self-evaluation	• Professional training	• Stress management	• Individual counselling
Interpersonal	• Peer feedback	• Support groups	• Creative supervision	• Group counselling
Work Place	• Formal surveys	• Professional development	• Job redesign	• Job changes
Organisational	• Performance monitoring	• Organisational development	• Quality assurance	• Employer assistance

Adapted from David Decenzo, *Personnel/Human Resource Management*, Prentice Hall of India Ltd., 1993, p. 521.

QUESTIONS FOR DISCUSSION

1. Define stress and explain the factors responsible for causing stress.
2. Explain in detail various sources of stress in relation to Organisational Behaviour. How would you rank these sources in the order of producing various degrees of stress?
3. Job stress can have physiological, psychological and behavioural effects.
4. What are the symptoms of stress?
5. Contrast type A and type B behaviours.
6. Are type B individuals less effective than type A's?
7. Explain the strategies for preventing stress.
8. What individual difference variables moderate the relationship between potential stresses and experienced stresses?
9. What is burnout? Describe the symptoms and causes of burnout.
10. Describe the process of reducing burnout.

17

Organisation Change and Development

DEFINITION OF CHANGE

Management prefers to accomplish their activities as planned. But unfortunately the change is inevitable and demands alteration of existing relationships. Organisations desire change in order to remain competitive with the changing environment. The extent change is planned uncertainty and unpredictability.

These changes do not greatly violate the traditions and *status quo* expectations of the organisations. They occur in piece-meal and one by one in terms of slight adjustment to the existing system. They do not bring dramatic results to promote enthusiasm. They do not represent significant departure to the past and provoke resistance.

Revolutionary changes are rarely introduced except when situation becomes highly intolerable having no other option. The revolutionary changes are rarely introduced only when the situations are warranted.

Changes are made by the organisations with a purpose of achieving something that might otherwise be unattainable. Through planned changes organisations reach new frontiers of progress quickly towards a given set of goals. Edgar Williams lists out three reasons for designing planned change:

(i) To improve the meaning for satisfying somebody's economic wants.

(ii) To increase profitability.

(iii) To contribute for the social well-being.

Planned change is the intentional attempt by an organisation.

Types of changes

Proactive change. Proactive change is something that is desirable and management vitiates it in the larger interests of organisation. Proactive change is identified by the management.

Reactive changes. They are changes introduced when some body demands for it. This change is proposed and pressed for by the outside forces.

Strategic change. This is a change in the very mission of the organisation. A single mission may have to be changed to multiple missions.

Structural changes. Decentralised operations and participative management style have been in force to meet the situation to enable the organisations for making the spot decisions. The structural changes have shifted authority and responsibility to lower levels of organisations.

Process oriented changes. These changes include use of machines, computers, robotics, etc., in the processing operations. This means replacing the personnel making heavy capital investment for machines and operational changes.

People oriented changes. Any organisational change affects people in some form or the other. The changes are directed towards performance improvement, group cohesion, dedication and loyalty to the organisation. These changes develop a sense of self-actualisation among the members.

Environmental forces that affect organisations

Change means the alteration of *status quo*. Many organisations change to strengthen the organisations. Economic and social environment is so dynamic that without change the organisations will be unable to survive in the new environment. Management should constantly monitor the environment and better utilise the resources to become competitive in the market. Successful organisations make changes in their philosophy, policies and strategies as the need be. Change involves creativity, innovation and realignment within organisation. Barney and Griffin state that the reason for organisational problems is the failure of managers to properly anticipate or respond to internal and external forces of change.

External forces. The external environment affects the organisation directly and indirectly. Since organisations do not have control over the external forces, the only way out left to management is realigning itself with them and aware of changes in the direction of these forces. Following are the external forces that affect the organisations:

1. Business and economic environment
2. Political stability
3. Cultural and market environment
4. Industry demand
5. Availability of resources
6. Sociological factors
7. Social norms
8. Government controls and policies
9. Legal forces
10. Technological developments
11. Competition
12. Shareholders' ambitions
13. Customers' likes and dislikes.

Business and economic environment. Management has to predict what is likely to happen in general and to its major segments. This requires a study of five-year plans forecasts of items such as the gross national product, industrial production, consumer purchases, retail and wholesale prices, employment and government expenditure. The prevailing economic situation can give many pointers to what is likely to happen in the future and what plans should be formed for the future growth of the organisation.

Political stability. Business environment is also affected by the political environment and stability of the government, local and national. It is also influenced by the international environment which might arise the questions of the necessity of import licenses, exchange control and so on. If the political stability is ensured managers can assume greater certainty in the conditions that are likely to prevail in the future.

Cultural and market environment. In India many religions, communities, castes and sub-castes with a number of languages being spoken are coexisting. Again management should take social and market setting into consideration. A product successful abroad need not be successful in India, it depends upon utility, necessity in India's cultural and market setting.

Industry demand. The sales volume of an organisation is obtained from total industry sales. Any alteration within the industry would reflect on the firm. The competitive conditions within the industry are constantly changing. This naturally affects the future probable sales of the company. The entry of new manufacturers into the industry affects the market share of the company. An organisation can redesign its entire line of products to secure bigger market share changes in the forthcoming period.

Availability of resources. Another important force that affects the organisation is the availability of capital, labour and other resources. Indian capital market is passing through crucial changes with the deregulation of CCI (Controller of Capital Issue) and evolution of SEBI (Stock Exchange Board of India). Liberalisation has opened up the investment opportunities to NRIs and FIs in both high tech and non-routine industries. Talent people are not in plenty. India has to depend more on technicians abroad.

Sociological factors. This includes prediction of future population with respect to sex, age, size, location and other characteristics relevant to the society. The relative emphasis placed by different segments of society on personnel needs, entertainment and so on also change over a period of time. Aspects like sex ratio, standards of living, composition of urban and rural population, literacy factor would certainly decide the future of the company. So management should consider them and change accordingly.

Social norms. Another important uncontrollable force is social norms. An organisation must operate within such social norms and the responsibilities placed on businessman regarding their obligations to society in general the customers the shareholders and the employees. In terms of long term interests of an organisation the manager must strictly act within the norms prescribed by society. Failure to do this might result in further government control such as price controls.

Government controls and policies

In all countries to a certain extent, through legislation exists such as price controls, Industries Development and Regulation Act, 1951, taxation policies, import restrictions and export entitlement, etc. In these ways, legislation seeks to make trade and industry serve social justice and foster a competitive environment.

Technology. Technology is the prime factor for changes in organisation. According to Handy, the rate of technological change is greater today than any time in the past. Knowledge explosion and revolutionary changes in information technology have made no logical advancement.

Competition. Competition can influence a change in an organisation by the price structure and product lines.

Shareholders. They can influence organisations because they can take action against the Board of Directors if they feel that the board is not acting in their best interests.

Customers. They have been known to change their loyalty for better quality product and better service.

Internal forces. Pressures for change also occur within the organisation. They are:

1. Managerial deficiencies
2. Shortcomings in the existing system
3. Domino effect
4. Ineffective company policies and programmes
5. Poor resource allocation
6. Sources of raw material
7. Others.

1. Managerial deficiencies. Knowledge explosion and change of technology calls for dynamism in the managerial personnel. Changes in managerial personnel is a routine matter, executive refinement, transfers on promotion, and exit of some managers create vacuum. So management should train the existing ones to raise to the expectations. With change a new manager brings his own ideas and begins to examine the existing organisation structure. Thus filling the top vacancies by new personnel offers a strategic opportunity for re-examining the entire structure.

2. Shortcomings in the existing system. Loopholes existing in the system such as gulf between manager and staff, poor communication, unmanageable span and poor coordination between the departments inhibit the need for change until a catastrophe occurs. A rational organisation thinks to change before crisis occurs.

3. Domino effect. It is one in which one change touches off a sequence of related and supporting changes. For example creation of a new department may cause the introduction of new managerial positions, reallocation of tasks, etc. So other departments may have to realign their structure, tasks, staffing, etc. Failure to consider the potential domino effects lead to the problems of coordination and control.

4. Ineffective company policies and programmes. Basic policies constitute a framework within which the organisation should work. These policies and programmes are to be updated from time to time in the light of development that occur.

5. Poor resource allocation. Resource allocation should be flexible. An inflexibility prevailing in the system of capital allocation will cause hurdles to the development. Capital invested in fixed assets get locked over long period. Hence resource allocation should be made rationally.

6. Sources of raw material. Inadequate raw material supplies cause shocks to the existing organisation. The manager should ensure required items in required quantities at appropriate time. Failure to arrange the raw material resources cause hardships to production.

7. Others. Among others the following forces demand for change they relate to inconsistency in methods of work, procedures, work standards, changes in authority status, responsibility.

Some other forces may also erupt because of—

(i) Employees' share in decision-making.

(ii) Employees' desire for higher wage payment.

(iii) Higher employee expectation for satisfying jobs and work environment.

(iv) Employees' demands for effective organisational mechanism.

Process of change

Once the need for change and goals are recognised and accepted management should attempt the process of change. According to Kurt Lewin the following are three important phases for change:

1. Unfreezing
2. Changing
3. Refreezing

Unfreezing the situation. Lewin believes that change should not come suddenly as sudden change leads to destruction. Management must prepare the minds of people for change, so that members will be ready to accept the change. And if there is any resistance it can be neutralised. According to Sechein, unfreezing is the process of breaking down the old attitudes and behaviours, customs and traditions. This can be done through meetings, bulletins, etc.

Changing or moving to the new condition. When the members are prepared for change their behaviour patterns have to be redefined. H.C. Kellman has proposed 3 methods of reassigning new patterns of behaviour.

(a) *Compliance*: Compliance is achieved by strictly enforcing the reward or punishment for desirable or undesirable behaviour. Thus, strict enforcement will ensure change.

(b) *Identification*: Many public organisations use celebrities as role models in advising young people not to try drugs (say). Identification occurs when to identify themselves with some given role models whose behaviour they would like to adopt.

(c) *Internalisation*: Members are left alone look within themselves and they are given freedom to learn and adopt new behaviour to succeed in new circumstances. Soul searching brings about a new dimension to the philosophy of existence and then bring about changes in behavioural patterns that are not considered socially. Internalisation means changing thought process in order to adjust to a new environment.

Refreezing. It occurs when the new member becomes normal and replaces former behaviour. If this takes place permanently 'Refreezing' is said to be complete. Management should see that this new behaviour does not diminish or extinguish. This should be understood that change is not a one time attempt but a continuous process, since the environment is changing continuously. Hence the process of unfreezing, changing, refreezing is a cyclical process.

Phases of organisational change

Change takes places in phases, till the change becomes an accepted part of the organisation. Rarely the change or new idea is accepted in one attempt. Changing system/practice/procedure is a cumbersome process. Planning is done by expert group and implementation is made by different group. The dangers of failure can be minimised if concerned people are involved in planning, evaluation and by good communication among all the people who will eventually be touched by the new practice.

Change is a continuous process and following eight phases are proposed here as framework of organisational change:

(i) Initiation
(ii) Motivation
(iii) Diagnosis
(iv) Information collection
(v) Deliberation
(vi) Action proposed
(vii) Implementation
(viii) Stabilisation

1. Initiation. Initiation is the phase of vocalisation of the need for change. The idea may be mooted at the level of top management basing on the observations or recommendations at the level of corporate management.

2. Motivation. In this phase, people are motivated to involve in detailed thinking about the proposed change and different dimensions of the change process.

3. Diagnosis. It is an attempt to search for the main cause of the symptoms encountered.

4. Information collection. Information is collected in such areas as indicated by the diagnosis.

5. Deliberation. In this phase, several alternatives generated for change are evaluated.

6. Action proposed. It is the phase a new action is proposed.

7. Implementation. Implementation is concerned with translating the proposal into action.

8. Stabilisation. The change under proposal is internalised and made a part of the organisational life.

It is necessary to understand the psychological process behind every phase of change which are shown in the Table.

TABLE: Showing changes and behavioural outcomes

Stage of adoption	Psychological process	Behavioural outcomes
1. Initiation	Arousal	Readiness
2. Motivation	Selectivity and stimulus perception	Hearing about innovation
3. Diagnosis	Exploration	Searching for information
4. Data collection	Orientation	Collection of data
5. Deliberation	Cognitive reorganisation and reinforcement	Discussion and planning
6. Proposal	Expectancy	Presenting a proposal with pay off and detailed planning and acceptance by the group
7. Implementation	Acquiring new learned drives	Extended use of the innovation
8. Stabilisation	Generalisation of learned behaviour	Change of attitude

The underlying psychological process at the initiation phase is arousal, resulting in readiness and characterised by dissatisfaction with the present state of affairs. Readiness is the result of several environmental factors.

In the motivation phase, the individual sees or hears about the innovation or new idea proposed. The underlying psychological process is selectivity and stimulus perception.

Diagnosis phase has underlying process of orientation and

exploration reflected in the behavioural characteristics of searching for more information about the practice.

In deliberation phase individual sees a number of patterns as if he were looking at a kaleidoscope. These shifts in relationships are reflected in the behaviour of the individual who is weighing the pros and cons of adopting the practice and who meets people to check with them about his perceptions.

In action phase, the response is the result of expectancy of results.

The stabilisation phase characterised by the change of attitude, there is generalisation of the learned behaviour and inhibition of older modes of behaviour.

The process of transformational change

Change assumes different dimensions and in complex organisations change is demanded by both external forces and internal groups. The process of change is a transition from the present to the future. Change is complex and has to be continuously monitored.

When an organisation undertakes to respond to a new challenge, it needs to re-examine and redefine its mission, create a vision for the members for mobilising the energies of members of the organisation go into the future. Such a change is called transformational change. Beckhard has suggested four types of changes as transformational:

(i) A change in what drives the organisations.

(ii) A fundamental relationship among organisational parts.

(iii) A change in ways of doing it.

(iv) A basic change in means, values and reward systems.

The prerequisites and the steps involved in transformational change

Beckhard has suggested 9 prerequisites for success (Table A) and 8 steps (Table B) in the process of transformation change. The role of the top executives is critical in transformation change.

TABLE A: Prerequisites for successful transformational change

1. Commitment on the part of top leaders.
2. Written description of the changed organisation.
3. Conditions that preclude maintenance of the *status quo*.
4. Likelihood of a critical mass of support.
5. A medium to long term perspective.
6. Awareness of resistance and the need to honour it.
7. The conviction that the change must be true.
8. Willingness to use resources.
9. Commitment to maintain the flow of information.

TABLE B: Steps in transformational change

1. Designing the future state.
2. Diagnosing the present state.
3. Extrapolating what is required to go from present state to the transitional state.
4. Analysing the work that occurred during the transitional state.
5. Defining the system that is affecting the problem.
6. Analysing each member of the critical mass with regard to readiness and capacity.
7. Identifying the power relationships and resources necessary to ensure the perpetuations of change.
8. Setting up an organisation system to manage the transformation.

Kurt Lewin's force field analysis of planned change process

Kurt Lewin a psychologist has developed a new way of looking at change. It is constructive and scientific in its approach and a useful tool. According to which he identified two types of forces that balance change such as 'driving forces' and 'restraining forces'.

Change is not a casual event but a systematic effort to balance two forces operating in opposite direction. Change occurs only when one set of forces dominate other set of forces.

If both act equally, things will not change. Lewin states that change occurs only when:

(i) Both forces are not equal in strength.

(ii) One set overpowers the other set.

(iii) If, strength of any one set reduces.

To bring change the manager should study the forces existing in the field and estimate the strength of each force. He also should identify which is driving and which is restraining. This evaluation helps him to weaken restraining forces and strengthen driving forces. Thus he can make the path very clear before implementing any change.

Manager should diagnose the forces and understand relevant forces on which to concentrate before controlling the situation. When manager wants to bring change, he should educate the people on driving forces and weaken restraining forces so that people will cooperate wilfully. Herbert *et al.* suggests that strategy of reducing restraining forces is better than trying to increase the driving forces. In practice both strategies of reducing the restraining and increasing the driving forces ensure best results.

Sources of resistance for organisational change

Changes are resisted by people. People tend to resist new (social or technical) system. Homeostatic forces expect organisations to maintain equilibrium by correcting themselves. When the changes are minor the adjustment will be automatic, but when the changes are major, resistance takes place. People often expect rewards with change otherwise, they resist. Change is not always for the good of the people. Hence resistance is also not undesirable. Managers have to precisely define the objectives, purpose, results of change.

Understanding the pointers of resistance to change is the basic step in designing a programme to help an organisation for change. These are most common causes for resistance.

1. Ignorance. When people have insufficient knowledge, they are uncertain about the causes and effects of change. The ignorance of benefits of change is causing resistance to change.

2. Desire for security. People often want to retain the *status quo* even when they know the past practices are inferior. Faster desire for job security is making employees to resist the changes such as computerisation, down sizing, etc.

3. Fear and lack of ambition. Another source of resistance to change is unwillingness to learn new skills on the part of employees. Employees fear inability to learn the skills. This fear is especially prevalent in old workers who have developed their skills over a long period. Some workers simply may not want to exert the energy, time, and mental effort required.

4. Informal group pressures. Organisational changes have some impact on informal networks in the formal organisation. A change in social relationships can provoke a great deal of resistance. Managers often overlook this source of resistance because the informal network is not the focal point of organisational change. This is often unplanned, the spillover effect can cause resistance to change.

5. Evading power bases. The fifth source of resistance to change results from its effect on personal power bases. When people expect their status or power to decline they show resistance. There are power and status considerations in the change process itself, such change often invites criticism from other employees and provokes workers to question their own abilities and self-worth.

6. Potential loss of job security. Advance technologies have made the concern for job security and becoming strong source of resistance. A change that can eliminate jobs is a big threat to employees.

7. Personality conflicts. The resistance is also caused by personality clashes. These conflicts often are the result of misunderstanding, lack of trust and past resentments.

8. Habit. Human being is a creature of habit. Man relies on habits and when confronted with change, the accustomed ways become sources of resistance.

9. Economic factors. Another source of resistance is that changes will lower one's income. Changes in job or tasks arouse economic fears then they won't be able to perform the new tasks when pay is closely tied to productivity.

10. Selective information processing. Individuals imagine their world through their perceptions once they have entered this world, these perceptions resist changes so individuals are guilty of selective processing of information in order to keep their perceptions intact. They hear what they want to hear and ignore the information that challenges the world which they have designed.

Selective information processing

Fear of the unknown

Habit

Economic factors

Security

Sources of individual resistance to change

Structural inertia

Informal group pressure

Threat to established resource allocations

Limited focus of change

Threat of established power relations

Threat to expertise

Sources of resistance to change

11. Structural inertia. People who are hired into an organisation are chosen for it. They are then shaped and directed to behave in certain ways. When an organisation is confronted with change, this structural inertia acts as a counterbalance to sustain stability.

12. Limited focus change. Organisations are made up of a number of interdependent subsystems. One cannot change without affecting others. If management changes the technological processes without modifying the structure of organisation to match, the change in technology will not be implemented successfully.

13. Threat to expert persons. Specialised are threatened by the changes in organisations. The introduction of personal computers, which allow managers to gain access to information directly from a company's mainframe is reducing the importance of computer experts.

14. Threat to established power relationship. Any redistribution of powers can threaten long and established power relationships within the organisation. The introduction of participative decision-making or self-managed work teams is the kind of change that is often seen as threatening by supervisors and middle managers.

15. Threat to established resource allocation. The groups in the organisations that control resources, often see 'change' as a threat. They tend to be content with the way things are, sometimes change mean a reduction in their budgets or a cut in their staff size. Those who are benefited from the current allocation of resources often feel threatened by the changes that may affect future allocations.

16. Lack of adjustment nature. The most important factor of resistance to change is lack of adjustment nature. Change affects one's position and authority relationships adversely, then he resists it. For each change one has to change in many ways which an employee dislikes because they present numerous problems.

17. Level of satisfaction. Every change will have impact on the level of need. Satisfaction is affected by the change, the employees resist.

18. Emotions. Emotional reasons are of class interest. For example, if management treats labour as a different class, labourers will resist any change by the latter.

19. Vested interests. Change produces some disturbances and dislocation. For example if an organisation creates new units in smaller towns, people have to move from cities to towns and face problems. As a result of this they resist change.

Coping mechanism to overcome resistance to change

Unless resistance is overcome management cannot implement change and derive results out of it. Management has to overcome by possible means some of which are discussed below.

1. Education and communication. Resources can be minimised by educating employees through communicating necessary information, timely. If employees receive facts and get cleared misunderstanding, resistance will subside.

2. Participation. It is difficult to convince people who do not participate in decision-making. So management which proposes changes should involve people for discussion and give them opportunity to understand the practical aspects of change. The employees who are involved in decision-making will contribute more and work with more commitment.

3. Facilitation and support. Change agents offer supportive efforts such as employee counselling, training, resistance when employees' fear and anxiety are high. Though these methods are time consuming managers should try with them.

4. Negotiations. When resistance comes from individuals who are strong, the managers have to negotiate with them and necessary pay packages could be offered to them. This way of negotiation will certainly enable in preventing the resistance for change.

5. Manipulation and cooperation. Manipulation refers to twisting the facts by withholding information. These manipulations make the employees to accept a change. Co-option is a form of both manipulation and participation, it seeks to 'buy off' the traders by giving them a key role in the decisions of change. These tactics become backfire if they feel they are tricked. It will reduce the credibility of the managers.

6. Coercion. When employees resist for change, management may adopt methods of coercion such as transfer, cancelling promotion, negative performance evaluations, and poor letter of recommendation.

7. Commitment. The employees will be made to extend voluntarily the commitment and involve in the process of change. Basically the employees should have confidence in the idea of change. The decision to commit oneself is a dynamic process. It grows slowly along with relationship.

8. Involvement. It is the process by which the affected employees are made to understand the change. It includes finding out from the members how they interpret the proposed changes and what they think about them. As this process goes the level of resistance tends to decrease.

9. Leadership. Leadership role is vital in the process of overcoming resistance for change. A leader has to create a climate of psychological support for change. An effective leader tries to time a change to fit the psychological needs of his followers. A weak leadership presents change on the basis of impersonal requirements but a strong leader uses personal reasons for change.

10. Willingness for the sake of the group. Some persons though personally resist change but be willing for the sake of group. So the management has to isolate such groups and try to induce the group to involve itself in the change process and accept the change.

11. Timing of change. There is appropriate time for introducing change as timing has considerable impact. Right timing always will mean less resistance. So management has to choose a time when the organisational climate is favourable for change.

12. Working with the total system. Resistance to change can be reduced by helping employees to recognise the need for change, to participate in it, and gain from it. Management's responsibility for change is five-fold:

(i) Make only useful and necessary change.

(ii) Change by evolution and not by revolution.

(iii) Share the benefits with employees.

(iv) Diagnosis the problems after change occurs and treat them.

(v) Recognise the possible effects of change and introduce it with adequate attention to human needs.

13. Management is primarily an initiator of change. Union acts as a protector to workers and as a restraint on management. Unions as a matter of policy favour improvement through technological change and will approve a change if that is carefully planned to protect members' interests. So management should maintain sound relations with unions.

14. Security. Job security is essential in any process of change. Management should ensure security, seniority rights, opportunity for advancement, grievance system, etc. All these help employees to feel secure in the process of change.

15. Share rewards. Another measure to secure support for change is assurance of rewards in the changed situation. Employees will not be enthusiastic to accept change if it does not benefit them. Rewards give employees a sense of progress with a change.

16. Use of group forces. It is necessary to study group as a means of change. Change is the integral part of groups and it is imperative to study the group as a medium of change. Group is an instrument for bringing strong pressure on its members to change. So changes in group behaviour will change the individual behaviour. The idea is to help the group which join management to encourage desired change. The power of group depends upon the strength of the members attachment with it. So management should influence group to bring change.

Role of group dynamics in coping with resistance of change

It is necessary to study group as a means of change. Change is integral part of groups and it becomes imperative to study the group as a medium of change. Through groups many things about change can be made clear such aspects as the reasons for change, benefits of change and how the benefits will be shared among the members. For this purpose continuous dialogue is necessary. Free flow of information helps people to understand the real picture of the change and many misunderstandings may be avoided. Research studies also support this aspect. Darwin cartwright has mentioned the following characteristics of group as a means of change:

1. Strong sense of belonging. Group members should have a strong feeling of 'we' in their minds. Then only group can be effectively used as a change agent.

2. Group prestige. Group should be attractive to the members so that it can exert influence on individual members and members adapt to the needs of the whole. A cohesive group is desirable for the organisation to act as means of change.

3. Attitudes, values and behaviour. Group will be successful in changing the attitudes, values and behaviour. For examples a union leader can influence over rank and title regarding the strikes and lock-outs, etc.

4. Individual prestige. Association with a group gives 'prestige' to the members in turn the members feel 'status' in society. Prestige does not necessarily accompany authority, so members since enjoying prestige and status, they sacrifice for the sake of group and accept changes proposed by group.

5. Deviations from group norms. Normally members follow group norms and any deviation from the established norms encounter strong resistance. In group interaction, the idea homoeostasis should be taken into account.

6. Shared perception. In a group when members share perception, change is needed and change can be easily implemented. The source of pressure for change lies within the group.

7. Shared information. For a purposeful change facts should be passed onto the people. Here group helps management in doing so. Since information quickly passes among group members, management should use group as a means of change.

Strategies using group as an agent of change

1. Group contact. Management if proposes to introduce any change it should be in touch with the group as it offers the following advantages:

(i) Through group it is easy to communicate to many at a time.

(ii) Group can get at the basic problem very rapidly as compared to the single individual.

2. Participation. Management should invite participation of employees in the proposals of change. And management should give opportunity to all the concerned to share their opinions and options. Thus management should allow meaningful participation of all concerned and invite options. It would be prudent if management takes workers' representatives into confidence before implementing the change. Thus management must make the employees as agents of change rather than party to resist it.

3. Training for change. Training for change helps in implementing the change. Role playing psychodrama and sensitivity of group training programmes provide understanding of behaviour thereby the people can establish climate basing on mutual trust which essential for bringing organisational changes successfully.

Action research process in organisational change

Action research refers to a change process on the basis of systematic collection of data and then selection of a change action based on what the analysed data indicates. It provides scientific methodology for managing planned change.

The process of action research consists of five steps: diagnosis, analysis, feedback, action and evaluation.

Diagnosis. The manager gathers information about problems, and needed changes from members of organisations. He asks questions, interviews employees, review records, and listens to the concern of employees. Just as a physician enquires an ailed patient, manager puts questions to employees.

Analysis. The information is analysed to identify the key problems, information of primary concerns and possible actions.

Feedback. The target persons propose to be changed with, be involved in determining what the problem is and in creating solution. So the employees develop action plans for bringing about needed changes.

Action. The manager and employees carry out the specific actions to correct the problems that have been identified.

Evaluation. Finally the manger evaluates the effectiveness of the action plans. Here he uses the points of reference in the data gathered. He compares the changed practices with previous practices and evaluates them. Action research is problem oriented. The manager looks for the problem and determines the type of change. Manager involves employees heavily so that resistance to change can be reduced. By this way employees become integral part of change rather than agents resisting change.

Steps to manage change effectively

Change is not instantaneous and it involves formidable exercises on the part of management. Following are the steps to be followed for managing change:

(i) Recognise the forces demanding change.

(ii) Diagnose the problem.

(iii) Plan the change.

(iv) Implement the change.

(v) Follow-up

(i) Recognise the forces demanding for change. Change means alteration of *status quo*. Many organisations change to keep the organisations stable. Economic and social environment is so dynamic that without change the organisations will not survive. Management should constantly watch the environment and better utilise the resources to become competitive in the market. Barney states the reasons for organisational problem is the failure of managers to properly anticipate or respond to internal and external forces for changes.

Internal forces include:

(a) Managerial deficiencies.

(b) Shortcomings in the existing system.

(c) Company policies.

(d) Internal changes, etc.

External problems include:

(a) Business and economic environment.

(b) Political instability.

(c) Cultural environment.

(d) Industry demand.

(e) Social norms.

(f) Government controls and fixed policies.

(g) Technology etc.

The manager should recognise these forces before introducing change. Manager should identify those forces which requires serious attention. He should ignore forces that are not potential. This is a crucial step since time, effort and resources be better allocated to bring change.

(ii) Diagnose the problem. Next phase is diagnosing the problem. Various techniques such as interviews, questionnaires, observation, etc., are used depending upon the nature of the problem. Manager uses appropriate technique to diagnose the problem. Diagnose enables managers to perceive the gap between desired and actual performance and take necessary course of action.

(iii) Plan the change. According to Harold, all organisational changes could be classified into task related, technology related and people related. Planning of change is concerned with what to change, when to change, how to change and why to change. Changing organisation involves restructuring organisation, change of tasks, etc. Changing technology involves addition of new lines, new control systems, new methods, etc. Change of people involves new recruitment, new selection, training, transfer, etc.

Guidelines in planning change. Manager should take the following guidelines:

1. Make clear the need for change and provide a climate.
2. Encourage group participation in clarifying the changes needed.
3. State the objectives.
4. Establish broad guidelines.
5. Select appropriate strategy.
6. Leave the details for implementing.
7. Indicate benefits and rewards to people.
8. Materialise the rewards.

(iv) Implement the change. Identifying local points the manager should choose appropriate strategy to implement the change. An optimist says that it is seductive to think of an organisation as a large machine whose parts can be replaced at will. And an effort to change encounters three problems such as resistance, power and controlling. Managers have to adopt necessary coping mechanism to overcome the resistance to change.

(v) Follow-up of change. Management of change is incomplete without proper follow-up. The sole objective of any change is to maximise the results and better performance. Here the manager has to company the performance before and after the implementation of change. Management should analyse the factors for the performance gap and take necessary action wherever necessary. Management can also identify stress area and take follow-up action appropriate to the situation and problem.

The importance of change implementation

Change should become part of an organisation in which it is introduced. Change should be internalised and integrated. Just as a transplanted part in a body gets integrated with that body, so the case with a 'change' in an organisation. Implementation means institutionalisation of a change that has been accepted. Fullan has suggested three dimensions of implementing change.

1. Innovation. They refer to explicitness of innovation and degree of change.

2. Strategies and tactics. They refer to training, resource support, feedback mechanisms, participation, etc.

3. Adoption. They refer to adoption process, organisational climate, environmental support, demographic factors, etc.

Paul has seen implementation as a multidimensional process such as environment, strategy, process and structure.

1. Environment. It includes opportunity, needs, constraints, threats, scope, diversity and uncertainty.

2. Strategy. It covers service, client sequence, demand and supply of resource mobilisation.

3. Process. It envisages planning and allocation, monitoring and control, human resource development, motivation and compliance.

4. Structure. It confirms differentiation, integration of tasks, structural forms, degree of decentralisation and degree of autonomy.

The end result of implementation is the institutionalisation of change *i.e.*, change should be seen as a permanent part of an organisation. Thus it is structural in nature. It is more of procedural and working.

A model of implementating change

Implementation starts with planning and the process covers monitoring the change, taking action in relation to change and making necessary adjustments.

(A) Planning. It refers to planning the implementation of change. The following 3 dimensions are involved in planning of implementing the change. They are phasing, processes and strategies. And the manager should allow people to participate as many as possible.

Phasing. Depending upon the nature of change the implementation process has to be phased. Phasing may be temporal or spatial. Temporal phasing involves preparation of a plan introducing elements of innovation slowly form time to time and get stabilised. In this phasing changes are introduced one after the other and the whole system may be not implemented at one time. Spatial phasing refers to implementation of changes in some parts of organisations. If organisation is large, the management would introduce the changes in those parts of the organisation where acceptability is high. Sometimes management may introduce the change on trial basis. After verifying its effects, the modified change will be introduced in other parts of the organisation.

Processes. While implementing change, management should pay attention to various processes such as increasing capability of organisation, establishing norms of openness, developing creative leaderships to deal with the problems, self-reliance, etc. Implementation will be easy if these things are taken care of. Any change without attention to these aspects will not enable change.

Strategies. Due attention should be given to strategies of implementation. Huberman has suggested the following four factors of effective strategy:

(i) Change should be responsive to the needs of local people.

(ii) Change should be flexible and broadly designed to make use of all ideas and resources from inside and outside.

(iii) Change should use laws.

(iv) Change should be clearly planned basing on objectives.

(B) Monitoring. Monitoring refers to gathering of information on project inputs, outputs and on circumstances that are critical for the effective implementation of the project. The term according to United Nations (1975), refers to the process of routine or periodic measurement of programme inputs, activities and outputs undertaken deriving programme implementation. Thus the function of monitoring is to provide early warnings concerning shortfalls in inputs to enable programme manager to undertake timely corrective measure.

Measures for effective monitoring

1. Implementation team. To monitor effectively the implementation of change a team should be set up with a whole time director. The team members should be taken from different parts of the organisation who are known for creativity, positive and rational. The director should have high regard and enjoy necessary support from members. The members should feel concern for change.

2. Minimum control. In one sense monitoring is a control function getting all the necessary information from time to time in order to take decisions ensuring that the programme is carried out according to the design and completing the schedules according to the plans.

3. Review and feedback. Manager has to review the programme from time to time to know about the difficulties experienced by members in programme implementation. And also the manager has to provide feedback to the people on how well they are implementing the programme. This is a continuous process.

4. Dissemination of information. The implemening team will collect information about what is happening in various parts of the organisation where the change is implemented. This information may be disseminated from time to time. The team should develop strategies to disseminate information to appropriate part of the organisation suitably and timely. The team should use oral and written communications during seminars and meetings in order to discuss the problems of implementations.

(C) Action and adaptation. Organisation requires action and adaptation to implement change effectively. Pomfret has suggested flexibility to be taken care of while implementing a change. Action refers to the details of what is to be implemented. Adaptation refers to modifying the programme to make it suitable to the local conditions.

Dealing with consequences of change. Introduction of change produces negative results in the form of dissatisfaction and fall in productivity, etc. The management has to pay necessary attention and take steps to twist them. If the management does not deal with such consequences these symptoms may accumulate and result in rejection of change.

(D) Support. The top management should give necessary support to implement the change successfully. These measures include—training, resources, commitment, linkages, etc.

Training. People need additional skills such as collaboration, openness, problem-solving, patience, risk bearing, decision-making, collecting information, etc. These skills may not be adequate in all people at all times. During times of change, management should conduct certain training programmes to improve some skills said above.

Resources. Change requires support in terms of manpower, material and financial resources. Management should arrange additional facilities by way of manpower, space, furniture, equipment, transportation, communication network, etc. Thus management should be prepared for all these things to implement modifications and adaptations.

Commitment. People implement the change if the management wants it. In the absence of management support, things would not move in the direction sought. Hence involvement of top management is necessary in any change proposed.

Linkages. The implementation team should build up linkages with concerned consultants, departments, people (internal and external) including management. The development of internal linkages helps to provide necessary support for the change.

Proactive action strategy for change

Systems in organisation should be designed so as to be suitable to culture of the organisation and culture of the society. This is called reactive position. People spend major part of their life to learn and acquire new skills and attitudes. Major responsibility of organisations is producing that kind of culture that is necessary for future effectiveness of the organisations. Organisations should exhibit better culture than society culture, since, they have the advantage of getting better educated citizens.

A proactive strategy would involve the following steps:

1. Determine the direction. It should be clear to organisations where they want to go. The direction should be defined in terms of feedback, counselling appraisal career planning, openness and collaborative action. An open discussion about new directions will help the organisations to prepare people psychologically.

2. Share possible consequences. The team introducing 'change' should anticipate the problems and be prepared to deal with them. The management should communicate verbally and in writing the possible consequences to all the concerned.

3. Start from where you are. Each organisation has a tradition and the new system will be different from the existing. The organisation should know in what direction it has to move. It may be useful for the organisation to understand this and start from the level where it stands in terms of sophistication of the system.

4. Take one step at a time. The entire new system cannot be changed at a time. Organisation should prepare a careful plan to phasing various steps and introduce bit by bit so that the entire organisation will understood and accustom to it.

5. Prepare for the journey. Introduction of change requires preparation, the people need new skills, attitude and orientation to understand the change and implement it. In the absence of 'preparation' the change will become a failure and it is better not to introduce new system, at all. Hence management should do necessary ground work before launching new systems.

6. Be prepared for reversal. Changes may or may not produce positive results and changes may cause some disturbing symptoms in the organisation. Managers may report that feedback is not as good as they have anticipated, in the beginning. Such reverse situations should not arouse anxiety. It should be understood that reverses are likely and organisations should be prepared for this.

7. Develop internal expertise. A system cannot be developed with the help of external experts alone. Management should simultaneously develop internal experts with the new system. Either in the beginning or at the end and external help could be used but not in routine work. The new system is likely to fail if enough attention is not paid in developing such expertise.

8. Follow up. Following the implementation of the change. The implementing team should deal with the problems without it being in the way of implementation. When the change is followed up and doggedly and that steps are taken continuously to implement the change success will follow.

9. Have a compass and a speedometer. Monitoring mechanism in the implementation of the system is necessary. The implementation team should collect information about the progress of the system and in which direction it is going. Special meetings, interviews, questionnaires, appraisal forms could be distributed from time to time to have feedback and in turn to counsel the people in correcting their actions.

S-P-S-T model in developing culture change-management

Management of culture change needs attention in four aspects, *viz.* Structural elements, Processes, Strategy of change and Tactics to be employed. New culture should become a part of the organisation. The elements of each aspect are listed below:

S-Structural elements

1. Flexible structure. The structure of organisation should be flexible to accommodate changes.

2. Linkage building mechanisms. The organisation should have strong and positive links with unions, groups, markets, technologists, government, suppliers, etc. so that it can implement change without much effort.

3. Information system. The organisation should have timely information on every minute thing before misdeed occurs.

4. Reward system. Organisation should have proper reward system to its employees. Proper reward system will enable the management to implement the changes effectively.

5. Regular budget. The organisation should budget its requirements, expenditure, sales, production operations, etc. The budget system will help management to check performance continuously.

P-Process

1. Action research approach. It refers to what action is to be taken by whom and when management should be careful in such aspects, since failure is likely.

2. Mentoring. Management should shape the career of people by guiding them in times of change. Thus proper mentoring would enable the success of change and its implementation.

3. Process awareness and orientation. People should be educated to know about the process of change, if the process is not followed.

4. Counselling. Management should counsel people in matters of organisational, family and personal interest. During implementation of change, people face many problems. Hence proper counselling would enable the change and its introduction.

5. Norms. Norms tell members what and what not to do. In times of change company people are prepared to sacrifice without affecting norms of the company.

S-Strategy

1. Anchoring in using strengths. Management should identify its strength and use appropriately to overcome the bottlenecks in times of change.

2. Competency building. Implementing team of change should train up the people to develop competency. Competency through skills of decision-making, risk bearing, problem-solving, visionary, etc., could be developed through rotation of job and job enrichment.

3. Critical factor. Management should concentrate on critical factors of organisation. If critical factors are taken to control organisational success is sure. Absenteeism, power shortage, competition, technology change are some for example.

4. Sanction and support. Management should extend necessary support by sanctioning required authority and resources to the supervisors implementing the change.

5. Idea ownership. Management should own responsibility for failure and prepare for risks. It should not implement any change without knowing the 'idea' fully.

T-Tactics

1. Prepare for risk. The management should prepare for risks and take troubles before implementing change. It should not imagine that change is risk free.

2. One step at a time. Management should not introduce all the changes at a time. It should implement the changes one after the other, slowly.

3. Prepare for the journey. People need new spirit, skills, attitudes to understand the change and implement it. Management should take adequate preparation to train the people to be fit in the new environment.

4. Work together. Changing to new pattern of work will always be criticised by even like minded, so management should call people to work together.

5. Stop and review progress. When new system is implemented, the management should review periodically the progress made. And the experiences and problems of change should be rectified from time to time.

6. Keep up the spirit. The effectiveness of change depends upon the spirit with which people implement. Hence the management should have positive spirit to take risk of the benefit of the entire organisation.

7. Keep going. Management should not keep quite after implementing the change. It should keep the 'new system' going without halt.

Observational methods of change

Every one observes people, things and events. Observational method means watching things in its normal setting. For example top management meeting is observed and data is systematically recorded according to a plan. The observer may observe the behaviour of top executives and collect the data about interpersonal communication or decision-making process.

The method has been widely used in many branches of science and technology. Mendel, the originator of the modern science of genetics has adopted observational methods. Later this method of observation was replicated in many experiments. Science has built innumerable instruments for observation such as microscope to telescope. In medical profession observational methods are fundamental.

Properties of observational methods

1. Things under observation should be observable. Behaviours are observable and intentions are not. But they can be inferred.

2. Particular *Vs.* Whole. Particular behaviour, settings, events or things are observed but not the whole. For example one can make a movie shot by shot. A shot can be observed not the entire movie.

3. Relevant. The behavioural settings, events or things under observation should be relevant to the aims.

4. Qualification. The set of behaviours under observation are quantifiable. This can be had by multiple measures in different settings.

5. Natural. The person under observation should be in his natural setting as far as possible.

6. Dominant features. When observations make change the dominant features of the natural setting should not get tilted.

7. Choice. Observers make choices in selecting things or behaviours to be observed. They edit the observations before, during and after the event knowingly or unknowingly. The more explicit the choices the more the scope for improving the diagnosis.

8. Extensive. All information about the observed situation cannot be retained only the relevant and useful information can be retained or recorded.

9. Observed records are not data. All that observed cannot be a data. When the records are encoded, they yield data.

10. Experimental. For hypothesis testing, the observational methods employed become experimental.

When to use observational methods

Some of the following occasions indicate the use of observational methods:

1. When immediately needed.
2. When details are needed.
3. In the preliminary stages of investigation.
4. When any limitation has to be offset.
5. When there is over involvement of the subject.
6. When the subject is not aware of the activities since they are habitual.
7. When the phenomenon is fleeting.
8. When the subjects cannot describe their actions.
9. To bring better data on beliefs, values, attitudes, norms, etc.
10. When the data is needed on the environment in operations.
11. When data is needed on the intimate relationships between the person and the setting.
12. When phenomena are complex and multidimensional.
13. When laboratory induction is unrepresentative of reality.

14. When data from actual actions are more important than the thoughts.

What is to be observed

Some broad behaviour commonly observed are:

1. Non-verbal behaviour.
2. Spatial behaviour
3. Extra linguistic behaviour.
4. Linguistic behaviour.

These behaviours are classified into two:

1. Process dominant.
2. Content dominant.

Behaviour analysed by observational methods

I. Process dominant

Focused more:

(i) Non-behaviour	— Facial expressions
	— Exchange glances
	— Body languages
(ii) Spatial behaviour	— Interperson distance
	— Spatial relationship
	— Spatial perception
	— Architectural perception
	— Conversational clustering
(iii) Extra linguistic behaviour	— Vocal
	— Temporal
	— Interaction

II. Content dominant

Linguistic behaviour	— Interaction process
	— Member leader analysis
	— Behaviour scores system.

In the above exhibit, the only observed behaviour of organisations are mentioned. It should be clear that what is presented is the basic active ingredient of observational methods.

It is like grains of wheat whether one used it for seeds, breads or cakes is a matter of mode of working with those grains.

Modes and methods of observations

1. Interaction process analysis.
2. Interpersonal behaviour analysis.
3. Small group interaction analysis.
4. Group process analysis.
5. Time and motion work study.
6. Task analysis.

1. Interaction process analysis. It is based on poor assessment. Bale has formulated 12 interaction categories. Borgatta refined by deleting and adding some categories and formulated 18 category system. Using this Flankers, Paveek and Rao have analysed teacher behaviour and enriched classroom behaviour of students.

2. Interpersonal behaviour analysis. This takes into account different aspects of behaviour for analysis. Paveek and Rao have reported influence of teacher on the initiative dependence proneness, adjustment and group cohesiveness. Mann has analysed the other areas such as impulse, affection, ego state, authoritative relation, etc.

3. Small group interaction analysis. It focuses on members' communication among themselves.

4. Group process analysis. This method is useful when a small group is evolving from a collection of strangers towards becoming a small team. It is used to study some of the processes like inclusion, exclusion, exercising power, integration disintegration, cooperation conflict, leadership, cohesiveness, norms, customs and values in the group.

5. Time and motion work study. These are borrowed from industrial engineering discipline wherein behaviour on job with machine are studied. They have been used to analyse utilisation of machines on a shop floor and people spend their time on job. The job analysis, job description, reward and punishment, etc., are determined using these methods.

6. Task analysis. This analyses the activities and tasks performed by the employees in the light of goals to be achieved.

This helps in comparing the expected behaviour with actual ones and identify gaps and areas of change.

Survey feedback technique in organisational change

This method of data collection consists of using questionnaires supplemented by interviews and observation. The data are analysed and feedback to the management and employees for solving problems.

The questionnaires elicit data from the following major areas such as leadership organisational climate and satisfaction.

The dimensions under leadership are:

1. Managerial support
2. Goal emphasis
3. Work facilitation
4. Interaction
5. Peers support, etc.

The dimensions under organisation climate are:

1. Communication with company.
2. Motivation
3. Decision-making
4. Controls within
5. Departmental coordination
6. General management

Satisfaction contains the following dimensions:

1. Satisfaction with company policies
2. Satisfaction with supervisor
3. Satisfaction with job
4. Satisfaction with work groups, etc.

Steps involved in the survey feedback are:

1. Organisation members at top are involved in planning.
2. Questionnaire is administered when diagnosis is focused.
3. Data and feedback to the top management team and down through the hierarchy.
4. Data discussed in the presence of head of the organisation and his subordinates.

5. Plans are made for constructive changes.
6. Feedback meetings are held with a consultant who acts as a resource person and prepare the superior for meeting.
7. Chief executive officer sees the results of the survey first and initiates to share the information.

Projective methods

It is a well-known psychological phenomenon that motives and emotions are projected on to some object. This property is utilised in this method. The more ambiguous a stimulus the greater the projection. When the stimulus is ambiguous the subject chooses his own interpretation. Thematic appreciation tests, role playing, sentence completion, writing a story, playing with dolls and toys are some examples of testing projective methods. The projective tests are categorised on the basis of types of response.

(a) Association
(b) Construction
(c) Completion
(d) Expression

Association technique. It requires the subject to write, tell the first thing that comes to mind when presented with a stimulus. **Word association.** It is another such method when the subject is asked to respond with the first word that comes to mind when he is presented with a word list.

Construction technique. It requires the participant to develop a story on unclear pictures, shown for few seconds.

Completion technique. It requires the person to choose an item that appears to him relevant from among several items.

Expressive technique. It is like the construction technique but the emphasis is on the process of construction *i.e.*, the manner in which it is done not on the end product. This technique is used to bring out the hopes, fears, aspirations and apprehensions both at national and individual levels.

Archival methods and unobtrusive measures

Every organisation acquires information on various matters such as absenteeism, turnover, repairs, costs, complaints etc.

The information is not readily available in the required form but it is there in some form or the other. This information exists in some location undefined that has no boundary. This source of information is called 'archives' web said to collect the information, it is not necessary to rely on a respondent for obtaining facts. The facts in existence are tale telling stories and speak themselves.

For example fingerprint on the dagger, number of cigarettes smoked as an indication of tension in meetings. This information already in existence is not utilised. The information is called 'archival' data. This does not disturb anyway the person. It is not influenced by anybody. Strictly speaking the data do not have a respondent to tell.

Archival data is easy to recognise due to their 'factness' principles of both deductive and inductive logic, are in operation in dealing with a 'archival data'. The investigator has to identify his question first. Answers to the questions can be obtained from the realities.

Content analysis

Content analysis is a method of studying and analysing communication, information or any symbolic behaviour in systematic manner. Content analysis is a technique for making inferences by systematically and objectively identifying specified characteristics of messages. In this analysis, content of the information is coded where data is transformed into units such as: (a) Defining the universe, (b) Categories of analysis, (c) Units of analysis, and (d) System of enumeration. These are briefly described below:

(A) Defining the universe. On the basis of hypotheses the variables are decided. Relevant information is determined. One has to outline the relevant source of data in the universe. The categorisation of universe depends on the variables and hypotheses.

(B) Categories of analysis. Categories into which content analysis are classified below:

Categories are:

1. Subject matter
2. Direction

3. Standard
4. Values
5. Methods
6. Traits
7. Actors
8. Authority
9. Origin
10. Target
11. Location
12. Conflict
13. Ending
14. Time

Categories 'how it is said'

1. Form of communication, medium of communication. Example: newspaper, radio, television, speech, etc.
2. Form of statement.
3. Device, propaganda method used.

(C) Unit analysis. It refers to units such as words, theme, characters, items, and space time measures.

The word: It is the smallest unit.

The theme: It is a difficult unit, it is a proposition about something.

The character: It is mostly used in literacy analysis.

The item: The article, film, book or radio programme is characterised.

The space time measures: They are the actual physical measurement of content such as number of paragraphs, number of minutes of discussion.

(D) System of enumeration. This means how number could be assigned to the units.

Frequency: Count the number of objects in each category.

Ranking: It is the ordinal measurement judges can be asked to rank the objects according to a specific criterion.

Rating: Techniques like Thurstone's technique of paired comparison can do it and content units are usefully compared.

Relationship between transformational change and organisational development

Organisational Development depends on the recognition of the fast pace of organisational change and the need for organisation to respond to it effectively. OD is rooted in 60s and 70s when changes were not rapid. As such OD has focused and planned one time transformational change. Various OD approaches are shown here:

OD Strategies

FOCUS

	JOBS	Interpersonal Exchanges	Work groups	Whole organisation
Emphasis on Structure	Job Redesign	Communication Pattern	Autonomous work group	Survey feedback
	Flex-time		Team building	Action research
	Job enlargement	Transactional Analysis		
Emphasis on Process	Job enrichment	T-group Process Consultants	Conflict Resolution	Management Grid

The sequential process involves 8 phases:

(a) Motivation

(b) Initiation

(c) Diagnosis

(d) Information collection

(e) Deliberation

(f) Action proposal

(g) Implementation

(h) Stabilisation

Key roles in managing change

Change is a team work where different people involve simultaneously or collectively. Various persons perform different functions. These roles are:

1. Management
2. Internal consultants
3. Implementation of team
4. Chief implementers

5. Task forces

6. Consultants (outside)

1. Management. Management members include executive cadre persons who are at the helm of affairs and making policies. Corporate management legitimises the change and extends support. The changes proposed by management will be resisted by employees who generally feel it difficult to practice new things. Here management should invite discussion and motivate them. Management if necessary invite consultants to orient or train the starter in addition to incentives for those who invite changes.

2. Consultants (internal). Some people from inside are experts in the field. They should play the role of counterparts and help co-employees in implementing the policies of organisational changes.

3. Implementation of team. In order to ease the implementation of changes a team could be formed. The expert members may be drawn from various parts, sections of the organisation.

The team should collaboration with each other by taking decisions on consensus (or majority) basis. The members should respect the feeling of others. The team will work as a communication channel between policy makers and implementers. It clarifies the doubts of people and gives feedback to the decision-makers. The team also reviews the progress of the change from time to time for effective implementation of changes. If necessary they suggest modifications so that implementation cannot be hastened.

They also formulate plans and policies for smooth functioning of the organisation. This makes the change programmes realistic. This group is only recommendatory.

4. Chief implementer. He will be the chairman of the implementing team with executive responsibility. He takes the responsibility of monitoring and ensuring proper implementation. He will scan the environment and identify blocks coming in the way of successful implementation of changes. He collects information through interviews and questionnaires and discusses them with the team implementing.

He not only bears the responsibility of execution but mobilises the resources required to various departments in implementing the changes. The implementer should have confidence in the proposed changes and be systematic with necessary flexibility in his dealings with people. He should be resourceful, imaginative and creative to tackle the problems of change. He should be acceptable to the system. He should maintain rapport with all people. And he should be known for qualities of implementation.

5. Task forces. Task forces may be formed for execution of specific change. Task forces are constituted for each activity. Task forces help in using resources, experts, equipment available for implementing the changes.

6. Consultants (external). Outside experts in the field may be consulted when changes are proposed. It is necessary to hire them where internal experts lack the perceptions of the problem. Functions of the consultants are:

(a) *Implanting function*: They should supplement the internal experts. They also should adjust with the existing functional executives and give them orientation.

(b) *Transcending function*: Their role is very creative. They are not bound by the constraints of the organisation. They keep the future of the organisation in their mind and tone up the men, machines and matters.

Generate alternatives. Utility of the consultants lies in their ability to develop alternative courses of action to find solution to the problems. The consultants with their knowledge in the field and experience all over the industry will find solutions effectively.

Facilitating. The consultant is a facilitator. He understands reality and helps people in developing various roles as the change programmes expect.

Shock absorber. Being change, the people face unpleasant experiences and management needs feedback on matters of implementation and consequences. The internal people may feel it difficult. But the outsider consultants can take such risk and absorb the shocks created by the changes. They can confront realities and cope with the changes.

Resource sharing. The outside consultants with abundant experience and knowledge share them wide the internal and functional authorities so that the knowledge can be utilised for effective implementation of changes.

Resource building. Consultant helps in building internal or external resources like time, manpower, money and materials by reducing wastages and utilising optimally the resources.

Self liquidating. As soon as his purpose for the organisation is over he *i.e.*, the consultant will go back. He should not make the organisation dependent on him. The organisation should make use of the consultant by making proper communication with him at every stage in the change process.

Models of change

There are several models of change. A model is an integrated effort with several relationships involved in it. A comprehensive way is to look at the main emphasis in producing the change at individual level.

Individual is the driving force behind any change in an organisation. If individuals get motivated, change is easy. Individuals change when they learn new things and only when they get non-threatening feedback and also when their motives change.

1. *Change as a learning process*: Man learns when he is dissatisfied with the present state. He learns new process, implements, assess its advantages and then adopts it. But rate of change varies from person to person or group to group. Individual change depends upon his initiative, motivation, information, deliberation and stabilisation mainly. Also individuals according to research do not change equally or at the same rate. The individuals are classified into the follow groups, innovators, early adopters and early majority to adopt change.

2. *Change through feedback*: Individuals change if they get feedback on their behaviour. The feedback need to be objective and non-threatening.

3. *Motivation change model*: Individuals engage in certain activities because of their dominant motive or psychological need. A person with affiliation motive will be competitive. Thus

motivation *i.e.* motive of a person is important to change his behaviour. A management pundit has suggested the following proposition to acquire motives.

4. The man as an individual believes in that he can develop a motive the more likely he is to succeed in educational attempts.

5. The more an individual perceives in developing a motive is consistent with the demands of reality the more likely he is to succeed in educational attempts.

6. The more an individual in educational attempts the motive the more likely he is to develop it.

7. The more likely is to occur in thought and action if an individual can like the newly developed network to related actions.

8. More likely to influence his thought and actions if a person conceptualises his actions in his life.

9. The motive will influence his thoughts if an individual perceives the motive as an improvement in the self-image and cultural values.

10. The more an individual to achieve his goals if the motive influences his thoughts.

11. Changes in motives are likely to occur and persist if the new motive is a sign of membership in a new reference group.

12. The newly formed motives influence more if the record of his progress to achieving goals is more.

13. Changes in motives are more likely if he is respected by others in an interpersonal atmosphere.

Organisational change through efficiency

One of the approaches used for organisational change is role efficiency. The progressive management should follow the measures given to change the organisation through 'role efficacy'.

Centrality. The more the people feel their roles are important in the organisation, the higher will be the role efficiency. It is not possible to enhance effectiveness unless the individuals feel important in the organisation.

Integration. The management should integrate the 'role and self' so that people use their knowledge very well. As long as people feel distance it is difficult to bring change.

Proactive. The employee if does something independently the management should give necessary encouragement. Otherwise the employee becomes mere reactive and does things mechanically. He will do things said to him and will be not proactive.

Creativity. The individuals should feel creative in their jobs and introduce 'new' things. Management should encourage creative people otherwise people do routine things.

Linkage. The employees should feel that they are interlinked with others and this feeling go a long way to increase the efficiency. As long as staff work in isolation it leads to functioning.

Helping. The people should feel that they receive 'help' whenever necessary. They should never feel that others are indifferent to him. Thus a perception of hostility decreases the efficiency.

Superordination. The 'people' should feel that they are contributing to some larger entity. They should also believe that they are benefiting the organisation.

Influence. The role occupants should necessarily feel that their voice or advice is taken into consideration in decision-making or problem-solving. Also the people should feel that they are able to influence the policies.

Growth. The position occupants in organisation have to learn new things and grow with organisation. If they feel that they are lacking opportunities of personal growth, their role efficacy will be low.

Confrontation. The roles have to confront the problems and find solutions. When problems arise the people should not try to avoid them.

QUESTIONS FOR DISCUSSION

1. What is change and define it? Explain the types of changes prevailing in the organisations.
2. Describe in detail the steps in the change process.
3. What are the environmental forces that affect the organisations?
4. Explain the process of transformational change and the pre-requisites and the steps involved in it.

5. What are the sources of resistance for organisational change?
6. Explain the coping mechanism to overcome resistance to change.
7. What is the role of group dynamics in coping with resistance of change?
8. To what extent do you think the human resistance can be addressed through group dynamics?
9. Describe action-research process in organisational change.
10. Discuss how a manager manages change effectively.
11. Briefly explain the importance of implementation of change.
12. Explain in detail the model of implementation of change in an organisation.
13. What are the steps involved in proactive action strategy for change? Explain.
14. Explain how the S-P-S-T model helps in developing culture-change management.
15. Discuss important diagnostic methods employing observational methods.
16. Explain the survey feedback technique in organisational change.
17. Describe how one can diagnose through projective methods.
18. What is meant by Archival methods and unobtrusive measures?
19. Discuss the content analysis and its importance.
20. What is the relationship between transformational change and organisational development?
21. Who play key roles in managing change?
22. Describe models of change with a focus on individuals.
23. Explain how to bring about organisational change through role efficacy.